The 20
Off th

The 20th Century
Off the Record

Gilbert Mant

Kangaroo Press

Acknowledgments

Neil McDonald, of the Charles Sturt University at Bathurst, is to blame for persuading me to embark on these occasional memoirs of people and places when I thought I was written out.

Others who have helped to refresh my memory and supplement my story include David Burrows, Bill Daley, Doug Denham, Alec Ezard, Tom Gurr, John Hilvert, Anne and John Hoey, Eric Jolliffe, Mari Mears and the staff of the Hastings Municipal Library, Port Macquarie. Special thanks to Yvonne Bartlett Hawes and Susan Brown for typing the manuscript and helping in other ways in its production. And once again, thanks to Carl Harrison-Ford for his skilful and understanding editing of my manuscript. The many books I have read or re-read are listed on another page.

I freely confess to lifting the Abominable Showman title for Chapter 12 from Billy Moloney's wonderful book of memoirs as manager of the Tivoli Theatre in Sydney and other showbiz engagements. He sent me a copy of his book, inscribed 'From one Abominable Showman to another'.

© Gilbert Mant 1994

First published in 1994 by Kangaroo Press Pty Ltd
3 Whitehall Road Kenthurst NSW 2156 Australia
PO Box 6125 Dural Delivery Centre NSW 2158
Typeset by G.T. Setters Pty Limited
Printed by Australian Print Group, Maryborough Vic. 3465

ISBN 0 86417 652 X

Contents

Acknowledgments 4
1 Livestock and Lamingtons 7
2 The Gorgeous Easts 10
3 The Columnist Circus 15
4 A Family Feud 26
5 Going to Gigoomgan 35
6 The Roaring Twenties 42
7 The Journos' 53
8 The Golden Ball 61
9 A Militant Pacifist 72
10 Truth, the First Casualty 79
11 The 'Grand Old' 92
12 An Abominable Showman 103
13 Last of the Bohemians 113
14 Georgiana 121
15 Dr Balsam's Pub Crawl 132
16 Bodyline and All That 150
17 How Being 90 Ruined My Golf 160
Bibliography 166
Index 167

1
Livestock and Lamingtons

The cow just did not want to be photographed. 'That back tit is facing the wrong way,' its owner complained. 'And her feet are not regular.'

It was the Wauchope Show on the Mid-North Coast of New South Wales and I was photographing the Best Uddered Cow for *The Land* newspaper. The cow was a Jersey, usually the most placid and docile of animals, though the bulls can sometimes become treacherous and savage. This cow was camera-shy. She stamped her feet petulantly as the owner tried to position her teats and feet for the vital shot. He was peevish, too, conscious that the cow was humiliating him in front of the big crowd in the dairy breeds judging ring. But at last the teats and feet were manoeuvred into their desired place and the picture was taken. You must understand that udders and teats are things of great beauty and profit to dairymen and the Best Uddered award is highly prized. Judges like the four teats to be pointing towards the ground; marks are lost if they point sideways. Udders should have good milk veins and good front and rear attachments to the body. No wonder my photographs had to be meticulously posed.

As the crowds dispersed, I thought to myself: What on earth am I doing at the age of 81, manipulating a cow's udder at the Wauchope Show? What quirk of fate has led me to gallavant around the Australian countryside photographing cows, horses, goats, pigs, sheep, dogs, cats, pumpkins, lamingtons, show girls, show presidents, sideshows and all the other things that make up a country show?

Eleven years have passed since I photographed my last cow's udder. At the age of 92, I am now persuaded to answer my own question as to what transformed me into an udder-taking cameraman. The immediate explanation is that after thirteen years as public relations manager of the Royal Agricultural Society of New South Wales, I retired to Port Macquarie on the Mid-North Coast. *The Land* newspaper in Sydney engaged me to cover local North Coast shows with stories and photographs and this I did for about ten years. I learnt, as I have said, to arrange cows' udders in the proper position for photographing. I did not have to learn about country life because my heart has always been in the bush.

We built a house beside the then desolate Lighthouse Beach. We argued that we could always go back to Sydney after a couple of years if we did not like it. We haven't liked it sometimes but we're still here after more than twenty years. I figured that if I did not keep my brain active I would quickly vegetate in the Port Macquarie paradise, living a life of fishing, golfing and mucking around doing nothing else.

Well-meaning people have often told me I should write my autobiography. My answer has been that I would not dream of being so vain or presumptuous. Only people as important as politicians, cricketers, footballers, film stars, fallen entrepreneurs, royal butlers and valets are entitled to do that kind of thing. So this book is not an autobiography. It does not begin at the beginning and the end has not yet come. I've lived through most of the twentieth century but this book does not purport to be a serious survey of the period. It is a collection of random pieces about the weird and wonderful people who crossed my path and the many paths I crossed as a working journalist for more than 70 years. Many of the stories were strictly off the record at the time. It is full of cliches and split infinitives and a fig for grammarians. I believe some cliches are matchless in describing certain situations and events, while some unsplit infinitives read and sound pedantic and cumbersome. Modern poets are warned that the numerous poems and verses quoted in this book nearly all rhyme, which is against the trend of things.

My credentials can best be summed up in an entry in the 1962 *Who's Who in Australia*. You cannot buy your way into that publication but if the editor was the best man at your wedding you have a fair chance of making it. So Alec H. Chisholm, noted author and editor of the 1947 edition, saw to it that I made the grade. I lasted into the 1962 edition, after which a new editor blue-pencilled me into oblivion.

MANT, Gilbert Palmer, Author: son of late William Hall Mant, Syd.; *b.* July 20, 1902, Syd.; *ed.* Syd. Gram.; staff Syd. *Daily Telegraph* 1925–30; Reuters Newsagency Lond., Canada, Aust. 1931–42; 2/19 Battn 2nd A.I.F. 1940–41; Reuters war cpt. Malayan campaign 1941–42; State Publicity Censor and Dep.-Dir. Dept. Inform. S.A. 1942–45; feature writer and columnist Syd. *Sunday Sun* and *Sun-Herald* 1946–56; P.R. manager R.A.S. of N.S.W. since 1956; *publications*, Glamour Brat 1941, Grim Glory '42, You'll Be Sorry '44, Gone Tomorrow '48; *m* Mar. 7, 1933, Marion D., d. late Rev. H. Carroll, 1s. 1d.; *recreations*, sport, gardening; *club,* Journalists' (Syd.).

An update to 1994 would read as follows:

Married (2) 1963 Yvonne B., d. late C. Hawes; retired R.A.S. 1969; feature writer *The Land* 1972–84; *publications,* Buttercup 1969, The Big Show '72, Show People '85, A Town Called Port (with John Moyes) '86, Soldier Boy '92, The Singapore Surrender '92, A Cuckoo in the Bodyline Nest, '92; *clubs,* Journalists' (Syd.), R.S.L. (Port Macquarie).

You'd need a cluster of cliches to deal with that kind of life, although it's all in the day's work with dozens of other journalists. It's a wonder more of them do not record their experiences. My cast of characters includes princes, a Queen Mum, a Pope, a cardinal, prime ministers, sportsmen, artists, authors, stage and film stars, soldiers, heroes, villains, mountebanks and some fascinating nobodies.

I can't resist a modest sense of satisfaction in mentioning the publication at the age of 90 of three books in 1992, a record of some kind. *Soldier Boy* was based on a remarkable collection of letters to his parents by Gunner John Duffell, a seventeen-year-old Australian soldier in World War I. *The Singapore Surrender* was a reprint of two books I wrote, about the disastrous Malayan campaign of World War II. *A Cuckoo in the Bodyline Nest* was the story of the notorious Bodyline Tour of 1932–33, of which I am the sole surviving cricket-war correspondent. *Soldier Boy* was rejected by three publishers before a lucky introduction by Gerard Thompson to David Rosenberg of Kangaroo Press, Sydney. KP went on to publish all three books, with success in Australia and the U.K. I was honoured to have *Soldier Boy* launched by World War II heroine, Nancy Wake, and *Cuckoo* by cricket legend, Alan ('Davo') Davidson. My age was a publicity bonanza. NINETY-YEAR-OLD WRITES THREE BOOKS IN A YEAR! headlines led to radio and television appearances. It did not go to my head because I was pragmatic enough to know that being 90 was my chief achievement, not my literary ability.

When John Moyes wants to annoy me, he jokingly refers to me as a 'living legend', a hackneyed bit of journalese, if ever there was. Well, I suppose being a living legend is better than being a dead loss.

2
The Gorgeous Easts

Many years ago I read a book entitled *Such Interesting People* by an American whose name I cannot recall. The title came from trite remarks made to him about the 'interesting people' he must have met as a journalist. The book was hilariously funny about the zany exploits of American journalists themselves in the 1920s and 1930s rather than those people they were reporting. I resolved to collect the equally hilarious adventures of Australian newspapermen and artists of those wild bohemian days in Sydney and Melbourne but, sadly, I never got around to it. Some, however, remain unforgettable.

There was Hugh Buggy, generally accepted as the originator of the word 'bodyline' to describe the bowling during the notorious English cricket tour of Australia in 1932–33. The best story about Hugh is based on the fact that he mumbled rather than spoke and had to be reinforced with an interpreter named Owen Hoy when telephoning stories to his newspaper. One day (so the story goes) Hugh identified himself over the telephone to an important bureaucrat by mumbling 'Buggy here'. 'And bugger you too!' the angry bureaucrat replied.

Massey Stanley was a prominent political journalist, capable of unusual performances. He is said to have once ridden an elephant up the steps of the old Parliament House in Canberra for a wager, having waited for a circus to visit the capital with his steed. The idea was to introduce 'one white elephant to another'. The story is apocryphal but anyone knowing Massey would not have doubted his ability to perform the feat.

Massey and I were 1902-ers, born in the reign of that royal playboy, King Edward VII. We had a private ceremony when one of us would exclaim without warning 'Our King!'—at which we would be obliged instantly to take off our hats (we all wore them in those days) and stand stiffly to attention for a few seconds. We both lived in the eastern suburbs of Sydney and often went home from work on the same bus. Massey's fiendish delight was to catch me unawares and defenceless sitting in a crowded bus with a newspaper and some parcels on my lap. Suddenly there would be a loud cry of 'Our King!' resulting in acute embarrassment on my part and amazement among other passengers as I tried to extricate myself for the ceremony.

There were other giants of journalism, prone to untoward behaviour at times. They included Brian Penton, Cyril Pearl, Syd Deamer, Eric Baume, Hugh Dash, Brian Fitzpatrick, Alex Macdonald and, at a later date, Francis James. By far the most flamboyant was Stanley East.

Stan was born in New Zealand, the son of an Anglican clergyman, if not a bishop; and like so many other New Zealand journalists, then and since, he migrated to Australia where he became a highly competent sub-editor on Sydney daily newspapers. He was a man of many parts. At some period of his career in New Zealand he had been a professional actor, taking the stage name of Owen Hardy because, he explained, he was usually owen money and cracking hardy about it. 'Not a feather to fly with,' was the way he described his chronic impecuniosity.

The Easts—Stan, his wife Milba, Tibby, Kenneth and Kura—occupied several flats in Sydney, finally settling for a small cottage in a quiet (but not for long) street near Bondi Beach. My six months as what was loosely called 'The Lodger' in the Bondi cottage are months that I look back on with a kind of fascinated horror.

This was the end of the Roaring Twenties, the last fling, so to speak, before the coming of the Depression. Sydney was in the throes of all kinds of public scandals. The razor gangs were rampant at Darlinghurst and in the 'Dirty Half-Mile' of the then Woollcott Street, bohemia was at its wildest and wooliest. These were the days of Dulcie Deamer, Lennie Lower, Brian Fitzpatrick, Jack, Phil and Ray Lindsay, and scores of other mad artists, poets and writers. The first and last Artists' Ball was held in Sydney Town Hall, a bacchanalian orgy that defies description even in these supposedly unrestrained days.

The Easts' parties at Bondi became legendary and soon Stan became known as 'The Bishop of Bondi'. The parties had a habit of starting late on Saturday night after work and continuing throughout the weekend, with waves of different sets of guests engulfing the cottage with vast quantities of food and liquor. The cottage would practically burst at the seams, with beer in the laundry tubs, card-playing in the kitchen and general entertainment in the sitting-room.

As the night wore on, Stanley would revert to his theatrical days when he paced the boards in such epics as *A Message from Mars* and *East Lynne*. His biggest punch-line was from some melodrama I cannot now recall. You must imagine him, a heavily built, rotund man with saucer-like eyes behind the horn-rimmed spectacles, striding up and down the room, thumping his hand on his breast and declaiming, 'Thank God, sir, there are such men in England today!' to the thunderous applause of the audience.

He would be followed by an old JCW actor named Val Atkinson, whose favourite recitation was a lugubrious naval poem, something about 'a dirty old cruiser, a filthy old cruiser, built sometime before 1902 . . .'

The noise of all this, of course, was deafening, especially as the dawn approached. Once or twice the neighbours complained to the police. The police, when they arrived, were invited inside, and that was the end of that. So the neighbours also wearily adopted the attitude of if you can't beat them, join them. So did the milkman.

The chief source of music at the parties was a pianola with hundreds of classical, musical comedy and jazz rolls to be played. The milkman always made for the pianola, striking concert pianist attitudes and gestures as he operated the keyboard and pedals. The noise penetrated as far away as the pavilion on Bondi Beach.

I recall one terrifying aftermath of a party when I awoke at about 3 a.m. to hear Stan stamping around the cottage sharpening a large carving knife on a steel and shouting 'I'm going to do The Lodger in first!' I suppose it was cowardly of me to act as I did, but I was certain it was only a drink-inflamed Owen Hardy at his melodramatic best and he would not carve up his wife and children after doing in The Lodger. I fled the cottage in my pyjamas and somehow found my way to Jack and Kit Quayle's flat in Clovelly. Stan apologised profusely afterwards but it was some days before I was persuaded to return to Bondi.

It was said that Lennie Lower based his immortal Jack Gudgeon of *Here's Luck* on Stan East, but I do not know how true that was. The morose Lennie did come to one or two of the parties, and he must have picked up a lot of atmosphere for *Here's Luck*.

I, The Lodger, was given a memorable farewell party when I went to England in 1930. It lasted approximately six days, police, neighbours, milkman and all. A human safari of relations, journalists and artists carried me and my luggage up the gangway of the liner and dumped me in a cabin, there to recover consciousness days later, at Hobart, I think.

A year or so later Stan and Milba startled everyone by winning £25,000 in the Queensland Golden Casket, a vast sum of money in those days. Soon they, too, fled to England, presumably to escape a horde of spongers and/or creditors. In London, the Easts rented a mansion in St John's Wood, near Lord's cricket ground, and there Stan achieved one of his life-long ambitions. He hired a real live English butler. His name was Watson and he played his part to perfection.

My first encounter with Watson was a baffling experience. In chauffeur's uniform, he turned up at our West Kensington flat at the wheel of a magnificent car. He drove us to the house in St John's Wood, quickly opened the car door, then without a word sprinted away to the back of the house. In some bewilderment we walked to the front door and rang the bell. It was opened almost immediately by Watson, dressed this time in immaculate striped trousers and a frock coat.

'Please come inside, sir,' he murmured respectfully, 'the master is expecting you.'

The master, also playing his part to perfection, ushered me into his 'library' (another fulfilled ambition) and flung open the door of a cupboard containing every conceivable type of alcoholic beverage.

The parties at St John's Wood were frequent but not quite so hectic as those at Bondi. But I remember one in particular. For some reason I can't remember, a team of gigantic South African international footballers attended the party. In the early hours of the morning they suddenly burst out into their war cry, some kind of Boer song.

This greatly incensed Stan, who was a veteran of World War I. With bulging eyes, he bellowed angrily. 'I will not have German songs sung in my house! Out of the house, all of you, before I throw you out with my bare hands!' There was a stunned silence among the guests. Then, the South Africans meekly looked for their hats and coats and departed into the night. Watson showed them out.

When the Easts returned to Sydney, Watson came with them to an old stone house they bought by the river at Wiseman's Ferry. But the butler was out of his element there and I believe he eventually went back to England.

Apparently Stan's hatred of German songs never left him, for at the age of 55 he joined up again in the army at the outbreak of World War II and became a sergeant. The war over, he worked as a sub-editor of the Australian News and Information Bureau in Canberra until his retirement. After that, I understand he became librarian and official historian of the Canberra Club. They tell me Stan turned into a benign old gentleman, though subject to sudden outbursts of histrionics when he would cry out passionately, 'Thank God, sir, there are such men in England today!' Stan died at the age of 81. I wouldn't be surprised if Watson was waiting at the Pearly Gates to show him in. I remember him affectionately as a good friend and a kindly landlord, though hot-tempered and unpredictable in his cups. He was a relic of a light-hearted, unregimented but brilliantly individualistic style of Sydney journalism that is never likely to return.

Sydney's brilliant humourist and columnist, Ross Campbell, contributed a memoir in *Nation Review* magazine after Stan's death:

> My only meeting with that legendary figure was in 1929, during the Wiseman's Ferry period. I was in a party of people who drove up from Sydney to spend an evening at the East manor. As we approached the house I was shown a spot where a relation had driven a brand-new car of Stan East's into the Hawkesbury, from which it was never retrieved.
>
> Stan received us cordially and poured drinks for us in his book-lined study. While doing this he peered frowningly at a set of the *Encyclopaedia Britannica*. Then he put his fingers in his mouth and gave a loud whistle, and shouted 'General Jackson!' A young man, who I think was one of the family, came into the room.

Stan pointed a finger at him and said, 'General Jackson, you've pawned another volume of the Encyclopaedia! Lord to Mumps is missing!'

Memories of the rest of the evening are blurred. I know there was a long game of poker during which several people were accused of cheating, a bottle was thrown, and somebody ran out and hid in a cupboard. We were driven out of the house at about 4 a.m. by a lady brandishing a rifle.

The evening was an unforgettable glimpse of a truly magnificent Bohemian establishment of the old inter-war school. But how Gilbert Mant adjusted himself to an extended period as a lodger with the Gorgeous Easts is beyond my grasp. He must be made of sterner stuff than I am.

No doubt there are plenty of 'characters' in journalism today but I fancy they are kept in tight rein by their computerised bosses. The black-and-white artists, I suspect, are as mad as ever.

3

The Columnist Circus

'My uncle, the fifth Lord Balsam, committed a ghastly contretemps at Balsam Castle one Christmas,' remarked my friend, Dr F. ('Call me Friar') Balsam, apropos of nothing.

The doctor flung open the surgery cupboard and poured out two slugs of pure (for medicinal purposes only) alcohol before continuing his story.

'Lord Balsam, who was pretty full at the time, was playing the part of Santa Claus and went down the chimney of the maids' bedroom at midnight instead of Lady Balsam's.'

'I bet that taught the old boy a lesson,' I murmured.

'Yes, indeed,' replied the doctor, with a slight leer. 'He made exactly the same mistake the following Christmas.'

Dr Balsam was the tailpiece and safety valve of my twenty years as a weekly newspaper columnist with the Sydney *Sunday Sun, Sun-Herald, Land, Coastwatch* and *North Coast Magazine*. Balsam was not everybody's cup of pure (for medicinal purposes only) tea but its deliberate deadpan type of humour appeared to amuse a lot of people. I have reason to believe that some people thought the doctor was a real person and I know that many members of the medical profession did not approve of such a disreputable specimen in their cult. But not my much beloved Vaucluse GP, Dr Colin Love (he married a Miss Bliss). Dr Love always inquired kindly after Dr Balsam when I visited him for a consultation. I must have produced more than 1,000 Balsam jokes, some taking hours to concoct. How daily comic strip artists keep up their gags is beyond me; I found it very hard work. Even today, so many years later, I am occasionally introduced to a stranger who will murmur, 'for medicinal purposes only'.

I can modestly claim to have been the first of a new rash of columnists in the Sydney press after World War II. My first full-page broadsheet column, 'The Way I See It', appeared in the *Sunday Sun* in October 1945 and continued without a break for thirteen years, spilling over into the *Sun-Herald* when the *Sunday Sun* was sold to Fairfax. Those years were among the most rewarding and enjoyable years of my journalistic life. My column evolved into a strange mixture of serious comment on issues of the day, with lighter gossip and Dr Balsam. Tom Gurr, my editor-in-chief, gave me a fairly free hand on comment. 'I'll make you a publicist, not a columnist,' he used to say. But Tom had a Black List and the whole paper had to conform to it. For instance, no comment on the price of gas in Sydney without reference to Sir John Butters, chairman of our owners, Associated Newspapers. You see, Sir John was also chairman of the Australian Gas Light Company. There was also a ban on certain individuals who had sinned in some way. In these days of republican–monarchist debate, it is interesting to note that there was still a general ban on anything likely to harm or bring the monarchy into disrespect. It was a voluntary self-imposed censorship by the Australian press, except for some scurrilous 'yellow press' publications. The war was only just over and there was still a euphoria of patriotism and victory in the air. The monarchy was sacrosanct. It would have been unthinkable to publish anything derogatory to the Throne, such as scandals of the Fergie or Diana kind. Any such stories would have been spiked immediately.

I needed to identify my column with some kind of a gimmick so I created Dr F. ('Call me Friar') Balsam. I confess freely that the catalyst was Dr Strabismus (whom God preserve) of Utrecht, an eccentric inventor, the brainchild of the incomparable J.B. Morton of the London *Daily Express*. Morton wrote his witty and satirical column, 'By the Way', for more than 40 years under the pseudonym of Beachcomber. It was noted for outrageous parodies, lampoons and occasional 'Talks with my Stomach'. His cast of characters included the rakish Captain de Courcy Fulenough, and Mr Justice Cocklecarrot, who was plagued by twelve red-bearded dwarfs. Politician Arthur Fadden gave me the idea of 'Call me Friar'. Fadden was an egalitarian sort of chap who got on particularly well with journalists. He urged them to 'Call me Artie' and it became a jocular subject with political writers and cartoonists. During the political turmoil in the early World War II years, Artie became Prime Minister of Australia from August to October 1941. The 'Call me Arties' were less frequent after he became Sir Arthur Fadden in 1951.

The Balsam jokes were sometimes as obscure as a cryptic crossword and I know that they fell flat on many readers. But I did not mind so long as a select few got a laugh out of them. Take this one, the solution of which can be found on page 166:

'I see that ear-piercing is the latest craze among Sydney women,' I remarked to my friend, Dr F. ('Call me Friar') Balsam.

'Yes, indeed,' said Dr Balsam. 'It reminds me of a strange ear-piercing operation I performed many years ago as a young doctor in Gilgandra.

'My patient was a heavily-built man with exceptionally large ears and I had great difficulty in performing the operation with my usual instruments. At last I had a brainwave and successfully pierced his ears with a vegetable knife.'

'What a bizarre affair,' I exclaimed.

'Not really,' said the doctor, with a bit of a smirk. 'You see, he was the local heavyweight boxing champion.'

The rash of Sydney columnists really broke out after the first appearance of David McNicoll's 'Town Talk' on the front page of the *Daily Telegraph* on 4 February 1946. It was a very well-informed column of people and events on American lines and was often used to break major hard news stories. Frank Packer had planned such a column for a long time and had sent McNicoll to the U.S. to get some hints from Walter Winchell, Drew Thompson and other American columnists. David McNicoll, in his eightieth year as I write, is now the doyen of them all, writing a weekly column in *The Bulletin* and causing a lot of controversy at times. Robert ('Buzz') Kennedy survived with a column in the *Weekend Australian* until his retirement in 1994.

The *Telegraph*'s lead was soon followed by the *Sun*, which launched Jim Macdougall who was to become a familiar figure on the Sydney scene with a whimsical touch to his pen and with a flower in his buttonhole. Jim columnized for more than 40 years under various managements before retiring in his nineties. The columnist circus grew with the addition of the *Daily Mirror*'s fictional 'Sydney Mann' and 'Granny' of the *Sydney Morning Herald*'s Column 8. The first 'Sydney Mann' was the talented Murray Sayle, who went on to make a name for himself in London and now operates from Tokyo as an international authority on Japan. The first 'Granny' was the brilliant Syd Deamer. (The *Herald* later dropped its 'Granny' image as not befitting one of the world's great modern newspapers.)

Most of the columnists were simply out to entertain, not to take up lost causes. Each one had his own different style. The telephone of Column 8's secretary ran hot with delightful stories from the suburbs, chiefly the North Shore. 'Granny' was adored by middle-class dowagers, not always aware of the witty and sometimes caustic interpolations Syd Deamer gave their messages about pet dogs and cats, flower gardens and other trivia. Jim Macdougall also had to have a full-time secretary to cope with the hundreds of people wanting to get their names in the paper or fly various kites in the business or entertainment world.

Columnists of the time were the darlings of the public relations firms, the swanky restaurants and nightclubs (these were the effervescent days of Romano's and Princes), the theatre and film publicity men and women. Week after week the same columnist circus would congregate at plush hotels to attend what was loosely described as a 'press conference' with visiting firemen, film and stage stars, authors, politicians, businessmen launching new products, sportsmen and various types of ratbags. The same old food, the same old drinks, the same old hand-outs. The cynics talked about 'free food, free drinks and the free "press".' Some of the plugs became so blatant that the newspaper proprietors clamped down on the use of names. Frank Packer was quoted as saying: 'If they want the names of their products mentioned, tell them to bloody well pay for an advertisement like everyone else.'

If there was any substantial payola attached to being a columnist in those golden days, it did not come my way. The most dangerous temptation was the opportunity to be on the 'free list' of a few theatres and restaurants. Of more material gifts, I still have only a cigarette box, shaped like a piano, given to about 50 ladies and gentlemen of the press at a nightclub function by Winifred Atwell, a very nice person in her own right. I've not much else to show in the way of payola. I took the cigarette box along to show Winnie when she performed at Port Macquarie shortly before her death. She was a warm-hearted woman and a great artist.

There's no doubt the old gossip columns were popular and suited the mood of the day; the telephone calls and the big fan mail proved it. An all-star international cast passed constantly through the 'press conferences'. The columnists quizzed, dissected and wrote their crisp paragraphs about Katharine Hepburn, H.G. Wells, Oscar Hammerstein, Vice-President Richard Nixon, Chico Marx, Randolph Churchill, the young Shirley Bassey, Frank Sinatra, Johnny Ray, Lord Attlee, Louis Armstrong, Nat King Cole, Field Marshal Montgomery, Vera Lynn and a host of others. I loved meeting these giants of their professions, as well as the go-getters, the phonies and the con-men. It all made wonderful copy.

The most vital person I ever met at these shows was American actress, Katharine Hepburn. Although I spoke with her for only about ten minutes, the memory is with me still. The blue flame of her eyes, the wit, the intelligence, the intense interest in what you had to say. Hepburn came to Australia to do Shakespeare with Bobby Helpmann. Another woman with a more tigerish magnetism was Shirley Bassey. I first met her when she came from England in her teens with a theatrical company. You could tell at once that she was something special. Bassey, in her later prime, did not just hold an audience, she gripped it so tightly with her marvellous voice and gestures that when she released them at the end of her song, they exploded into wild applause, almost in relief from a delicious tension. (At the age of 57, Bassey performed at the Sydney Hilton Hotel in March this year to a rave notice by *Sydney Morning Herald* critic, Bruce Elder. 'Bassey still has a fabulous voice, a great stage presence and enough excellent material to have the audience spontaneously hollering for more', he wrote.) Satchmo Armstrong took me aside to stress the importance of regular bowel movements. He assured me that copious doses of cascara night and morning was the key to physical well-being, though he phrased it in rather coarser language. 'Man,' he said, 'cascara is the elixir of life.' If it was cascara that inspired that magic trumpet and strangely exciting gravelly voice, then good luck to it. Which reminds me that Dr Balsam once had to diagnose a stomach complaint under the most difficult of circumstances.

'I was captured by cannibals in Darkest Africa while acting as medical officer to an expedition searching for a prehistoric beast known as the Great Mumbo-Jumbo,' said Dr Balsam, downing a double slug of pure (for medicinal purposes only) alcohol.

'Fortunately for me,' went on the doctor, as the fiery liquid coursed through his veins, 'the local witch-doctor had been unable to cure the cannibal chief's severe abdominal pains and I was promised my life if I could ease his agony.'

'What on earth did you prescribe?' I asked breathlessly.

'I advised him to stay off meat for a while,' replied Dr Balsam, with a cannibalistic smirk.

One thing the column taught me was the rather frightening gullibility of some newspaper readers. On two notable occasions, tongue-in-cheek leg-pulls were taken seriously. The first leg-pull centred around England's identical cricketing twins, Alec and Eric Bedser, in the 1940s. Alec was a star bowler, one of the few to tame Don Bradman at times, while Eric was of lesser ability. I manufactured a 'diabolical plot' by the Marylebone Cricket Club, England's cricket body, to send Alec to Australia secretly in disguise before the arrival of the official Test team which would include Eric. Eric's mediocre performances in minor matches would lull the Australians into a false sense of security and Alec would be switched for him in the Tests. Some idiot cabled this nonsense to London where the sensational *Daily Mirror* headlined it:

M.C.C. SWITCHED TWINS IN 'DIABOLICAL' PLOT, AUSSIE PAPER 'REVEALS'

A deep and diabolical plot to fool the Australian Cricket public was worked out by the pundits of the MCC in their St John's Wood sanctum before they sent the English team on tour.

So alleges Sydney *Sunday Sun* columnist Gilbert Mant, who maintains that Alec Bedser, the Surrey bowler now touring with the MCC team, is not Alec at all but Eric, his slightly less successful twin brother who was not chosen for the tour.

'The MCC are a diabolical clever collection of English sportsmen,' writes Mant.

'The whole thing is an elaborate plot and to my mind there is no doubt that the twins are being switched for the Tests.'

Asked to comment on the columnist's 'revelation', Mr A.F. Davey, secretary of Surrey County Cricket Club, told the Daily Mirror: 'It's too damn silly for words.'

There was uproar. The Australian Cricket Board of Control assured the MCC that it did not go along with the story. Letters of protest poured in on me from the strangest places. The entire ship's company of a Royal Navy cruiser based in Hong Kong expressed disgust over my allegations.

It should have taught me a lesson, but it didn't. My second leg-pull was based on a true story of World War II in 1943, just before the Allied invasion of Sicily and Italy. A 'double' of Field Marshal Montgomery was sent to Gibraltar to make the Germans believe the invasion was planned for southern France. The ruse inspired a best-selling book and a film. Montgomery visited Australia after the war and I attended his press conference at Victoria Barracks in Sydney. Afterwards I told my readers not to be fooled. It wasn't Monty at all, it was his celebrated double. Nobody in their right minds will believe this, I thought. But many did. In fact I received a serious letter of correction from a colonel of Military Intelligence at the barracks, assuring me that it had been the 'real' Monty. After that, I gave up leg-pulling, realising that leg-pulls on sensitive subjects such as health, religion and ethics could create serious repercussions to gullible readers. Orson Welles also gave up leg-pulls after he caused a nation-wide panic in America in 1935 by broadcasting a supposed invasion of Earth by Martians. Believing everything you 'read in the papers' is a dangerous and unwise pursuit, though not as bad in Australia as in Britain and America.

'The Way I See It' dealt with serious subjects, too. I received a big mail each week, both complimentary and downright abusive. If the mail flagged, I had only to comment on something religious and it would increase immediately. Then would come the anonymous letters, some too filthy to repeat. It was sickening to encounter such violent bigotry and hatred in the name of the Almighty.

There was one more friendly reaction, however, to a piece I wrote criticising 'Archbishops who live in their palaces while many of their parishioners live in abject poverty'. I can't remember what prompted the attack but, as an Anglican, I was referring to the Archbishop of Canterbury and his Lambeth Palace in London. Next thing, I had a telephone call from St Mary's Cathedral inviting me to have morning tea with His Eminence Cardinal Gilroy, Roman Catholic Archbishop of Sydney. I knew at once what had happened. The Cardinal had assumed that I was referring to him and his 'palace' at Manly which was, in fact, a very spartan Catholic seminary. I was only too keen to explain the mistake as I held the Cardinal in great regard. 'Bluey' Gilroy, as he was affectionately known to all denominations, was a fair dinkum Aussie cardinal, the first Australian ever appointed by the Pope. Before studying for the priesthood, he served with the Naval Wireless Transport Service in World War I. He saw the landing at Gallipoli in April 1915 from the deck of the transport *Hessen*. I was pretty nervous at meeting a cardinal but the hour-long talk was a delight and he accepted my explanation at once. Somebody brought in tea and scones and we talked on a variety of subjects in a large and very plainly furnished room. In the course of the conversation, I confessed that I tried to lead a Christian life but was not a regular churchgoer as I could not accept some of the fundamental dogma of my church. I thought he looked at me thoughtfully and hopefully for a moment or two. I think he then realised I was a lost sinner but nevertheless when we shook hands at parting, he pressed a small book of Catechism into my hand. I still have it but have not yet repented. Cardinal Gilroy (later knighted by the Queen as Sir Norman Gilroy) never forgot me. Over the years when we attended the same official functions in our various capacities, he always flashed me a toothy smile (he was fitted with rather prominent false teeth—now delicately called dentures in the same way as lavatories are called toilets).

Dame Mary Gilmore bombarded me with letters. Socialist poetess, writer and passionate defender of lost causes, she could be autocratic at times but at heart was a caring woman and I loved her. As well as receiving her letters, I often visited her in her flat at Kings Cross before it became a sleazy, sex-shop district. Country-born Mary edited the women's pages of *The Worker* for 23 years. They must have had large families in those days as one of her cookery recipes began with the words, 'Take one whole sheep...' Once in my column I misquoted a poem she wrote about llamas as follows:

> As he passed along a chasm he chanced to meet a yak
> Who had a sneezing fit and blew him off the track.

'For two pins,' wrote Dame Mary, 'I would come in and bash you! I nearly skinned both knees and broke my (literary) back over the last two lines. "Spasm, man, not fit!"' I kept bundles of her letters and passed them on to Dymphna Cusack, who was collecting them for the National Library in Canberra.

Whenever I am in Sydney, I make a pilgrimage to the Art Gallery of New South Wales to sit and look at Dobell's portrait of her. There's twenty dollars of my money in it as it was commissioned with public money by the Australian Book Society. The portrait caused nearly as much controversy as Dobell's one of Joshua Smith. It may look distorted to some eyes, but it *is* Mary Gilmore, not only in likeness but in its inner character portrayed by a painter of rare genius. Mary herself defended Dobell with these words:

> It is the painter and not the sitter who really counts. The great galleries of the world proves this. As an example, take *The Last Supper* by da Vinci. Who cares tuppence for the sitters? You do not even ask their names or what they were. I will mention only one other thing. Of course I know that, measured by the callipers, this portrait of me calls for adverse criticism. But there is another aspect by which to judge portraiture. No one is born without ancestors. At my first sight of this portrait, for one second I saw my father looking at me. Then the looker disappeared and the painting was there. After the unveiling (in 1957) a lady whom I had not earlier known came to see me. She said: 'When I put my hand over the lower part of the face the upper part was my grandmother Mackinnon'. To emphasise her point she said that twice. Her grandmother Mackinnon was my father's niece and my first cousin. If a portrait carries in it the likeness of one's

own people, however little, and whom the painter has never seen, that is real portraiture. If it does not do this it is merely camera. Our ancestors in us are not there.

I feel that I never made a more satisfying investment than my twenty dollars in the Gilmore portrait. I met Bill Dobell on a number of occasions but never got to know him well. He was a gentle, supersensitive man, easy to feel hurt.

North Coast-born Ion Idriess was another writer who crossed my path in my columnist days. His books about Australia and the islands have recently made a big comeback, after years of neglect. Idriess wrote nearly 50 books with a combined sale approaching a million copies. They included such bestsellers as *Lasseter's Last Ride, Flynn of the Inland, The Drums of Mer, Gold Dust and Ashes* and *The Cattle King*, now reissued in two volumes by Angus & Robertson.

I first met Idriess in the 1920s when he was peddling his stories and paragraphs to Sydney newspapers and magazines and having a pretty thin time of it. His friends called him 'Jack' for no apparent reason.

A gnome-like but rugged little man of Welsh extraction, he had led a wandering life across Australia—prospecting, station work, trochus-selling, pearling, cable-laying, sandalwood getting and what have you. After his break to become Australia's bestselling author, he was adopted by Angus & Robertson and given a room in their Sydney headquarters. There he would quickly write and write and write with a stubby pencil, revising his work three times and handing it to a typist. He was also a fanatical advocate of the Bradfield Plan to divert the waters of North Queensland over the Great Dividing Range and irrigate the Dead Heart of Australia. I wrote about Jack Idriess in my column, adding that he was a convivial fellow, fond of a drink at the nearby St James Hotel and always trying to pick winners at the races. Jack reported that in the week following the article, he received dozens of letters, including two from sly-grog sellers and eight from people offering to sell him 'infallible' betting systems. Jack commented: 'The part that intrigues me about infallible betting systems is what happens to the infallibility when the horse drops dead or breaks its neck at the last hurdle . . . that's what's happened to some of the horses I've backed.'

The biggest fan mail I ever received came when I went to the defence of Major Charles Cousens at the end of World War II in a case unprecedented in Australian legal history. To me, the Cousens case was another Dreyfus affair and I will always believe he was crucified by the political and military hierarchy. Before the war Cousens had been one of Australia's most popular radio announcers and the Japanese knew this when he was captured with other Australian troops at the fall of Singapore in February 1942. They took him under duress to Japan and he broadcast and wrote scripts for Radio Tokyo for the remainder of the war. At war's end he was arrested on General Douglas MacArthur's orders and charged with high treason in Australia. The prosecution argued he was a traitor who collaborated with the Japanese, likening him to 'Lord Haw Haw' the traitor who broadcast for the Germans. Cousens maintained he was a prisoner of war, forced to cooperate with the Japanese under threat of torture or death. He claimed that he had tried to sabotage Japanese propaganda and to broadcast information of value to the Allies. Many saw no difference between the actions of Cousens and those of 15,000 other Australian POWs, who built railways, roads and airfields for the Japanese under similar death threats. The high treason case against Cousens was dropped but a vindictive military Establishment stripped him of his commission and entitlements. He returned to radio and television, but his life was ruined and he died at the age of 60, of a broken heart, I think.

The Cousens trial created immense interest and controversy. I received hundreds of letters of support for my attacks on the federal government and military authorities for keeping Cousens waiting for more than a year before putting him on trial. Cousens paid a heavy mental and physical price from such a cruel delay of justice. It is true that I had a personal interest in 'Bill' Cousens, as he was known to his friends. I knew him before the war and served with him in the same battalion, 2/19th Battalion AIF. I know to this day that such a man could never have been a traitor to his country. Ivan Chapman has written a brilliant examination of this tragic case in *Tokyo Calling* (Hale & Iremonger).

The chief prosecutor at the Cousens trial was W.R. (Bill) Dovey, KC, a big and somewhat fearsome-looking man with a monocle, later to become a judge of the Supreme Court of New South Wales. I had locked horns the previous year with Dovey in my column during an inquiry into another controversial figure of the ill-fated Malayan campaign. Lieutenant-General H. Gordon Bennett, commander of the Australian forces, did not have to wait as long as Cousens for investigation. Bennett had escaped from Singapore, believing he should return to Australia to give first-hand reports on Japanese jungle tactics and fighting ability. He was snubbed by the military Establishment on his return and not given an overseas command for the rest of the war.

In November 1945 Mr Justice Ligertwood presided over a Royal Commission to enquire into the circumstances of Bennett's escape. Much of the argument centred on whether the terms of the cease-fire at Singapore requiring the troops to remain in their positions was a Japanese order directed to prisoners of war. After sitting for three weeks, Ligertwood found that in his opinion Bennett was not justified in relinquishing his command and leaving Singapore, but that his decision to escape was 'inspired by the belief that he was acting in the best interests of his country'. It was not the happiest of decisions for Bennett and controversy over his escape still lingers among members of the 8th Division. Dovey, KC, had been appointed as assistant commissioner to Ligertwood and it seemed to me that he was adopting a bullying and antagonistic attitude towards Bennett during the course of the trial. I said so in my column, suggesting that he was acting more like a prosecutor than an assistant commissioner. Well, I still tremble over the stinging letter I received from Dovey, KC. I could see him furiously adjusting his monocle as he tore strips off 'ignorant, meddlesome journalists', especially columnists, and general abuse of the press. It was an imprudent letter for an eminent advocate to write and he delivered himself into my hands when he ended it with, 'I am well aware that you will not print a word of this letter in your precious column'. Not print it! I printed every word of it and it made him look a little foolish. There was to be a rather comic sequel to this affair about ten years later during a cricket match at Randwick Racecourse, which I shall relate in another chapter.

The columnist years were enjoyable and rewarding. I tried to write with sincerity but was often hurt by criticism. Some cynics sneered that I was the 'voice of suburbia', to which I replied that there were a lot of readers and decent people in the suburbs. A little man named Frank Browne once gave me an awful roasting. Browne was an ultra-right-wing journalist who circulated a private weekly newsletter from Canberra with inside political, business and other information. he certainly had good contacts and many of his revelations were much too hot and defamatory to be handled by newspapers.

Frank Browne, once a professional pugilist, achieved fame in 1960 when he laid out the young Kerry Packer with a right hook, or something, during the fisticuffs battle for the control of Francis James' *Anglican* newspaper printery.

For some reason I cannot remember, I criticised General Franco, dictator of Spain, with a climatic 'Shake hands with Franco? I'd sooner shake hands with a snake'. Browne took to me as if I was a boa constrictor, accusing me of being a rabid Communist in disguise spreading pinkish leftist propaganda, etc., etc., etc. Now, I'm not a Communist, nor a Fascist, nor any ist. I'm so much middle-of-the-road that it's painful. There's no place for my sort in the political arena. I'm of the Don Chipp–Ted Mack variety. I voted Democrat for some time, then left them when Senator Janet Powell went to Iraq, which may sound a bit anachronistic. I may yet go back because of the charisma and commonsense of Senator Cheryl Kernot.

The criticism that really hurt me most came when I wrote a light-hearted novel, *Gone Tomorrow* (Angus & Robertson) in 1948. A book reviewer in the ABC commented: 'It comes as rather a shock to find that Gilbert Mant, who writes a pompous column in a Sunday newspaper, has written a novella of the most frippery nature'. He then proceeded to demolish it as being trite and unfunny. I did not mind the book being rubbished; it was the 'pompous' that hurt. So help me, I can't stand pomposity and hope it doesn't show up in this book. I've never ever had any tickets on myself.

Dr Balsam was available for weekly consultations for thirteen consecutive years, his surgery cupboard containing ample supplies of pure (for medicinal purposes only) alcohol. I remember particularly the last Christmas of our association. He was in one of his jolliest moods, having consumed a number of what he described as 'tiddlies' with his patients.

'It reminds me,' he said, 'of the Yuletides I spent as a child at Balsam Castle.

'My dipsomaniac aunt, the fifth Lady Balsam, used to take the whole staff and us children to the battlements and give us each a glass of cider. After it was drunk, we hurled the glasses into the moat. After years of this, the moat was well laced with broken glass.

'It resulted in the grisly murder of the Balsam butler. The fourth footman hated the butler so much that one Christmas Eve he dived into the moat, brought up some broken glass and gave it to the butler as crushed ice in a glass of whisky.'

'Wait a moment, doctor,' I said. 'Why did he have to go to all the trouble of diving into the moat when he could have broken up some glass in the pantry?'

Dr Balsam looked at me in annoyance. Then he gave a good-natured hiccough.

'A merry Christmas,' he drooled. 'I'll get you a whisky and water.'

'The same to you, doctor,' I said, adding 'No ice in mine.'

Dr Balsam as seen by the artist Lahm.

4

A Family Feud

There was an ostrich farm at Vaucluse and an emu behind a tall wire fence in Ocean Avenue, Double Bay, when I was born in Darling Point in 1902.

For those unfamiliar with Sydney, Vaucluse is a narrow isthmus between Sydney Harbour and the Pacific Ocean. Today it is tightly packed with the mansions and apartments of millionaires and millionairesses. The only hiding place for an ostrich would be to stick his head in the sands of nearby Watsons Bay. The same goes for Double Bay, sometimes known as Double Pay, and Bellevue Hill, the tycoon belt of Kerry Packer & Co. There was a dairy farm on the hill when I was a boy, and Chinese vegetable gardens in Rose Bay and lawn tennis courts in Double Bay. Today these places are the homes of rich old and young yuppies. The old Australian aristocracy ran a rigid establishment in those days. Only their names rated a mention in the 'society' notes; there was no place for any family tainted by trade or commerce, whatever their wealth. The old aristocracy are still in Sydney but seldom appear in the 'social notes', not wanting to be seen in such company, I presume. The lone emu in Ocean Avenue used to frighten the life out of me as a child as it charged up and down its enclosure, waving its long neck in anger and grunting and glaring at passers-by. I have no idea why the emu was there or what was its purpose in life except to frighten small boys.

My own little world was a short cul-de-sac called Marathon Avenue. It was on the top of a steep slope with access below to William Street, Double Bay, by the 76 steps of Breakneck Steps. These were the days of gaslight and hansom cabs. There were no refrigerators and the iceman cometh twice a week with great blocks of ice which he carried on his shoulder into the house, putting them into our ice chest with a pair of steel claws. Once a week the egg-and-butter man would call with fresh farm eggs in a basket. The local grocers, Mr Turner or Mr Hooey, would take orders in the morning and deliver the next day. All these tradesmen would linger for a friendly chat. As a foretaste of the multicultural Australian days to come, I remember periodic visits to the neighbourhood by an Italian organ-grinder and his monkey, a German band and an aged and wrinkled Chinese gardener carrying his vegetables across his shoulders with a bamboo pole. There was always a jar of ginger from him at Christmas time. We regarded these people as aliens from outer space in our strictly Anglo-Saxon world.

Next-door neighbours on the eastern side were the Allens, whose son of my age, George Oswald Browning Allen, was to become famous as Gubby Allen and link us together 30 years later during the Bodyline Cricket War of 1932–33. Opposite were the Merrivales, whose child was another George and addicted to straying far afield from the family mansion at the top of Breakneck Steps. I still recall the cries of 'Geor-gie! . . . Geor-gie!' from his frantic parents as darkness set in with no sign of him. George Merrivale was to become an ebullient and popular Sydney man-about-town.

Further up the avenue lived Valerie, a pretty child whose parents were prominent members of Sydney high society. I was about five at the time and she was five years older. Valerie always seemed to be following me around with a disturbing sort of huntress look about her and one day I learnt what it was all about. She enticed me into some bushes in her garden ostensibly to play hide-and-seek and propositioned me with a 'You show me yours and I'll show you mine' advance. She apparently had an obsessive desire to see what Adrian Mole would describe as my 'thing'. I put up some resistance but finally succumbed to her entreaties. I never got to see hers because I hadn't the slightest interest in it. Valerie's family moved to the North Shore shortly after this encounter and I never saw her again until more than 40 years later. Then we re-met at an official function in London. Valerie was married to an admiral in the Royal Navy. 'You must meet Gilbert,' they said. 'He comes from Sydney, too! Perhaps you've seen something of each other before?' Valerie and I looked each other straight in the eyes and neither of us blinked an eyelid. I laughed to myself afterwards and have often wondered if she remembered. I'm sure she did and probably laughed, too, despite being an admiral's wife. Come to think of it, I have a vague recollection that my young nursemaid, Alice, was also unduly interested in my thing, especially at bath times. I should emphasise, however, that neither of these two young ladies ever attempted to sexually molest me.

I have only one clear recollection of my father, 'Billy' Mant, and it is a painful one. We were a happy family so it was not unhappiness that caused me to 'run away' from home at about the age of six. Perhaps I was influenced by the runaway exploits of Georgie Merrivale. I ran away with another small boy from a neighbouring home but only as far as across the street down into a deep scrubby gully that ran the length of Marathon Avenue. When darkness fell and there were shouts of 'Gilbert!' and 'Charlie!' and other goings-on we were too terrified of the consequence to give ourselves up. Eventually cold, hunger and thirst prompted our surrender late in the night. We emerged sheepishly from the gully to face the warmth to come. I learnt later that my father had toured as far as Randwick and Rushcutters Bay in a hansom cab in search of his missing son. I got the thrashing I deserved.

If childhood memories of my father are only shadowy, they are much more vivid about my mother. I remember particularly occasions when she was going out to parties or official functions and would come upstairs to say goodnight to me. I thought this beautiful young woman in stylish evening dress was a princess as she bent over to kiss me. She was small and slender with opalescent eyes and two fringe curls of her dark hair lying over her forehead. She was one of the beauties of Sydney. A striking portrait of her when she was 26 by Mary Stoddard, a noted New Zealand artist, painted in 1899, still graces our sitting room in Port Macquarie. The portrait was exhibited, on loan for some years in the Art Gallery of New South Wales. It would not have much chance of getting in there nowadays as it would be contemptuously banished to the basement as 'photographic art'. It's just too much like her. I remember dinner parties at Marathon Avenue with people coming and going in hansom cabs. Among the guests were my father's fellow solicitor and close friend, A.B. ('Banjo') Paterson. He became my brother John's godfather and I have a signed first edition of *The Man from Snowy River and Other Verses*, published by Angus & Robertson in 1895, he gave my father. There would be much lively conversation and laughter and the clinking of wine glasses on these occasions. Sometimes after dinner there would be music around the piano. Mother had a sweet soprano voice and once sang to a capacity audience in Sydney Town Hall at a charity concert. My favourite was the 'Kashmiri Love Song' by Lawrence Hope (Adela Florence Nicolson):

Pale hands I loved beside the Shalimar,
Where are you now? Who lies beneath your spell? . . .

My father, William Hall (Billy) Mant was a prosecutor with the Crown Law Office in Sydney and took a prominent part in the celebrated Dean case in 1895. The Dean case was one of the most sensational cases and trials in Australian legal history. Dean, a Sydney ferry-master, poisoned his wife and confessed his crime to his solicitor, Richard Meagher, who kept the confession to himself and continued to defend his client. Meagher was struck off as a solicitor but made an extraordinary return to public life. He was eventually reinstated and became Lord Mayor of Sydney. Dean was condemned to death for murder, then pardoned and released after a Royal Commission, and later convicted of perjury, serving fourteen years in prison.

My father's early death remains somewhat of a mystery to me, though not a sinister one. My mother never talked about it and I heard various versions over the years. From all accounts, the marriage was a happy and socially exciting one. Billy appears to have been a bit of a playboy, proud to have such a beautiful and vivacious woman at his side. He was a keen racegoer and a member of the Australian Club and the Australian Jockey Club. He was extremely popular in social, sporting and legal circles. It all came to an end when he was suddenly taken ill early in 1910. He was granted extended leave from the Crown Law Office and went to recuperate in hospital in the Maryborough district of Queensland, founding home of the original Australian branch of the Mant family. George Mant, my grandfather, had settled there as a nineteen-year-old from England in 1856 to become one of Queensland's noted graziers and pastoralists.

Three months later, Billy Mant was dead at the age of 41. It was said to have been caused by asthma. A contemporary newspaper account of his death attributed it to a 'sharp attack of internal haemorrhage'. He was buried in the Anglican cemetery at Maryborough. Mother was 37. This is where the story takes on an element of mini-series drama.

The old Hampshire family of Mant derived their name from the French Mantes who went to England with William the Conqueror in 1066. There is a French town of Mantes and my grand-daughter, Jennifer Brown, on a recent working holiday in England, came upon a Mant Lane in the cathedral city of Winchester. George Mant was the son of George Joseph Mant, a colonel in the British Army stationed in India. George, Jnr, was born in Bombay in 1837 and went to Ireland and England with the regiment as a child. He was educated at Brighton Public School and the Agricultural College at Cirencester. He sailed to Australia in 1856 to join his uncle, Peter Dalgairns Anderson, and his partner, George Farquharson Leslie, at Gigoomgan, a large cattle station named after Aboriginal words for a 'place of white cockatoos'. Two years later, the new chum had so easily adapted to Australian conditions that he was admitted to the Anderson–Leslie partnership. By 1860 various other large leases had been consolidated into an area of some 107 square miles (27,682 hectares) at an annual rental of £186 9s. 0d. ($373). On 1 July 1866, a muster yielded 14,066 head of cattle.

In 1860, Peter Anderson took his bride, Ellen Palmer, to Gigoomgan. The following year George Mant established an unusual relationship by marrying Ellen's sister, Helen, thus becoming his uncle's brother-in-law. The Mants had eight children, four sons and four daughters. My father, William Hall, was the second son, born in 1869. Apparently Gigoomgan was a lively place in the early years. George was a champion cricket and tennis player and there was a constant stream of visitors to the homestead. But as the years passed by, he became intensely religious and a strict disciplinarian. He became an ardent member of the British Israelites Society which believed that the English were the Lost Tribes of Israel.

So when his son, William, married what my grandfather regarded as a 'flighty' young woman named Frances McCrae from Sydney, he was very angry. His disapproval grew over the years, strengthened by exaggerated stories of wild parties in Sydney. Frances was regarded at Gigoomgan as a Jezebel or the original Scarlet Woman for leading the boy from the Queensland bush astray. And when his son died at the early age of 41 grandfather Mant blamed my mother for it, or so it seemed. There was no help forthcoming from Gigoomgan when it became known that my father had left behind a load of racing and other debts. It was left to my father's many friends to go to the financial rescue of my mother. Grandfather was so unforgiving that when he himself died, two years later, in 1913, at the age of 76, it was found that he had cut off his erring son, William, without a shilling. In his Will, Gigoomgan was to be divided up among the family (minus William). A large sum of money was left to the British Israelites Society to help prove that the English were the Lost Tribes of Israel; to the widowed Frances Mant, nothing. The only concession he made to our family was a bequest of £500 each to my brother John (then thirteen), Gilbert (eight) and Dick (three) on attaining the age of 21.

So there it was. My mother, still beautiful at 37, was abandoned by Gigoomgan with three young children to support. She had been flung into a harsh world from the comfort and security of Marathon Avenue but she was determined to bring us up in the 'manner to which we were accustomed'. And so she did, with the help of friends and her father, Farquhar Peregrine Gordon McCrae, a retired bank executive. Poor Grandfather McCrae! No sooner had his daughter, Frances, been widowed than another daughter, Emily Kilgour, lost her husband at an early age and was also left more-or-less penniless. Grandfather and Grandmother took the two refugee widows and their five children under their wings in a huge house at Chatswood. One abiding memory of Rostrevor at Chatswood is that of Miss Cave, the 'lady help', a euphemism for a poorly paid sort of governess–housekeeper. Miss Cave was a rather plump young Lancashire woman with a cheerful disposition. We five children called her Scave and loved her. To our sorrow, Scave suddenly left us to marry John Watkins, a noted English-born artist many years her senior. Watkins later taught thousands of students in his Sydney school of design, colour, drawing and life classes. His voluptuous nudes were the talk of the town and guess who was his chief model? I ran across a more middle-aged-spread Scave a couple of times in later years and contemplated—who'd have thought our lady help at Chatswood had such a gorgeous body?

I don't think my childhood was desperately unhappy but it was certainly an unsettled and disturbed one. I can't put our moves and my schools in chronological order, but after my grandfather's death in 1913, we left Chatswood for Darling Point where mother ran Milroy, a boarding place for Sydney Grammar School pupils. We had seven country boys and a schoolmaster and, sadly, most of them were killed in World War I. Then there was a move to a two-storey semi-detached house in Albert Street, Edgecliff, where we took in 'paying guests', the genteel euphemism for boarders. I was shuttled from school to school, three preparatory schools before the big one, Sydney Grammar School. If you are wondering where mother got the money from, my fees were paid by a family friend Dr Norman (later Sir Norman) Kater, a prominent medico and pastoralist. I was a boarder at the age of nine at Chatswood Preparatory School (later Mowbray House) where I was bullied and taunted as 'Turkey Egg' because of my freckles. Later, I was a day boy there, a fellow pupil being Kenneth Slessor, to become one of Australia's finest poets. Then came Sydney Prep, somewhere in East Sydney under the control of a Mr Nimmo, then Edgecliff Prep with the redoubtable Miss Van. Nobody could ever forget Miss I. Van Heuckelum, daughter of Dutch parents who came to Australia in the early part of the century. She was educated in Holland and Belgium and then became a teacher and governess in the Australian bush. Teaching girls irritated her, so in 1911 she started her own boys school in an old-fashioned yellow stone building facing New South Head Road at Edgecliff. A straight-backed, handsome woman, she ran the school for more than half a century, preparing a long line of boys for the Great Public Schools, many of whom went on to distinctive careers in the professions, sport and the armed forces.

Miss Van terrified most boys but they loved her just the same. She had very forthright views on practically everything, especially education, and for some reason I have kept an attack she made in 1946 on what was then known as 'the wireless'. 'The wireless is the downfall of children,' she said. 'It is interfering with their homework. It is making them lazy, and they won't read. The wireless is killing good English. The English language is the most beautiful language in the world. If we can send our boys away with a love of good English and a desire to read, we'd feel we have achieved something. Wireless serials make our task much harder, and the only bright spot in the industrial strike this week was the curtailment of wireless programmes.' I wonder what Miss Van would think of the violence and sex of television today?

I was a 'muck-up' at Sydney Grammar School, being told by some teachers that I was ruining the fine reputation my brother, John, had left behind him at the school. I know now that lack of a father was partly responsible for my behaviour. I was interested only in English and History and was demoted to class 3E in the 'dungeons' of the school in College Street, which was about the lowest you could get in those days. I was on the receiving end of strangely worded punishments issued by the class master, 'Burg' Golding, to unruly pupils. When he said, 'Draw the card, lad!' it meant that you found yourself at school on Saturday morning, writing hundreds and hundreds of lines. I drew many Saturday cards and it distressed my mother. I felt ashamed of myself. I learnt one sharper lesson during a French lesson by W.H. ('Sav') Savigny. All the boys liked Sav, a gentle and kindly man, and some of us took unfair advantage of him. I overstepped the mark by shouting out 'Sarsaparilla!' when he was explaining the cedilla to us. This was too much even for Sav, who took me upstairs to the Lower School Headmaster, the dreaded 'Gilo' Giles, who expertly administered six stinging cuts of the cane on my hands. But I never offended again and am still a strong supporter of corporal punishment.

I remember Grammar also because of the crippling railwaymen's strike in New South Wales in 1917 at a critical stage of World War I. It was broken by volunteer labour from all walks of life. The railwaymen downed tools because they objected to a fresh system of time-cards; they claimed that this would lead to speeding-up and other undesirable things. I was one of a strong contingent of Grammar boys who cleaned locomotives at Everleigh Workshops. I saw the strike only in black and white—my brother, John, was with the AIF in France fighting the terrible battles of the Somme. To my young mind, I believed that nothing whatever should be allowed to impede the delivery of supplies to our troops. We lived in train carriages at Macdonaldtown, cleaning the locos with waste and kerosene. The big thrill was travelling one night in the cab of the Brisbane Express to Newcastle, being pelted with lumps of coal thrown by strikers as we tore at high speed under railway bridges. One of the strikers was an engine driver named Ben Chifley, later Prime Minister of Australia. Chifley was dismissed but reinstated, on appeal, as a downgraded fireman. I occasionally met Ben Chifley in later life but I never let on to him that the first money I ever earned was as a 'scab'. We called it quits in 1955 when I found myself on strike in a newspaper dispute. Despite my undistinguished career there, Grammar instilled in me a love and respect for tradition and (ultimately) discipline. I'm grateful for that.

We were accompanied to Albert Street by Aunt Emmie Kilgour and her two daughters, Jean and Gordon. They were all to leave when Aunt Emmie re-married to a Sydney solicitor. My mother was being wooed at the same time. She was to reject three proposals of marriage from well-to-do suitors when she was in her forties, still handsome and vivacious. I shall forever blame myself for those refusals of marriage. I was about seventeen or eighteen at the time and when she hinted at the possibility of presenting us with a stepfather, I was implacably opposed to it. I had no sexual experience or understanding of it at the time, but the thought of a strange man going to bed with my adored mother outraged and disgusted me. I believe my hostility influenced her to reject these opportunities of companionship and financial security.

All these traumatic things made me a psychological mess as I lurched into adolescence. Painfully shy and supersensitive about my freckles, terrified of girls, an acrophobic and a claustrophobic, I was glad to be taken away from school when I was sixteen because of rheumatic fever and sent to a 'dry climate' in far western New South Wales. Eight years in the bush should have straightened me out but they didn't, as is evident in this jingle published in *The Bulletin* in the Roaring Twenties when I was 22:

SHY

The flappers turn and giggle as they pass you by
They leave you on the footpath thinking 'Why, why, why?'
Other fellows make advances when they're sitting out at dances—
For you'll never make a lover if you're shy, shy, shy!
You'll never be a rival of the smooth-haired Sheiks
Unless your tie is faultless and your breath just reeks
Of brandy, gin and whisky and you can't help feeling frisky
If you're pounding out a Charleston in your new dress breeks.

You're nothing else but simple if your home's all bliss;
You're a poor romantic wowser if you think like this;
You may call a lady 'honey', give her all your ready money,
But your very best credential is a long, close kiss.
You must read the naughty novels that the bookstalls ban
If YOU can't get home blithered—well, your girlfriend can,
Extol a flapper's glories in some rather risque stories
And you're sure to be a 'darling' or a real 'he-man'.

If you're out of date and simple, and your clothes passe,
And you feel a decent pleasure in an old-time play;
If you do not beg or barger for a lady's jazzy garter—
Well, you'll be a lonely mortal with your own shy way...
Still, I'd let the flappers giggle as they pass you by,
I wouldn't bother thinking of the 'Why, why, why?'
If the fellows make advances when they're sitting out at dances—
For I guess you're mighty lucky if you're shy, shy, shy!

That was in 1924 and it lingers on; in 1992, when I was 90, I created some kind of record by chickening out of an invitation by Ray Martin to launch my book, *A Cuckoo in the Bodyline Nest*, on his *Midday Show*. I just could not face that live audience of blue-rinse-set ladies, the lights, Geoff Harvey's beard and the general brouhaha. As a book launch on the *Midday Show* guarantees a sale of many thousands of copies, my publisher took a dim view of my timidity but has since forgiven me, I think.

My mother lived until she was 90, a familiar figure in Double Bay, darting in and out of the way of buses hurtling down New South Road. She got knocked over once or twice but quickly recovered. Every Friday afternoon, after the week's school, the grandchildren would arrive at her small flat on the corner of Manning Road. There would be waiting cold drinks, cakes and the dainty little wafer-thin sandwiches she made. She would melt the butter beforehand so that the bread would be spread easily and not crumble. They called her Granny Mant or simply Francie. It was the afternoon when the Matriarch held court. They loved her but were a bit scared of her; we all were at times, ridiculous when you think of it, that such a tiny woman could exert such influence. When necessary, she rebuked the grandchildren for 'bad manners' or for showing bad 'form'. But she was no saint, having the human frailties of us all, and was full of contradictions. She was thoroughly feminine and fastidious and somewhat snobbish, yet surprisingly pragmatic when it suited her. She smoked cigarettes at a time when it was thought to be daring and unladylike. She loved music, books and what she pronounced as 'poyetry', especially Swinburne and the lovely poems of her double-cousin, Hugh McCrae. She had very little money so we sons paid the rent of her flat and subsidised her in other ways. We had a devil of a job persuading her to apply for the old-age (as it was called then) or widow's pension. She refused to live on state charity and it was only after brother John explained to her that we, as taxpayers, were paying for the pensions that she surrendered. Then she loved it and the security and independence the regular cheques gave her and what she could buy with them. She was immensely proud that her three sons had done well in life—John as a solicitor, myself as a journalist and Dick as a pioneer airman in New Guinea and a Qantas pilot and senior executive. She never lost her bitterness towards Gigoomgan for the way they had treated her and my father.

I found her lying on the floor when I called at the flat one afternoon. I telephoned Dr Colin Love and, good fellow, he came immediately. After he had made her comfortable, she looked up at him and said, 'Have I had a stroke, doctor?' 'Yes, Mrs Mant,' he said gently, and strangely it seemed to comfort her. I think those were the last words she ever spoke. She was taken to St Luke's Hospital in Darlinghurst and died a few days later. There is a bronze tablet on a wall inside St Mark's Church, Darling Point, placed there by her three sons, lovingly and gratefully.

5
Going to Gigoomgan

Going to Gigoomgan was the big annual event in my young life. I went there during every Christmas holiday from the ages of about ten to sixteen. It was a three-days train journey and every moment of it was exciting to a city boy who loved steam trains.

When we lived at Chatswood, I would be taken by my mother to Hornsby station to await the arrival of the night Brisbane Express. Even the sight of that locomotive coming into view like a dragon breathing fire and smoke was an excitement. Mother would bundle me aboard a sleeping car and hand the conductor half a crown (two shillings and sixpence) to ensure that I would safely negotiate the border changeover at Wallan Garra onto the narrower Queensland-gauge railway. The journey was a constant joy and thrill. Despite warnings, I would lean out of the open carriage window to watch the head of the train snaking around a curve in the distance, with smoke and steam from the panting locomotive, and some coal smuts in my eye in consequence. Some kind woman passenger would remove the smuts with the curled corner of a white handkerchief, and a rebuke. Uncle Charlie (my father's elder brother) would be awaiting my arrival at Brisbane. Next day, I would be forwarded by rail to Maryborough and into the care of Dr Garde, a family friend. Then would come the Gayndah Mail en route to the Brooweena siding. It was a long, slow journey, travelling at about ten miles an hour and stopping at all stations. Many of the passengers would be cattlemen returning to their stations and their conversations introduced me to a new world.

Uncle George (my father's younger brother) would be waiting at Brooweena with a buckboard and two horses in the shafts. Uncle George, a large and easy-going bushman, put me at ease at once. Gigoomgan was about ten miles to the south, the buckboard having to negotiate several steep creek crossings on the way. Then we would come over a rise and there was the homestead beside the big bunya tree and beyond it a long grassy slope down to the creek, a watery avenue between a corridor of willow trees. The homestead was almost dwarfed by the bunya tree which was reputed to be hundreds of years old. The building was mostly of ironbark slabs, with a tall chimney arising from the outsize kitchen.

The kitchen was the nerve centre of Gigoomgan. There was a long, wide wooden table in the centre of the room and around it eight sawn-off logs serving as seats. The seats were smooth and shiny as the result of thousands of sittings by Mants and countless visitors. There was a substantial wood-burning stove, alight day and night, with a giant cast-iron kettle and pots on it. There were a number of gun-holes in the walls, relics of attacks by a fierce tribe of Aborigines who inhabited the district in the early days. The kitchen was separated from the main part of the building by a long roofed corridor with slab flooring. It led to a large sitting room and bedrooms with high ceilings. My grandparents and two spinster aunts lived in this section of the house.

Gigoomgan was a small self-contained community with several timber cottages for family members, a store, stables, blacksmith's shop, grain sheds and stockyards. Some rude locals referred to it as the Ants' Nest. I stayed in one cottage with my godmother, Aunt Mabel, who had married the station overseer (unhappily, as it turned out). I remember that there was always a long, thin sapling in a corner of the hallway to kill or frighten away any trespassing black snakes from their lair under the cottage. Every building at Gigoomgan had similar weapons on hand. Another bigger cottage was occupied by Uncle George, who ran the station, and his tall, plump and cheerful wife, Bessie. They had two small boys, Barty and Reg, and wild country kids at that. There was another smaller hut which housed a mysterious little man with a long white beard named 'Uncle Willie'. I've never discovered who Uncle Willie was, he does not appear on the family tree. I do remember that each evening an aunt would take him a double tot of Queensland rum and Uncle Willie would disappear into his hut with it like an elderly ferret.

Both my grandparents terrified me at first sight, though I grew used to them and vaguely realised they wanted to be kind to me. I give them full credit for not enlightening me about the family feud and the Scarlet Woman of Sydney who was my wicked mother. I knew my grandfather on only two holiday visits as he died after my second visit when I was eleven. He had a long beard (like Moses, in my childish mind) and wore on his head a circular shaped velvet affair rather like a fez without the tassel. He appeared to me to be stern and domineering, though he could not subdue his wife, who had a very strong character of her own. Grandmother was a plain-looking, stout woman usually dressed in black taffetas with a jabot trim around her neck, and she encased her hands in fur muffs during cold weather.

Life was somewhat crude and austere at Gigoomgan, with few creature comforts. They killed their own meat and for a few days fresh meat was enjoyed by everyone; then there would be interminable meals of salt beef for weeks on end. Grace was said before meals and at night we would gather in the big house sitting room for Bible readings and other serious pursuits. These were wretched evenings for a small boy 1,000 miles away from his mother and I did not look forward to them. The room was dimly lit by kerosene lamps and had a depressing air about it. The walls were lined with calico and one imagined black snakes slithering behind it. I watched in fascination as the geckos darted to and fro on the walls and ceiling chasing insects attracted inside by the lamplight. Then I would be brought back to earth by my grandfather's monotonous English voice as he propounded on some Biblical theme, perhaps the Lost Tribes of Israel. Apart from the geckos, there was another thing that fascinated me—my Aunt Mary had a moustache, an unmistakeable black wisp of a moustache. I had never seen a woman with a moustache before but I did not like to ask anyone about it. I could not help myself taking secret looks at it and wondering about it. I suppose it must have caused Aunt Mary a lot of private anguish but I was too young to understand such things.

If the nights were stuffy and austere, the days were magic. Nobody was bothering about my freckles and I was no longer imagining that people were looking at me. I learnt to ride a horse and crack a stockwhip. I went mustering with Uncle George and the stockmen. There were wild rides after cattle through the timber and across Karri Flat, a vast expanse of grassland like a Canadian prairie. We galloped after kangaroos and scrub wallabies. We camped out at night sometimes, boiling the billy and chewing at our salt beef sandwiches and yarning over the camp fire under the stars. We rode out to the out-station, Marodian, managed by Morrie Lewis, who had married my Aunt Ethel and produced a brood of children. All my Mant and Lewis cousins were younger than I but we were good mates. I became accustomed to the rougher things of bush life. I watched the slaughter of bullocks for our meat. I watched as Uncle George gelded the young horses and cattle with a razor-sharp penknife. The colts squealed in agony, the bull calves bellowed, there was blood everywhere and the blue cattle dogs greedily devoured the severed testicles as soon as they were thrown into the dirt. I watched the stallion, Memorist, serving mares in a small enclosure.

I often rode out with Billy, a full-blooded young Aboriginal stockman and we talked a lot but not about black and white. He asked me many questions about the Big City down south. He had never seen the sea, although it was only about 50 miles to the east from Gigoomgan as the crow flies. One thing I remember about Billy is that when he had a headache, he did not look for aspirin. He would pluck a stalk of the tough and sharp spear grass from a clump and jab it up his nose. His nose would bleed instantly and his headache would disappear. Billy was no relation to the small colony of blacks camped by the creek below the homestead. They were a bedraggled lot, leading aimless and apparently hopeless lives. My grandfather gave them regular rations of tea, sugar and flour, otherwise Gigoomgan had no association with them and no interest in them. I am ashamed now to confess that I scarcely regarded them as human. I apologise now but that's the way it was then and we white children were not taught otherwise. I knew nothing of black massacres in the past, only that there were gun-holes in the kitchen used to frighten off marauding black savages.

I remember other random happenings. A retired Brisbane businessman friend of the family named 'Old Mr Carrington' used to visit on fishing excursions occasionally. Gigoomgan was fed with many creeks, especially the Munna, which was almost a river. There were a lot of fish in the Munna, principally freshwater jewfish, resembling catfish, mullet and sometimes a ceratados, a rare lungfish which came to the surface for air at intervals. Old Mr Carrington caught a lot of fish and in one particular section of the Munna once landed 25 jewfish in a day. He was given the dubious honour of having the spot named after him. To this day, it is known as Carrington's Hole.

When I was fifteen and holidaying at Gigoomgan, a pretty nineteen-year-old governess from Brisbane arrived to teach the George Mant boys, Barty and Reg. I fell instantly and violently in love with her. It was a case of infatuated calf love on my part and I'm not sure whether it was a case of genuine affection on her part or whether she was having secret fun at my expense. At any rate, we used to ride off together into the paddocks and exchange a chaste kiss or two in the privacy of a creek bank. I remember once lying with her with my head resting on the bosom beneath her blouse. Apart from feeling that it was a soft and comfortable place to rest my head (in fact, I fell asleep) there was no sexual experience to it whatsoever. Nothing of that nature ever took place between us and the affair ended in high drama. Harry Pascoe, a burly eighteen-year-old stockman, taunted me one day with an allegation that the governess had been going to bed with the new overseer. Like a Sir Galahad, I rushed angrily to the defence of my lady's virtue and challenged Harry to a fight. With much reluctance, seeing he was about four times my size and twice my height, he agreed to meet me at 5 p.m. on the following day to fight it out on the banks of the creek below the homestead. Fortunately for me, my uncle got wind of the affair and he soon put a stop to it. Harry and I shook hands. Shortly after that, the governess suddenly and mysteriously returned to Brisbane. I was broken-hearted but soon recovered. I wonder today whether the governess was sent away because they thought she was seducing me or whether the overseer had indeed been indulging in a more than calf-love interlude with her.

Those holidays at Gigoomgan gave me an abiding love for the Australian bush and its people. I wanted nothing more than a property of my own, with horses, cattle and dogs, away from the city where people noticed my freckles and stared at me. It did not turn out that way but the love for the bush has never diminished.

These are some of the things I remember about Gigoomgan and the things I have been told about my family. Whether they are the truth about my grandfather and his vendetta against my mother, I do not know. I never saw Gigoomgan again until 60 years later when I made a sentimental return visit to it. The homestead block was then owned by my cousin, Reg, and his wife, Kath. They had built a modern home a few hundred yards away from the old homestead. The bunya tree was still there but the old place, with so many memories for me, was beginning to fall down after more than a century. The calico in the sitting room was peeling off like cloth from an Egyptian mummy. Reg was sad about it but was unable to maintain it and historical societies were unwilling to preserve it. Reg asked me to inspect the documents and books still in the old 'office'. He sought my advice about their preservation and told me to take what I wanted for myself.

The great prize for myself was the Family Bible. It was in wonderful condition except for the covers which I had lovingly restored by a Sydney bookbinder. The Bible was printed in 1798 by John Burge, printer to the University of Cambridge. It contains the 'Old and New Testaments: translated out of the Original Tongues; and with the former Translations diligently composed and revised, by His Majesty's Special Command. Appointed to be read in Churches.' The letter 's' is printed as the 'long s', resembling an 'f'. The Bible has a handwritten dedication to 'Sarah Mant—The gift of her mother Sept. 1804'. Sarah was the sister of my great-grandfather George Joseph Mant and the Bible must have been taken to Gigoomgan from England by my grandfather in 1856. A little further back in the Mant family tree is the name of the Rt Rev. Richard Mant, Lord Bishop of Down and Connor and Dunmore in Northern Ireland for 25 years from 1823 to 1848. The bishop was a prolific writer and I took away with me three volumes of his sermons, a book of poems which ran into five editions, and two 500-page volumes of *Holidays of the Church*, published in Oxford in 1831. This massive double-decker is described as 'Scriptural Narratives of our Blessed Lord's Life and Ministry and Biographical Notices of the Apostles, Evangelists and other Saints: with replexions, collects and metrical sketches'. Some of it is heavy going at times. There was also a memoir of the Bishop by his son, Ven. Archdeacon Walter Bishop-Mant, published in Dublin in 1857. A number of Bishop Mant's hymns can be found in the Anglican Hymn Book. The best-known is No. 161, the first stanza being:

> Bright the vision that delighted
>   Once the sight of Judah's seer;
> Sweet the countless tongues united
>   To entrance the prophet's ear.

Another rather surprising set of books I took away were four first editions of *The History and Adventures of Gil Blas de Santillane. Newly Translated from the*

French of M. de Lasage. To which is prefixed some account of the Author's Life. Illustrated with Copperplate. M. de Lasage appears to have been a poor-man's Rabelais as there are some very rude parts in his books. (Was Grandfather Mant a secret pornographer?)

The richest prizes of all from an historical point of view were a large number of copies of handwritten Gigoomgan daily journals, account books, letters and so forth. I put them all into suitcases and took them to the State Library of Queensland in Brisbane where they accepted them eagerly. They seem to me to be priceless accounts of early Australian history. Take this daily journal record of a lively Christmas Day at Gigoomgan in 1854:

> Fine, warm day ... The timber splitters all drunk. Carberry took up an axe to knock Heffernan down, accusing him of having stolen his chicks, also hit Beilby with a spade on the head. Heffernan then drew his knife.

On 4 April 1854, Mr Anderson wrote to a Mr Mader in Sydney:

> Sir, — Wishing to get a Photographic Machine, I have been recommended to you. Will you be kind enough to let me know if such is to be got in Sydney, and the value of it. It must be a simple construction so that an inexperienced hand may use it by practise.

In September 1854, Anderson wrote to his partner, Leslie, in Sydney:

> When I was in Wide Bay, I got a warrant for the man whom I left here when I was away and who bolted after having drunk all the grog—10 galls.

As late as 1860, hostile blackfellows had made it necessary for gun-holes to be bored in the slab walls of the homestead. On 5 September, grandfather Mant wrote to a J.O. Bligh Esq:

> As I have reason to believe that the blacks are mustered with mischievous intent and are assuming a very threatening tone towards myself and my neighbours, I beg that you will make a point of sending up a detachment of your police with as little delay as possible.

After 120 years, Gigoomgan passed out of Mant control with the death of my cousin, Reg, in 1978. I've never seen it again and the *Sydney Morning Herald* published some jingle about it in later years.

> Out of the past I recall the days,
> The Queensland life and the Queensland ways,
> When the man who limped for a scrub-dash fall —
> Well, he wasn't a man, at all, at all.
> It was life and laughter and love and songs
> It was Gigoomgan where my heart belongs.

The hardest day was a day of thrills
When we ran the steers through the Wombat hills,
The timber crashed to our pelting pace,
There was only the joy of the break-neck chase,
Hurtling horse and a bellow ahead,
And we followed the ways that the cattle led!

And yet there were moments as fine as that
When we chased a 'roo on the Karri Flat,
When we spurred and galloped and flogged the plain
With our heels jammed in and a tightened rein
The winds were lilting and clean and sweet,
There were drumming tunes in our horses' feet.

Life has a habit of running in grooves,
Still I treasure the song of those pounding hooves,
The life, the laughter at Gigoomgan
Where a man, to live, had to be a man —
And the only regret that those days recall
Is, perhaps, that I wasn't a man at all!

6
The Roaring Twenties

The Roaring Twenties was the description given to the decade of the 1920s. It was an era when the youth of the world ran wild after the trauma and dissolution of World War I which ended in 1918. At first disapproving, soon older people joined in the fun and kicked up their heels. The roaring started first in America and Britain and came to Australia later. The young rebels were called Flaming Youth in America and Bright Young Things in Britain. Teenaged girls were called 'flappers' but I have no idea what they were flapping. It was a world revolution in manners and morals, though the new liberation and permissiveness would seem absurdly puritanical by today's standards.

The old moral codes against drinking, smoking and talking about sex went out of the window. Naughty words no longer shocked, though the four-letter words were still banned in print, film and theatre. The flappers began wearing skirts nine inches above the ground, revealing shinbones. Then, greatly daring, they moved up to the knee. The female bosom went out of fashion and the breasts were flattened tightly against the chest. Corset, girdle and brassiere manufacturers went broke. Similarly, hairdressers and milliners went into recession with the short-hair craze, first the bob and then the shingle, and big hats gave way to cute little cloche numbers. The cosmetics industry, on the other hand, boomed as women took to lipstick and beauty culture.

One American observer, Frederick Lewis Allen, explained it this way: 'The women of the decade worshipped not merely youth, but unrepressed youth, they wanted to be—or thought men wanted them to be—men's casual and light-hearted companions; not broad-hipped mothers of the race, but irresponsible playmates'. So modesty, reticence and chivalry became old-fashioned. 'Nice' girls began smoking and drinking in public and getting 'blotto' (drunk) at dances, where the violin and its plaintive melodies had given way to the sexy saxophones and beating drums. The couples danced cheek to cheek and the older matrons pranced around madly doing the Charleston, a lively sort of polka. Cocktail parties and mah jong parties were all the rage. The Austrian psychiarist, Sigmund Freud, fanned the sexual revolution with his theory that distortions in infantile sexuality were the root of the neuroses of the adult. Uninhibited sex life was 'liberating', sex control was downright dangerous, he preached. The Flaming Youths and the Bright Young Things became eager disciples. A wizened little Frenchman named Emile Coué was another cult figure of the 1920s, though without any particular sexual implications. Coué was the precursor of today's 'motivators'. He had people of all ages all over the world repeating aloud his get-well physically and mentally formula of 'Day by day in every way I am getting better and better'. Although numbers of people seemed to be getting worse and worse, Coué-ism had a long run.

It is not to be imagined that the antics of Flaming Youth went unchallenged. The churches and other groups were vocal in their condemnation of the laxity in public morals and manners. Bills were introduced in some American Bible-belt states providing fines and imprisonment for those who wore on the streets 'skirts higher than three inches above the ankle' and forbidding women wearing evening gowns which 'displayed more than three inches of her throat'. An ordinance was actually passed in Norphlet, Arkansas, in 1925 which contained the following provision: 'Section 1—Hereafter it shall be unlawful for any man and woman, male or female, to be guilty of committing the act of sexual intercourse between themselves at any place within the corporate limits of the said town . . . Section 3—Section one of this ordinance shall not apply to married persons as between themselves, and their husband and wife, unless of a grossly improper and lascivious nature.'

The Roaring Twenties came to Australia a little later than the rest of the world but with all the rebellious elements of the U.S.A. and Britain and just as rumbustiously, if not more so. Cocktail parties and mah jong parties became the rage. Young and old indulged in Freudism and Coué-ism. Copies (if you could get one) of the outrageous *Married Love*, by Dr Marie Stopes, of England, were kept under lock and key. Dr Stopes broke all sexual taboos by asserting that women actually enjoyed sexual intercourse, using such forbidden words as 'foreplay', 'clitoris' and 'orgasm'.

I was working in the bush for the first few years of the 1920s, on the Monaro, the South Coast and the western wheat country. I drifted back to Sydney in 1924 when I was 22, not knowing what to make of my life and causing my family much worry. I lived with my mother at Edgecliff and tried to exist as a freelance writer. I wrote topical verses, paragraphs, articles and romantic short stories of the Mills and Boon variety. The *Woman's Mirror* (published by *The Bulletin*) was my main target. I sold them four allegedly humorous serials. My output was so prolific that I also used the name of Lois Palmer (who once received an enthusiastic fan letter). I picked up other odd jobs here and there. One of them was an extra in one of Australia's earliest major feature films. It was *The Mystery of the Hansom Cab*, based on the novel by Fergus Hume, a popular mystery writer of the time.

It was produced and directed by Arthur Shirley and filmed at Spencer's Studios, perched on top of a hill near Rushcutters Bay overlooking what are now the New South Wales Lawn Tennis Association courts. The company advertised for young men and women in the possession of dinner jackets and evening dresses to appear in a ballroom scene. Not many young men possessed dinner suits in those days, so I borrowed my older brother's outfit and became a film star. About a hundred of us, men and women, danced gaily around the studio as at a fashionable ball, with repeated shouts of 'Don't look at the cameras!' The make-up in those days consisted of putting large amounts of yellow or bright flesh-coloured grease paint on all parts of the exposed body. We danced in the glare of ten huge and powerful violet-ray arc-lamps. The effect of the lights was most painful and tears poured down my cheeks for hours afterwards. Experienced actors anointed their eyes with chopped up potato peel to ease the inflammation. Fourteen years later, the possession of a dinner suit enabled another young man of 22 to earn some money the same way. He was Edward Gough Whitlam who appeared in Ken G. Hall's production of *The Broken Melody* in 1938. The difference between me and Gough was that his name appeared in the official cast list as a 'man in nightclub'. I got no billing whatsoever as a 'man dancing'.

One day in 1925 when I was 23, on impulse, I walked into the offices of the *Daily Telegraph* in Sydney and asked for a job. The hire-and-fire man was Alec H. Chisholm, one of Australia's best-known editors, authors and ornithologists. By some lucky chance, he remembered reviewing a small book of verse and short stories I had self-published some months before. It was a prime example of 'vanity publishing' and was a complete flop, but Mr Chisholm had liked parts of it. On the strength of that, he gave me a trial run as a newspaper reporter. I took to it like a duck to water and I've been a journalist ever since.

At the *Daily Telegraph*, I struck an instant rapport with Jack Quayle, the paper's resident cartoonist and creator of a daily comic strip, *Casual Connie*. Jack was about ten years older than I but it did not seem to matter. You just make friends or lovers regardless of age. Tasmanian-born Jack was a clever black-and-white artist, later to create a popular racing strip character, Perce the Punter. I performed so well at the Telly that I was able to buy a second-hand blunt-nosed Morris Cowley motor car, an open affair with a 'dicky seat' at the back. I called it Mary and soon she was to acquire fame. Jack put Gilbert and Mary in the Casual Connie strip and we were to win first prize at the inaugural Journalists' Ball in 1928. Sitting in a toy replica car, I was escorted by police from the *Telegraph* building to the Wentworth Hotel at the other end of town where the ball was being held.

About a year after I joined the *Telegraph*, Jack embarked on one of his periodic separations from his wife, Kit. He suggested that we might share a flat at Kings Cross until the rift was healed. I was anxious to get away from my mother's apron strings so I agreed. I suppose that was when I first became a Flaming Youth and it's a wonder I have survived to tell the tale. We took a flat in a cul-de-sac off Wollcott Street, notorious as the Dirty Half-Mile. The street (since renamed) ran down the hill to Rushcutters Bay and was chiefly the address of brothels, sly-grog joints and other dens of vice. It was not a healthy street to frequent late at night as Sydney was being terrorised at the time by the Darlinghurst razor gangs. These were dangerous days and nights when vicious thugs roamed the streets with safety razor blades embedded in pieces of cork. The face slashings, especially of prostitutes, were horrendous.

The brothels of the Dirty Half Mile were about the only places where you could buy after-hours grog in those six-o'clock-closing of the hotel days. As prospective clients, Jack and I were given formal introductions to some of these houses of ill fame by Hugh Buggy, a crime and sports writer on the *Sun*, known as the Damon Runnyan of Sydney. Hugh was very popular with these creatures of the night who loved publicity in the newspapers. You were fairly safe in the company of Hugh in excursions to the underworld in search of crime stories. He introduced us to 'Mad' Bill Quinn, said to have been a murderer. He had a mass of electrical equipment, with wires running everywhere, in his one-room flat at the top of William Street. 'Mad' Bill Quinn claimed he was experimenting on a 'perpetual motion' invention that would revolutionise the world. We also met the beautiful Betty Carslake, said to have been a finalist in the Miss Australia beauty contest until it was discovered she was a top prostitute. Afterwards she worked in the migration department at Australia House in London, but came to a gruesome end. Her razor gang lover slashed her beautiful face from ear to ear in a jealous rage and Betty Carslake disappeared into gangland legend. Then there was the glamorous Rosaleen Norton, self-styled 'Witch of Kings Cross', who attracted a coterie of weirdos to her flat. She drew lewd pictures in the Aubrey Beardsley style and lived with Gavin Greenlees, one of our journalistic colleagues. Jack and I became regular clients of one particular brothel up the street owned and operated by Marie, a middle-aged, stony-faced woman said to have had a 'dark' past, though we never discovered the nature of it. It was accepted at Marie's place that you were only after beer and were not expected to seek the professional services of her girls. There were about six of them, all with fancy names such as American June and Big Madge.

As a black-and-white artist, Jack Quayle was part of the bohemian life of Sydney. The bohemians were a mad lot at any time, the Roaring Twenties just made them a little madder. There were two sets of bohemians—the intellectuals led by the Lindsay brothers and a sort of second division led by a bald, fat man named Sam Rosa. He operated from Theo's Club, in Oxford Street, I think. Sam called himself the King of Bohemia and probably dabbled in black magic. If Rosa was the King of Bohemia, Dulcie Deamer was unquestionably the Queen of Bohemia. New Zealand-born Dulcie was a beautiful and vivacious woman in her thirties; a prolific and talented writer. Her views were daring for the age and so was her behaviour. She was the belle of the first Artists' Ball in the Sydney Town Hall in 1923 which developed into a bacchanalian orgy. Dulcie pranced around the dance floor as Eve, dressed in a leopard skin and little else. The carousal went on into the early hours of the morning, the basement of the Town Hall was awash with grog and drunken revellers. The drunks were still staggering disgustingly around in the streets after the sun came up as ordinary people were going to work. The good people of Sydney were not amused; if that was typical of intellectual and artistic life, they wanted nothing of it.

The bohemian group with whom I became involved on the fringe with Jack Quayle had as its elder statesmen such poets, writers and artists as Norman Lindsay, Hugh McCrae, Christopher Brennan, Robert Fitzgerald, Eric Bedford, Elioth Gruner and George Lambert. These poets are forgotten today, drowned in the new-wave poetry. You will find a memoir of Hugh McCrae in Chapter 13 of this book. The young literary and artistic lions, all in their twenties, were led by Norman Lindsay's three sons, Jack, Raymond and Phillip, Kenneth Slessor, Unk White, George Finey and others. Jack was the erudite one of all the brilliant Lindsays. He was to write more than 150 books including autobiographies; history and biography; historical novels set in the Ancient world, Italy and England; twelve contemporary novels; eight collections of poetry; and translations from Greek, Latin and Russian. His brother Phil was a popular writer of historical novels. His *Here Comes the King* about Henry VIII was made into a blockbuster film with Charles Laughton in the leading role. The other brother, Ray, was an artist whose large colourful canvases of pirates and historical subjects never quite made it to the top but earned him a living. It was extraordinary how generations of the Lindsay family, male and female, inherited literary and artistic talents of an exceptional order.

The bohemians made merry in the Roaring Twenties but they also produced much good writing and good painting. Most of the action took place in Darlinghurst. It became the Latin Quarter, the Montparnasse, the Chelsea of Australia, though Kings Cross was not the sleazy, sex-shop cesspool of today. The three Lindsay brothers stuck together sharing flats at Woolloomooloo, Kings Cross and Bondi.

The merry-making did not divert Jack Lindsay from his crusade for a literary renaissance to develop Australian culture beyond the pioneering levels. With Norman Lindsay and Ken Slessor, he found a financial backer for a quarterly literary magazine called *Vision*. Its aim was to attack 'all forms of Modernisms and abstractions in art', and it explained its objects in its first issue in May 1923:

If you are tired of glutinous chatter about Chelsea artists—or reports from passionate spinsters on their souls—or studies in the rectangular nude by futurist tradesmen—or the poetic drops of the weekly Celts—or the smacking honesty of the monthly sea-dogs—or the album-cleverness of the young ladies and gentlemen who write vers libre

If in short you are tired to being modern, and want to be alive—

Then take heart. *Vision* may help you yet. *Vision* is the only magazine in the Continent with a definite literary standard. *Vision* will show you what is true and what is false. *Vision* will bring you gaiety and indignation. You will probably not like it—at first.

Vision was successful for a while, with Norman Lindsay's stories and poems by Hugh McCrae and Slessor, but the critics were divided. A *Vision* anthology, *Poetry in Australia*, shocked Dora Wilcox in the *Daily Telegraph*: 'Ring the changes on the theme of animal lust . . . no book of verse so dirtied the paws of the primitive beast has ever before been published in Australia'. On the other hand, the *Sydney Morning Herald* hailed it as a 'milestone in Australian letters . . . Gone are the days of the poems of the gum trees, the kookaburras and the stock rider'.

I'm not sure whether I was a renaissance man or not but I was in delight with the English poets of the day such as John Masefield, A.E. Housman, G.K. Chesterton, Walter de la Mare, John Drinkwater, Francis Thompson, W.B. Yeats and James Elroy Flecker. You seldom hear these names now. I was besotted by Flecker, whose 'War Song of the Saracens' is the most exciting poem I have ever read. The first stanza:

> We are they who come faster than fate: we are they who ride early or late;
> We storm at your ivory gate: Pale Kings of the Sunset, beware!
> Not on silk nor in samet we lie, not in curtained solemnity die
> Among women who chatter and cry, and children who mumble a prayer.
> But we sleep by the ropes of the camp, and we rise with a shout, and we tramp
> With the sun or the moon for a lamp, and the spray of the wind in our hair. . .

Flecker's poetic drama, *Hassan*, was staged in London in 1923 and hailed as the best of its kind written in England since the great Elizabethan days. It had a haunting verse theme of the Golden Journey to Samakand. I often recite the 'War Song' to myself and also the first line of a poem about Darlinghurst by Mervyn O'Hara, a minor poet of our group:

> The moon sailed down on Darlinghurst upon a sea of stars . . .

The words conjure up in my mind the loveliest silvery pictures of a heavenly galleon.

Kenneth Slessor possessed the greatest emerging talent of them all, influenced and encouraged by Hugh McCrae (in 1948, McCrae was to dedicate his *Story-*

Book Only 'To the poet I am most jealous of—Kenneth Slessor'). An incident in this period was to inspire Slessor's most famous poem 'Five Bells', the subject of a fine mural by John Olsen in the Sydney Opera House. Among the bohemians was Joe Lynch, a wild young socialist who jumped from a ferry in Sydney Harbour and was drowned. Joe's death was described by Phil Lindsay: 'Loaded with bottles, he had been to some North Shore party with his brother, Frank, when, tired of the slow progress of the ferry—or perhaps, of life itself—he had sprung up, saying he'd swim there quicker, and, fully dressed, dived overboard. A deck-hand had leapt in after him, and lifebelts were thrown. They saw Joe, said Frank, wave cheerily and strike out for Milsons Point; then he vanished in the moonlight. Perhaps a shark got him, or a mermaid—as some said—or the load of bottles in his greasy old raincoat tugged him to the fishes; no one can tell, for the body was never found.'

In his autobiography Jack Lindsay saw the elegiac element in Slessor's 'Five Bells' poem as marking the rapid development of his art:

> He was to use his idiom, conversational and yet highly coloured and concentrated, in his poems on the explorers, the sea captains, that added a fresh dimension in Australian Poetry, recapture the spirit of adventurous voyaging into unknown seas and making the voyage at the same time an exploration of strange dimensions of experiment. His inner conflict was between his keen sense of enjoyment and his sense of overwhelming loss. In 'Five Bells' and these other poems he finally resolved the conflict and won his full poetic stature. And this achievement of his, I think it will be clear, was firmly rooted in the phase of Australian cultural development which had been ushered in by the wild bananas of *Vision*.

I did not see much of Jack Lindsay in those days; he went to England in 1926. But his brother, Phil, and I were firm friends, to be reunited years later in London when he and I both went there in search of fame and fortune. Phil's historical novels were extraordinarily authentic in detail because he seemed to have an instinctive knowledge of the past. If you were walking with Phil along a London street you could tell that he was remote from the present; he was seeing it as if it was in the fifteenth or sixteenth century; the people, their clothes, their voices, the noises, the sights and the smells. He seemed to have an uncanny familiarity with the past, quite separate from what he could have picked up in books.

While the bohemians held their wild parties in cafes and flats, other Flaming Youths frequented the Ambassadors, Sydney's most fashionable nightclub in a basement in Castlereagh Street. It was the haunt of the rich, the snobs, the demimonde, stars of stage and sport. They would not have known poetry from a pick handle. There they danced the Charleston, drinking and eating and singing

'Yes, We Have No Bananas' with the band. The head waiter was an Italian named A.O. Romano, who later established one of Sydney's most elegant and fashionable restaurants bearing his name and he owned the great racehorse, Bernborough. I kept a foot in both camps and often went to the Ambassadors. There one night a very drunk man from an adjoining table lurched towards me. 'How are you, Norman, old boy!' he spluttered.

'I'm not Norman,' I said. 'I'm Gilbert.'

'What rot! You're Norman Lindsay! Don't play games, Norman, old boy! I'd know you anywhere! You know I'm George Lambert, don't you?'

It was indeed George Lambert, one of Australia's most eminent portrait painters of the day, whose *Across the Black Soil Plains* is still a popular exhibit at the Art Gallery of New South Wales. When I got home that night, I looked at myself in the mirror. Yes, side-face, there was a faint resemblance to the great Norman Lindsay. I took to wearing a fringe of hair across my forehead, hoping that people would look in my direction and say 'Look! There's Norman Lindsay!' Nobody ever did, but whenever I met George Lambert in his cups afterwards I made the first move by saying 'Hello George! It's Norman.' He would respond enthusiastically and shake me warmly by the hand.

One incident of those mad young days shocks me somewhat. It occurred after Hugh McCrae had introduced me to the delights of Guy de Maupassant and I had bought a ten-volume set of his stories at a second-hand bookshop in Oxford Street. One of the stories, 'Madame Tellière's Establishment', told how Madame Tellière and some of her girls had been taken for a holiday in the French countryside. I told Jack Quayle about it and suggested, 'Why don't we take Marie and a couple of the girls for a run in Mary next Sunday?' 'Why not?' Jack agreed, 'We could go to Manly. I'll get a few pies and Marie can bring the beer.'

And go we did after some difficulty in squeezing them into the dicky seat of the car. Marie and her girls were dressed in their Sunday best, American June carrying a green parasol. We set off for Benalong Point to catch the vehicular ferry across the harbour to the North Shore. We had our pies and beer on the beach at Manly, one of the girls removing her stockings and going for a paddle in the surf. We exchanged small talk about the weather and local gossip but strictly no mention of business affairs. Mary behaved well both ways without breakdown and we delivered them safely back to Wollcott Street, slightly sunburnt but thoroughly refreshed for the resumption of professional work on Monday. The girls seemed to have had an enjoyable day but it had been pretty boring for us. I guess we did it for a bit of a gag so that, on being asked by colleagues what we had done in the weekend, we could reply nonchalantly, 'Oh, we just took a madam and a couple of girls to Manly for some pies and beer'.

The Bulletin published some doggerel of mine about it all:

We splashed at silly pictures and we boiled our pots of rhymes,
  The police knew all our habits and they winked their eyes at times,
Our hunting ground was Darlinghurst, we made it share our joys,
  Many a joint around Macleay Street knew the wild Bohemian Boys!

We abode in dusty attics, two-roomed flats around the Cross,
  Visitors on Friday evenings often staggered in to doss,
With some dead marines and crayfish—some headaches when we woke!
  And not a drop to drink because the boys were always broke!

Oh, we seldom paid the butcher and we never paid the rent;
  Our financial ways were crazy; God knows where the money went!
When we parted with a picture or a rhyme for Lsd
  'Twas a time for loud rejoicing and for going on a spree.

Jazz and song and outright bedlam made the rafters fairly roar,
  When an irritated tenant would come knocking at the door,
How we'd hush before embarking on another burst of noise!
  Oh, you couldn't damp the ardour of the wild Bohemian Boys!

There were little alley cafes that were grog shops on the sly;
  If we left with bulging pockets no one asked the reason why.
Saveloys would furnish supper after midnight in the street,
  And I fear our voices sounded as unsteady as our feet.

We'd go singing through the shadows, minus collars, ties and hats,
  Making nightmare pandemonium in more Bohemian flats,
There was bound to be some party that would greet us with a cheer
  If we had the proper password—an unfailing one was 'Beer!'

Now I own a Campsie cottage and a wife and kids as well,
  But the moon's a witch at midnight and she makes your fancy dwell
With pensive yearning sometimes on these harum-scarum joys
  On a night in wild Bohemia with the wild Bohemian Boys!

The decade of the Roaring Twenties ended in October 1929, with the Big Crash on Wall Street. Its effects came to Australia later, ushering in the decade of the Great Depression, an economic and human calamity beyond the comprehension of present-day Australians, comfortably sheltered by the benefits of the Welfare State. Thus ended the Age of Ballyhoo.

The memory of the Roaring Twenties lingered on. One day, in 1930, I wandered, lonely as a cloud, into a pub in West Kensington, London, and there was Phil Lindsay sitting at the bar with a glass of beer on the counter and looking melancholy. We embraced and sat together and talked about Australia with tears in our eyes and, in particular, about Darlinghurst and the wild bohemian boys.

'I'm going to write a poem about it—right now!' I said. So we went to a table and, with Phil's help, I produced 'Oh to Be in Darlinghurst', which *The Bulletin* duly printed under my name:

> It is cold and I'm rheumatic
>   In my little Chelsea attic,
> There's a fog that's groping 'round the window-pane;
>   It is Christmastime in Chelsea
>   But I'm thinking of my Elsie,
> And I want to be in Darlinghurst again!
>
> Up the hill of William,
>   Round about the 'Cross.
> Darlinghurst's awake, dear,
>   Grief and gold and gloss.
> Then the morning after;
>   Bedlam in a flat,
> Could I hear the laughter,
>   I'd go home for that!
>
> Oh, I ought to feel ecstatic
>   In my little Chelsea attic,
> It's the status that I wanted to attain;
>   But the Chelsea poets' chatter
>   Daily falls distinctly flatter,
> So I want to be in Darlinghurst again!
>
> Marching up Macleay Street,
>   Singing Christmas songs,
> Darlinghurst's the Chelsea
>   Where my heart belongs!
> Up the hill at William,
>   'Round about the 'Loo...
> What? They haven't altered
>   Eaton Avenue!
>
> Do you wonder I'm dramatic
>   In my little Chelsea attic?
> It's a castle that was never built in Spain;
>   I admit I made a blunder
>   And I want to be 'Down Under'
> With the wildest lads of Darlinghurst again!

Round about Macleay Street,
   Fill a glass with beer;
Drink a toast to Gilly,
   Exiled over here;
Up the hill at William
   Where the tramcars start,
Darlinghurst's the Chelsea
   Tangled in my heart!

7
The Journos'

Journalists are a weird mob and journalism is a weird profession, or should we say trade, and it goes back a long way. One of the earliest newspapers, the *Acto Diurna*, is said to have been started by Julius Caesar about 50 BC. It contained announcements of marriages, deaths, military appointments and so on, and was posted up in public places. News-sheets as commercial undertakings followed the invention of printing and were introduced in 1609 in Germany. The first newspaper in English, *The Weekly News*, edited by Nicholas Bourne and Thomas Archer, appeared in 1622.

It has come a long way since Caesar edited his copy and the mistake the public make today is to regard newspapers as some kind of altruistic organs of information and entertainment. A modern newspaper in our capitalistic system is a commercial commodity as is a loaf of bread, a glass of beer or a suit of clothes—the more you sell, the more money you make for your shareholders. It is usually controlled by press barons and multinational advertisers out to make healthy dividends. So why is it that so many people regard a newspaper as being something invented for their personal convenience and enlightenment? People still accost me at times with indignation about something they have seen in the press, as if it were my fault.

Attempts have been made from time to time to produce newspapers with items such as Julius Caesar might have issued, without advertisements. They have all gone broke. Few people want to read about good or happy news, it's too dull—they go for the sex, the crime, the corporate and private scandals and the violence. And, besides, without advertising revenue, the cost of production is uneconomic. The very people who constantly criticise newspapers and journalists are the ones who contribute to the mass circulations.

There's no doubt that news and the public can be manipulated by newspaper proprietors printing only what they want to print, and bowing to the demands of advertisers at times. The media influence on politics is powerful and political bias can be cleverly disguised. There are reputable and serious papers, of course, but if they did not report the gross and the ugly and get on the bandwagon of current scandals, they would go broke, too, and so would their shareholders.

Australia is fortunate in not having the utter gutter press of America and Britain, though some Australian magazines are making a brave showing in that direction. The journalist 'reptiles' of the royal watchers in England are on their way to almost single-handedly destroying the British monarchy. In an earlier age, Humbert Wolfe satirised these creatures with:

> You cannot hope to bribe or twist
> (Thank God!) the British journalist,
> But seeing what the man will do
> Unbribed, there's no occasion to.

Let it be said loud and clear that although the press (and the rest of the media) has frequently abused its freedom with slanted stories and misleading headlines, the alternative of a state-controlled media is far more dangerous and must be resisted at all costs. For all its faults and self-indulgences, the press is still the chief guardian against public and private corruption and scandals, cruelty and injustice. And there is much to be said on the credit side. As well as exposing evils, it sponsors good causes, uncovers heroes as well as villains and provides essential information of the Julius Caesar type such as the weather, the markets, finance, the law courts, the churches, sporting and entertainment fixtures. There is a whole library of books about the evils of the written word of the press, though fewer about the evils of the spoken word. The academic critics put forward ardent pleas for a more responsible press, with a commitment to perform a more serious socially critical job in the fields of culture, education and politics. That's all very fine but the question is: Who's going to buy papers of that sort?

Is it any wonder that journalists are a weird mob? They lurk behind the scenes of politics, big business, crime, sport, entertainment, writing many stories that can never be printed. They see life in the raw from the inside, more often the seedy side. It makes many of them cynics and disbelievers, few retain much idealism or faith in human nature. They know they are not held in high regard by the public (who nevertheless rush to buy the papers they write for). People in trouble with the law or debt-collectors disguise their true identity by describing themselves as 'labourers' or 'journalists'. They are called nasty names by public figures who claim they have been 'misreported'. The ultimate epithet was uttered by former Prime Minister Sir John Gorton. He is on record as having described journalists (presumably those of the Parliamentary Press Gallery at Canberra) as 'slimy white things that crawl out of sewers'. Conrad Black, the Canadian Press baron who conducts the Fairfax group of newspapers, was warned about the militancy of Australian journalists. He seems to be getting along with them but has noted that alcoholism seems to be endemic. You should not be surprised that many journalists have been driven to drink because of the nature of their work.

Bearing all that in mind, it was only natural that journalists should form a club to get away from it all. And journalists being journalists, it was also only natural that there would be all kinds of troubles and complexities. A Sydney Press Club was formed in 1911 with premises in Hamilton Street. It became fraught with internal disputes and feuds. In 1937, the defection of a journalist member of the board of directors resulted in journalists losing control of the club to the associate members. The journalists of Sydney rallied together and, after litigation, a new club, the Journalists' Club, was granted a licence in 1939. The New South Wales Teachers' Federation offered the third floor of Federation House in Phillip Street as club premises at a nominal rent of £1 per month until the club established itself financially. By July 1939 the club had 100 Australian Journalists Association members (yours truly being No. 66). The newly elected Prime Minister of Australia, Robert Menzies, gave it his official blessing by attending an inaugural dinner at Pfahlert's Hotel on 29 July.

The club stayed at Phillip Street until 1958 when it moved to its own premises in Chalmers Street, adjacent to Central Railway Station. Since the end of 1940, its doors have never been closed, operating on a 24-hours-a-day, seven-days-a-week liquor licence to cater for its journalist and kindred trades workers. Its associate members included lawyers, actors, musicians, politicians, public servants, businessmen and what have you, an extraordinary mixture of professions and trades, politics and religions. The club's original charter to 'promote literary, artistic, scientific culture and research' has been followed over the years, with awards for literature and art.

The club has been addressed by such guests as a Pope, cardinals, archbishops, Governors-General, prime ministers, premiers, national and international leaders in the fields of literature, art, music, religion, film, theatre, radio, television, commerce and sport. Although its thunder has been stolen somewhat in recent years by the National Press Club in Canberra, the Journos' still hosts a regular round of distinguished people. The VIP Visitors Book contains the names of eight Australian Prime Ministers—Menzies, Curtin, Whitlam, Chifley, Holt, McMahon, Fraser and Hawke. Others include Noel Coward, Sir Edmund Hillary, Danny Kaye, Helen Keller, Norman Lindsay, Rupert Murdoch, Sir Ralph Richardson, Paul Robeson, Alfred Hitchcock, Dame Sybil Thorndyke, Katharine Hepburn, Kath Walker, Harold Larwood, Morris West and dozens of others of a world-wide section of eminent people. The name of Prince Philip, the Queen's husband, is not in the book but he visited the club in Phillip Street during World War II when he was serving as a young officer in the Royal Navy. He was taken there late one night in 1945 by his friend, Sydney photographer Joe Fallon. Philip was serving in HMS *Whelp* with his Australian officer friend, Michael Parker, of the same age and spirit. It was Philip's final bachelor fling before marrying Princess Elizabeth. He and Parker, both bearded and dressed in identical uniform, took each other's identity in pranks at parties in Sydney and Melbourne.

When Pope Paul VI announced his intention of visiting Australia in December 1970, the Journalists' Club, via its president, Don Angel, invited him to address the Australian mass media through the facilities of the club. The letter to the Pope ended with, 'I respectfully draw your attention to the signature. Signed ANGEL, president.' It did the trick. The Pope held a highly successful media conference under club auspices at the Wentworth Hotel. Afterwards he accepted from the hands of Don Angel the gift of a toy kangaroo on behalf of the media.

The postwar decade until the coming of television in 1956, which revolutionised all aspects of our lives, saw the golden era of radio drama. The Colgate–Palmolive plays had a huge audience, as did ABC plays. 2GB was just down Phillip Street from the Journos' and the actors and disc jockeys made it their green room. Their names were of the household variety, such stars as Peter Finch, Rod Taylor, Grant Taylor, Lloyd Lamble, Ron Randall, John Meillon, Chips Rafferty, Alex Archdale, Jacky Carpenter, Denis Collinson, Eric Parrant, John Dease, Gordon Chater, Terry Dear, Dick Fair, Jack Burgess, Michael Pate and many others. There were all sorts at the bar. In one corner Peter Finch and Alex Macdonald might be holding forth; in another corner the president of the Teachers' Federation might be arguing with two top Communists of the day, Ernie Thornton, of the Ironworkers' Union and Jack Hughes of the Federated Clerks' Union. It was a noisy place, day and all night, with hardly room to move in the small bar area.

On the other side of Phillip Street towards King Street was the small Phillip Street Theatre where many wonderful shows were staged (remember this was before the days of television). It was there that the great Laurence Olivier (or was it his beautiful wife, Vivien Leigh?) 'discovered' Peter Finch, launching him for future Hollywood superstardom and to bed with Vivien. Those were the golden years of the legitimate theatre in Sydney, supplementing the radio plays. Among the actresses (they call themselves actors today, which seems to me sexist) were Gwen Plumb, Ruth Cracknell, Neva Carr-Glynn, Dinah Shearing, June Salter, Wendy Blacklock, Lyndell Barbour, the Perriman sisters, Muriel Steinbeck, Margo Lee, Thelma Scott, Hilda Scurr and so many other talented players. Some were often seen in the Journos' but only in the dining room, accompanied by a male club member. They were not permitted to drink in the bar area. Women members of the Australian Journalists' Association were also barred, as they had been granted only honorary club membership, with no access to the bar. The reason given for not granting full membership was that there was insufficient space to make reasonable accommodation available. Mind you, it is only fair to point out that women were not welcome in any Sydney hotel public bar in those days, one of the reasons for the ban being that they would be exposed to too much bad language. The ban on AJA women members remained after the club moved to its commodious three-storied building in Chalmers Street, causing much bitterness and controversy. It was to be a further fourteen years before women were granted full membership in 1972. It was a strange example of male chauvinism, seeing that journalists pride themselves on being broad-minded and supporters of the equality of the sexes.

It would be an understatement to describe the Journos' merely as an 'unconventional' club in those early days. In fact, it was regarded as a 'bloodhouse' in more conservative circles. There came a period when it was decided to 'upgrade the club's image'. I was persuaded against my better judgment to stand for election to the board of directors on a sort of 'reform' ticket. I served for two terms but did not enjoy it very much as I am not much of a reformer. The idea was to cut down on the incidence of late-night altercations between members and other untoward behaviour. I found it uncomfortable to sit in judgment on colleagues and sentence them to varying terms of banishment from the club. One member, for instance, used to sleep on a billiards table after all-night drinking sessions. When told to cut it out under the new image-upgrading, he protested, '. . .and what about the people who wake me up playing billiards?' It was difficult to know what action to take against a prominent press photographer who, incensed by the treatment he was getting from it, picked up a poker machine and threw it out of the window on to a vacant block of land adjacent to Martin Place. And there was the matter of the hats and braces. In those days, it was not socially acceptable to wear hats indoors, even in lifts crowded with people, or to wear exposed braces. These habits were cherished by several of our oldest members, including a famous New Zealand cartoonist named Brodie Mack. They put up a fierce fight but the ban was enforced. Strange to think that today not many men wear hats and exposed braces are considered trendy in some fashionable circles.

One day a giant international Rugby League forward, belligerent in drink, was suspended for six months for a late-night fracas in the club. He defied the ban one afternoon and, somewhat the worse for wear, walked into the club and demanded a drink from the bar steward. I happened to be there at the time and the steward looked at me appealingly as a board member. This big hulk of a man put his ham-like hands on my shoulders and asked me what I was going to do about it. I managed to stammer something to the effect that if he did not leave the club premises immediately I would telephone the police to eject him. His grip tightened and I thought my last hour had come. Then suddenly and inexplicably he broke away, burst into tears of repentance and meekly left the room. I was praised afterwards for standing up to him. The truth of the matter was that I would have fallen down in terror but for his tight grip on me.

The board was never officially informed about a ritual that took place early every morning in the days when Sydney was serviced by trams. The last tram to Watsons Bay (or should we say the first tram?) left the club each day at 2 a.m. That is to say, the tram would stay parked at nearby Queen's Square while the driver and conductor adjourned to the Journos' for a few refreshers. At the appointed time, the crew and the few regular club passengers for the Eastern Suburbs would totter around to Queen's Square to board the tram. On occasions, it was said, a club member would take over the driving of the tram, a frightening prospect when one considers the precipitous nature of the tram line from South Head Lighthouse down to Watsons Bay.

In the course of time the image-upgrading campaign ended at the Journos'. Nobody was allowed to sleep on the billiards tables any more, or wear hats or exposed braces inside the club. Otherwise everything went back to normal, as I suppose is the case today.

When he was not on walkabout in the Red Centre or the Top End, black-and-white artist Eric Jolliffe was often seen in the Journos'. Eric was the creator of *Saltbush Bill*, an immensely popular strip cartoon, featuring outback life. *Saltbush Bill* is still going strong after more than 50 years, though now in the form of Jolliffe's *Outback* books. Strangers to the Journos' were sometimes startled on first introduction to Eric Jolliffe. Suddenly a phalanger (small flying squirrel) would dart out of Eric's pocket, run swiftly up one arm, across his shoulders and then down the other arm into the other pocket. Eric had two of them and they were as tame as mice and just as mischievous.

In 1948, Eric accompanied A.P. Elkin, professor of anthropology at the University of Sydney, during a seven-week National Geographic Society expedition to the Northern Territory under the auspices of the Australian Department of Information. With them as an adviser went a rugged bush philosopher named W.E. (Bill) Harney, who had recently retired as a patrol officer and Protector of Aborigines with the Department of Native Affairs. The party travelled 1,000 miles by truck to the Roper River, visiting mission stations and Aboriginal settlements. After the Roper, they travelled a further 1,000 miles around Arnhem Land and the northern coast.

Eric brought Bill Harney to Sydney and the Journos' once or twice and I would rank him as the most unforgettable bush character I ever met. With rugged features and a leathery face, Bill was a sort of pre-Hogan Crocodile Dundee, with a never-ending swag of bush yarns and philosophies. At the time he cared for between 8,000 and 10,000 Aborigines in their tribal areas. His headquarters were at Katherine and he patrolled an area of 250,000 square miles, taking in the Barkly Tablelands, Arnhem Land and Bathurst and Melville Islands. The Aborigines called him Ebumbarboo, meaning 'Rock-Head'. 'If they had a word for Pumpkin-Head, they'd probably call me that,' he told me. Bill's job was to see that rations were properly distributed to the Aborigines, settle their many tribal disputes and generally act as godfather to them. He travelled by plane, boat and truck and was sometimes away for two months at a time. Bill was a natural storyteller and had the gift to put them down in words. His first book, *Taboo*, had just been published when I met him and he went on to write nine more, including collections of bush ballads and verse. He had a remarkable knowledge of Aboriginal languages and ways of life. He wrote many magazine articles and appeared on radio and television. It was fitting that his last official posting was as Curator of Ayers Rock from 1957 to 1961, before he retired to his Dreamtime in 1962. Here are a few of his bush philosophies:

> The secret of life is not money but to learn to live without it.
> A house is a gaol—give me the open bush.
> The only reason I come to the city is to become damned pleased to get back to the bush.

'I can't write for nuts,' Bill said to me once, 'but I can tell stories.' To which I replied that many a pretty writer has failed because he lacked that very gift. In *Who's Who in Australia*, Bill described his recreations as 'anthropology, taking life easy'. His only club was the Bread and Cheese (Melbourne).

Eric Jolliffe, by the way, is now 87 and living at Bateau Bay but not exactly in retirement. As well as producing his *Outback* books and an annual Jolliffe calendar, he took up watercolour painting at the age of 82 and recently held a successful one-man exhibition at a Kurrajong art gallery.

Another visitor from the Red Centre was Albert Namatjira, the great Aboriginal artist, and I still remember it with a touch of sadness. They dressed him up in a suit and brought him by air to Sydney to meet the new Queen Elizabeth II on her Australian tour in 1954. His minders took him to the Journos' for some reason or another. He was the most gentle and shyest of giants, with soft but troubled eyes and a quiet, deep voice. He was uncomfortable in his clothes and surroundings, and I felt unutterably sorry for him. Fame had brought trouble to his simple life and it was soon to take on the elements of a Greek tragedy.

Namatjira was a full-blood member of the Aranda tribe. After earning a living at a mission out of Alice Springs carving mulga-wood plaques, he was suddenly 'discovered' as a talented painter of Australian gum trees amid Red Centre landscapes. It was not long before a Namatjira painting was worth hundreds, if not thousands of pounds and he was hailed as another Hans Heysen. The blessings were mixed for Albert, who was not allowed to vote (or drink) but expected to pay income tax. When he tried to buy a house in Alice Springs in 1951, he was refused permission on the grounds that Aborigines were not allowed into the town after dark.

Albert returned to the Northern Territory after meeting the Queen and in 1957 was made an official Australian citizen as a reward for his growing international reputation as an artist. This was ten years before all Aborigines were given (I regard the word 'granted' as condescending) full citizenship in 1967. Namatjira's citizenship only deepened his problem of trying to live according to two sets of cultures and laws. He was now legally entitled to purchase liquor and, under tribal laws, was expected to share his possessions with his relatives. About 500 'relatives' moved in to share the spoils. In October 1958, Namatjira was arrested for supplying them with liquor and sentenced to six months gaol. There was a national outcry, the sentence was reduced and he was released after two months. But the distress of it all had taken its toll on the old black painter. Two years later, on 8 October 1959, Albert Namatjira died at the age of 59, a broken and bitter man. It was commonly thought that his bitterness was directed at the treatment he had received from the white man, but Eric Jolliffe believes it was disillusionment with his own tribe that broke him up.

I have fond memories of the Journos' and they kindly made me an honorary member in my second childhood. It was a lively place, full of lively and interesting people. I have inconsequential recollections of it, such as dear old Jack Hatch, who was regarded as the Club Earbasher. Jack played the cornet in a Royal Australian Navy band before becoming a journalist, a most unlikely transition. The trouble with Jack was that he just could not stop talking. People would retreat in mock terror when they saw him coming in their direction. He was at his most dangerous when cornering a victim to explain why he did not deserve to be called an earbasher. I remember Jack holding forth one day at a table laden with drinkers at the Journos' and a member pleading, 'Jack, I'll give you ten bob to shut up for five minutes'. Big John Yeomans leapt to his feet and exclaimed, 'Don't take it, Jack! You can do better!' Jack left journalism to establish a duck farm of all things.

I'm not against progress (it would not make any difference if I was) but I don't think I'd enjoy being a computerised journalist today. A Sydney colleague tells me how he clocks in each day to his computer by pressing a switch and it prints out: *Enter your log-in name.* He taps out *Charlie Jones* and the computer greets it with *Good morning, Charlie Jones!*

I've got this horrible feeling that one day my computer would learn to talk, with a polite *Good morning, Gilbert!* and then at some later date, *Good morning, Gilbert! Don't bother to come in tomorrow—I don't need you any more.*

8

The Golden Ball

The *Sun* building in Elizabeth Street, backing into Phillip Street, had a huge ball painted in gold leaf on top of it, symbolising the *Sun* newspaper was 'Above All For Australia'. It was known as the Golden Ball. The ball is still there, but the glitter and the gold had worn off to a dull grey when the Government Insurance Office bought the building in 1956. The building was the home of the *Daily Telegraph Pictorial* when I worked there in the late 1920s. Next door was the New South Wales Leagues Club, with its bars, billiards tables and poker machines. The club was the bane of the life of Bill Tonkin, the *Telegraph* editor. He called it 'The Menace'. It was obvious that the close proximity of a club like that and a team of journalists was bound to result in a union. Bill would cry despairingly, 'Where's Gilbert?' or 'Where's Blue?' — 'Send someone into The Menace and tell them to come here immediately or they'll be fired!'

In the course of time, the *Telegraph* was taken over by the Packers and moved to a new location in Castlereagh Street. About twenty years later, after the end of World War II, I found myself back on the same floor at the Golden Ball where the *Sunday Sun* was produced under the editorship of Tom Gurr. The Leagues Club was still next door, though much bigger, with more bars, billiards tables and poker machines. But Tom did not have to worry about sending messengers into The Menace to round up his staff, as Bill Tonkin had done. From Tom's office, he looked straight across Phillip Street into the third floor of Federation House and the billiards room of the Sydney Journalists' Club. As most of his staff were members of the Journos', you could say that Tom had complete control of them and knew exactly where to find them.

There was plenty to write about in the *Sunday Sun* during the immediate postwar decade of victory euphoria and, ultimately, disillusionment. The wartime blackmarkets in liquor, housing and other commodities continued to flourish. Exorbitant 'key money' was demanded for the purchase or rental of houses or flats, to the detriment of returned servicemen and the enrichment of unscrupulous landlords and real estate agents. There were years of headlines from 1951 to 1954 out of the Royal Commission in New South Wales Liquor Laws when Justice A.V. Maxwell uncovered unimaginable bootlegging rackets and conspiracies between breweries, hotels and mobster-run nightclubs. There was the usual quota of scandals, murders, kidnappings and general mayhem. The youth revolution continued with crazes such as rock-and-roll, jitterbugging, the twist and yo-yos. In sport, Don Bradman scored his 100th century in 1947 and in 1948 led the Australian side to England to notch the unique record of remaining undefeated throughout the tour.

The big one in 1954 was the political defection of Russian spy Vladimir Petrov. It reunited my wife and me with our old Adelaide friends, George and Edith Ligertwood. Now Mr Justice Ligertwood of the South Australian Supreme Court, he had been appointed as one of the three judges of the Petrov Royal Commission. The Commission developed into what one commentator described as a B-grade movie. Spies, counter-spies, false beards, kidnappings, coded messages left in tree trunks, other secret material written on toilet paper, Petrov's beautiful wife, Evdokia—the Petrov story had it all, alternating between melodrama and farce. Evatt, Bialoguski, Lockwood, Dalziel headed a large cast of characters and there were angry scenes in court.

The Ligertwoods used our house as a retreat. Often they would arrive in a Commonwealth car for dinner or just to talk. George Ligertwood was such a scrupulous man of integrity that he was uncomfortable in using a Commonwealth car for private visits. I assured him that they went with the job and that nobody could possibly begrudge him such a convenience. If you think that he ever spoke about proceedings in court or the people concerned, you have another think coming. There were no scoops or leaks from 'Your Honour', as I called him, and none expected. I detected, though, that His Honour was somewhat shocked and disgusted by the outlandish and theatrical performances in the crowded Darlinghurst courthouse. The proceedings received saturation media coverage and there were stories (since debunked) that Menzies had conceived and stage-managed the whole thing for political purposes.

I shared a large room with Kenneth Slessor and Ray Robinson at the *Sunday Sun*. Ken was writing leaders (editorials, they call them now) for the daily afternoon *Sun*. He was a bit of a dandy in some ways and very methodical in everything he did. He appeared to make drafts of his leaders in pen or pencil before the final version. Having finished his leader, he would prepare to depart by arranging his pens, finely sharpened pencils, Indian rubber and reference books into a symmetrical pattern on his desk. Every day they were meticulously positioned in exactly the same place.

By then Kenneth Slessor was firmly established as one of Australia's finest poets, with an international reputation, and a small coterie of admiring disciples in Sydney. He was a Jekyll-and-Hyde writer; not only did he write exquisite verses but was also a prolific writer of comic verse and prose, especially when the editor of the irreverent *Smith's Weekly* in 1935–39. He was made editor-in-chief for four months at the end of 1939, when the circulation of *Smith's* had begun to slide. George Blaikie in his *Remember Smith's Weekly?* describes Slessor's efforts to save the dying paper as 'one of the epics of newspaper history. He not only edited the paper but wrote the front pages, the leaders, the satire, the verses to go with the weekly caricatures, the film reviews and answered the telephone to all who wished to register a grouch against the paper.' Ken was shy and modest. He was easy enough to get on with, if you knew his temperament, but when upset, would turn puce in the face and stutter with anger. He was a *bon vivant*, greatly enjoying food and wine. Slessor went off to the Middle East as an official Australian war correspondent in World War II, there to have blazing rows with the Australian commander-in-chief, General Sir Thomas Blamey, over censorship and other matters. After the war he returned to journalism and the *Sun* and, reputedly, never wrote another serious poem for publication for the next 25 years when he died in 1971. I find it hard to believe that a poet of Ken's calibre could have suddenly turned off his poetry like a tap and I suspect that he would have written many more beautiful lines for his private satisfaction and contentment.

I remember that room at the *Sunday Sun*, particularly after the first issue of a new weekly magazine entitled *People*. The title was the brainchild of our editor-in-chief, New Zealand-born Tom Gurr. The first issue was written by members of the staff, without bylines, my contribution being a profile of the eminent Sydney surgeon, Mr Harry Winsor, and his revolutionary treatment of 'blue babies'. The star feature was 'A Study in Scarlet' by Tom Gurr, a brilliant story of Sydney's underworld, featuring two of its most melodramatic characters, Tilly Devine and Kate Leigh, bordello madams and sly-grog operators. These two scarlet women engaged in fierce feuds and Tom painted a vivid picture of the scene.

A couple of days after the first publication of *People*, Ken Slessor was working away at his leader, and I was preparing my weekly column 'The Way I See It', when a large and florid woman with a wide floral hat on her head, and carrying a copy of *People* in one hand and an umbrella in the other, burst into the room. 'Where's the bloody bastard who wrote this story about me? Where is he?' It was Kate Leigh and she continued her stream of invective. 'I'll knock his bloody head in!' she screamed. 'Where is he?' Ken, who did not like 'scenes' or unpremeditated violence, hastily arranged his pens and pencils into their symmetrical shape and quietly slipped out of the room. I was left to confront this raging harridan. I played the part of the village idiot; I had no idea who had written the story; the editor was out of the town; etcetera, etcetera, etcetera. Kate gave me up in disgust and charged down the corridor where she confronted the acting-editor of our women's magazine, hitting him over the head with her umbrella. Uttering more obscenities, she managed to penetrate to the editorial holy-of-holies and terrify Tom's secretary. With great presence of mind, she said the editor was out of town and would Miss Leigh please put her complaint in writing. Eventually Miss Leigh gave up and departed the scene in high dudgeon.

Tom Gurr, now retired, was a gifted and innovative journalist and editor. He began his Australian career with the *Melbourne Herald*, when he ran its newsreel division. When it was amalgamated with Cinesound, he was put in charge of the operations of that famed newsreel organisation for two years. After sub-editorial work for the Sydney *Daily Telegraph*, he became editor of the *Sunday Sun*, then editor-in-chief of the paper and its many magazines. Three of them—*Pix*, *People* and *Sporting Life*—were his own creation.

Kate Leigh's assault on the *Sunday Sun* is as clearly remembered today by Tom Gurr as it is to me. He confesses that he borrowed the title of 'A Study in Scarlet' from the Sherlock Holmes story and wrote his story with some close knowledge of his two leading characters. Tilly Devine, in fact, once had Tom to afternoon tea at her Maroubra home. This is his story:

> Matilda ('Tilly') Devine was a bottle-blonde London whore who was wed by Jim Devine, AIF private, in 1916 and who came to Sydney as a Pommy war bride. Jim was a good-natured bludger and Tilly was in everything with a quid in it. One day, talking to a member of my staff, she discovered that I knew about film-making and would I come to afternoon tea? So, one fine afternoon I drove to the Devine cottage in Torrington Road, Maroubra.
>
> Now, at this time, Sydney society was graced by blonde Nellie Cameron, product of a private girls' school and a graduate of the tough end of town. The company she kept had earned her, after the termination in death of members of her gallery of criminal associates, the title of Angel of Death. Her most recent swain was one, Guido Colletti, a handy man with a razor when it came to battle and a jealous man, too. At about the time of my invitation to afternoon tea, word had got around that Colletti was 'looking for' Sweet Nellie so she was taken to the shelter of the Devine menage.
>
> I was received in the friendliest manner. We discussed the storming of the Devine home on a very recent night. Mr Colletti had arrived, after a telephone warning, by taxi. It was to be Nellie or else! Shouted threats. Guns. A rifle shot killed the innocent middle-aged taxi driver. The raiders had departed. No Nellie. During the telling of the tale, I was served with cucumber sandwiches and tea by Tilly. Also present was the establishment's Man Friday, a wizened little man called Les. Enter Nellie and girl friend, back from the beach. The ladies retired to dress. Left me and Man Friday.
>
> Conversation returned to the battle of Torrington Road. So the cops had no guns as evidence of the taxi driver's slaying? 'Nah,' smirked Les. He lifted the lid of the upright piano and brought out the rifle. The dumb cops, said Les, had no ear for music . . . At a subsequent meeting, I declined to be the Devine

cinematic producer and underwriter of the enterprise. I said they might find an undertaker more useful.

It's a pity Tom did not produce 'A Study in Scarlet' on film—it might have been an underworld classic.

I remember that room at the *Sunday Sun* for another bizarre reason. In a corner of the room on a pedestal was a huge and very old *Webster's International Dictionary*. We all frequently consulted it and one day, browsing through it, I came upon the word 'merkin', with the unexpected meaning of 'false pubic hair'. We all giggled about this extraordinary product, wondering why anybody would want to use a merkin, anyway. A couple of days later, Emile Mercier came in with his weekly cartoon or joke block for the paper. Mercier was in great vogue at the time. Of French extraction, he was the son of a baker in New Caledonia and had come to Australia in search of fame and fortune. His distinctive Aussie-Gallic humour had caught on in his rather gawky drawings, which often included a weird-looking cat, dog or fish lurking in corners.

I showed Emile the dictionary on this occasion and the following Sunday his cartoon appeared with a drawing in one corner of a repulsive-looking fish with the word 'MERKIN' underneath it. We all had a good private laugh about it until the editor received a letter from an irate mother of a fourteen-year-old schoolgirl who, in studying for her exams, had come upon the word merkin in an old dictionary. The mother expressed disgust at the action of a family Sunday newspaper in publishing such filth. There was an office inquest and I copped the blame but received a heaven-sent reprieve. Some impulse made me inspect the dictionary again and I made the face-saving discovery that as well as meaning false pubic hair, merkin also meant a mediaeval French army cannon. A dignified letter was written to the shocked mother that merkin meant a mediaeval French cannon, after which Mercier had named his imaginary fish. Nothing further was heard of the matter, though Tom Gurr kept an even closer scrutiny of Emile's drawings afterwards, screening them for hidden indecencies and rudery. I still have in my possession the original of a Mercier drawing banned by the editor of the *Sun-Herald*, after the amalgamation of the *Sunday Sun* and *Sunday Herald* in 1953. It shows a man arm-in-arm with a woman with an ample bosom walking past a newspaper placard about the Melbourne Cup. ' 'Ullo!! Looks like Charlie's struck the big double at last!' an onlooker remarks. It would not raise an eyebrow today, even if the big double were drawn topless. Every now and then Mercier would include a ricketty old building named Mant's Manse in a drawing. Once he depicted a Balsam & Co draper's shop window displaying 'Stiflingly Stylish Mant's Pants'.

Every Friday at the Golden Ball we would go up to the accounts department

"Well, here y'are! A fiver a week for the house, of course, the rowboat at the usual four bob an hour rate!"

Emile Mercier's impression of 'Mant's Manse'

where a young pay clerk would give us an envelope with our money in it. He was said to be a very good cricketer and his name was Richie Benaud.

The enforced demise of the *Sunday Sun* as an entity was a sad affair for journalists. It had been built up by Tom Gurr into an entertaining, informative and influencial newspaper with such outstanding journalists on its staff as Colin Simpson, Ray Robinson, Jack Paton, Syd King, Alan Dexter and many others, and was home of the immortal Ginger Meggs. Early in 1953, our proprietors, Associated Newspapers Ltd, put on a sumptuous dinner at Ushers Hotel to celebrate a Sunday circulation of 500,000, a landmark in Australian publishing history, far ahead of any other newspaper in the Commonwealth. Not long afterwards Associated Newspapers were taken over by Fairfax. The *Sunday Sun* was merged with the *Sunday Herald* (150,000) into the *Sun–Herald*. We moved to a new Fairfax building in Broadway (Alcatraz, we soon called it) and life was never quite the same again.

The face of downtown Sydney began to change rapidly in that first decade after the war as the bulldozers moved in and new skyscrapers reached for the sky. Among the victims were to be many old and famous hotels, redolent with stories of old Australia, soon to be replaced by a new multicultural Australia. Among these were the Australia, Ushers, Belfields, Assembly, Durban Club, Metropole, Newcastle and Aarons.

The Australia had been the social hub of Sydney for half a century or more. The Long Bar, the second longest bar in Australia, was the haunt of both city and country drinkers. The fashionable rendezvous was its palm-fronted Wintergarden which took up practically the whole ground floor. There was to be seen everybody who was anybody, as the waiters dashed to and fro with drinks. There was a barber's shop downstairs where I used to get my hair cut by Mr Hubble, the last of the comb-and-scissors men. A two-shilling piece tip would be accepted discreetly when the operation was over. The Metropole was almost exclusively a countryman's hotel, packed to its limits during the Royal Easter Show or the spring racing carnival. On your right as you entered Ushers from Castlereagh Street was the New Guinea Bar. In the 1930s, that was where the stories were for a journalist. Standing at the bar, you would meet prospectors, government district patrol officers, gold millionaires, pilots who dared the turbulent skies of New Guinea in small piston-propelled aeroplanes flying gold to the coast, and all kinds of other adventurers. The Assembly was a journalists' pub, being close to *Smith's Weekly* and a particularly thirsty mob of black-and-white artists.

Geoff Cahill, in retirement at Port Macquarie, recalls that Herb Blaterwick, the genial mine host at the Assembly, took a fatherly interest in journos to the extent of making a 'tick book' from Monday each week. A similar situation was in place at Dr Moreau's Tudor Hotel in Phillip Street, while journos on dog watch were given rare accommodation at Herb Donnison's Royal Hotel in King Street. The *bête noire* of all journalists was six o'clock closing but Herb overcame this by providing late workers with a key to the top bar which was not manned. The drill was to either put money for drinks into the till or an IOU. In later years Herb told Geoff Cahill that it was a most profitable bar, with no defaulters. In fact, clients became so confused that they left notes for more drinks than actually consumed. 'We Depression folk were chronically broke,' Geoff recalls. 'One boost was Harold Brokenshire's magnificent silver cigarette case. It had a hockable value of three pounds at the pawnbroker's. I would say, 'Hey, Broke! May I borrow your cigarette case until next Friday?' 'Sorry, Geoff! Neil Murray has it. It goes to Freddie Folkard after Friday, then to Gibbo.' That cigarette case was shuttled around like a pass-out check at a theatre—sometimes Broke did not see it for twelve months.

The gradual disappearance of these old pubs was the precursor of the changing habits of Australian drinking, especially the old-fashioned Aussie beer-drinker. Wine-growers had launched a big public relations campaign to eradicate the word 'plonk' for describing their product. Beer gardens were replacing the revolting 'six o'clock swill' and, for the first time, women were being admitted to bars. Barmaids were changing, too; younger women were taking over from older women. New restaurants with Continental chefs and menus were opening as European migrants poured into the country.

One of the last of the big hotels to fall under the jackhammer, in 1964, was Aarons in Gresham and Pitt Streets towards Circular Quay. It had been the mecca for generations of wool, sheep and cattle men, shipping magnates and clerks, cabinet ministers from Macquarie Street, government servants from the nearby Education and Lands Department buildings, and itinerant groups of rural and metropolitan newspapermen. There was a masculinity about the spacious old Gresham Street bar with its 30-foot high ceiling, substantial oak bar counters, shelves, doors and cedar panelling. And the mouth-watering rump and fillet steaks in its dining room were world-famous.

I wrote a lament for Aarons for *Nation*:

> The end of Aarons [it said in part] will accelerate the death of the old-time unrepentant Australian beer-drinker. The schooner and pint man is dying out, in the city pubs at any rate. He was the man who actually *liked* what was once called the 'six o'clock swill'. He enjoyed fighting his way to the bar and drinking with a 'school' of mates. It was an Australian way of life that horrified overseas visitors, but he didn't care. He would have found no contentment in a quiet English pub, sipping nut brown ale at a table and listening to the gossip of the village. For him the crowded, noisy impatience of a Sydney bar, the exuberant shout of a Lennie Lower's 'Here's Luck!'
>
> If the present trend of pub destruction continues, I can see the emergence of a Sydney counterpart of Mr Humphrey Pump. For those unfamiliar with Chesterton's *The Flying Inn*, Mr Pump was the last English innkeeper when all Western Europe went 'dry'. However, under the laws of England, it was still possible to sell or give away liquor if you were in possession of an inn sign—and Mr Pump had the last sign in England. So he and his Irish friend, Captain Patrick Dalroy, careered all over England carrying the sign of The Old Ship, being chased by policemen, members of parliament and Chesterton's 'great big black teetotallers'.
>
> It may come to that in Sydney. When all the real pubs are closed down, I can see an Australian Humphrey Pump planing the sign of the last 'Coo-ee Arms' in the middle of Macquarie Place, surrounded by an excited crowd of emancipated beer-drinkers. The cries of 'Here's luck!' will be heard as far away as Observatory Hill. Then the traditional enemies will appear and the Australian Mr Pump will grab his sign and flee towards Circular Quay, pursued by them all: Brown Bombers, Boys in Blue, members of the Water Board, the Milk Board, the Ladies' Temperance Union and the rest. Farewell, Aarons and all the other vanished pubs of Sydney!

My article resulted in an indignant and somewhat hurt response to *Nation* from two members of the public relations section of the Water Board, John Brennan and Phil Dorter:

The Water Board is blamed for many things but Gilbert Mant's suggestion that it would join in hounding the last hostelry out of town is a slur most unjust. For roughly 25 years two journalists we know inhabited the old *Bulletin* in lower George Street, where, as Mr Mant laments, the pubs are now falling like the flowers of the forest before those great glassy-eyed skyscrapers. In their time, the Lion was the first to go—a pleasant old pub across the road from the City Bowling Green, headquarters of the Royal and Ancient Paspalum Bowling Club. They noticed its passing with regret, but without foreboding. As they recall, the Star was the next casualty—otherwise known as Sneddon's or the Bulletin Pub. They suspected then that the writing was on the wall. Then the Victoria fell and they panicked—it was time to move. They cased the city and decided that the Water Board, atop Brickfield Hill, was beautifully set about with excellent hostelries which seemed assured of reasonable longevity. And so they sought sanctuary from lower George Street. In the half-decade they have sheltered there, no nearby hostelry has been sacrificed to so-called progress, while downtown the Euston and Aarons have fallen to the wreckers and the beery, cheery old Plaza has transformed into what they neither know nor like.

Who, by the way, but old *Bulletin* men would know the secret route to Aarons—down to the composing room, through the stereo, down through publishing, a leap over Hamilton Street, through an insurance building (one of the first 'glass houses'), a dash across Pitt Street, into another commercial building, down the passage, turn left and into the bar! It was a maze that would have pleased Chesterton's 'rolling English drunkard'; certainly it fascinated privileged friends, and frustrated searching wives and debt collectors. All gone now. Sometimes these two ageing journalists make a sentimental journey from Brickfield Hill to lower George Street to see if Claude Fay's Metropolitan and Jim Buckley's Newcastle still stand where they stood. They do, but our friends fear for them as they return to Buckfield Hill where Lee Dowling's Lismore shelters comfortably under the south wall of the Water Board where, across the road, the Edinburgh flourishes with, further along Bathurst Street, the Royal Standard and the Hyde Park. In nearby Liverpool Street, the North Star and Century still endure, while in Park Street, the Town Hall, Coronation and Criterion are beacons to good company, and the Castlereagh and the King's Head nestle on each side of Sir Frank's [Packer] edifice.

No, the Water Board offers no threat to these genuine inns, it dwells amicably among them, some of the staff no doubt contributing to their welfare after the whistle blows. It also provides the raw material to make the glorious stuff—12 gallons of water to every gallon ale—and the sewerage maintenance workers stay respectfully out of the sewers until the hotel flush dies down at about 10.30 p.m. And, finally, it is indeed commendable that, whether by accident or design, the board's new building now reaching for the sky, imperilled not a single pub.

Nation gracefully allowed me to acknowledge this letter:

I'm very pleased to accept the assurance of John Brennan and Phil Dorter that the Water Board offers no threat to the pubs of Sydney and I regret that so far the Milk Board has remained silent. It is a sobering thought, however, to learn that 12 gallons of water go into every gallon of ale. One is tempted to remark 'No wonder Sydney's beer's so b____ crook', but I'm content to echo Chesterton's poem about an immortal Biblical drunkard:

> And Noah, he often said to his wife when he sat down to dine,
> 'I don't care where the water goes if it doesn't get into the wine'.

A former cellarman at Aarons named Jim Buckley went on to conduct one of Sydney's most unusual hotels, the Newcastle in lower George Street. When Jim realised that many of his regulars were journalists, advertising men, PR men and art lovers, he established an art gallery in his pub. Soon the walls were covered in paintings, at first amateurish and then dominated by professional work of some of our best artists. A little Englishman named John Allcot was a regular drinker and exhibitor of wonderful paintings of ships and the sea; he was, in fact, one of Australia's leading marine artists. The exhibitions were officially opened by leading art critics or public figures. The Newcastle was always packed with people at lunchtime, the long-haired bohemians rubbing shoulders with smartly groomed business executives and professional men and women. All talking shop at the top of their voices. The Newcastle was a second home to author Xavier Herbert on his visits to Sydney from the Northern Territory. Another visitor from the Top End was Alan Stewart, a former public relations man for the Australian Gas Light Company who had established a tourist buffalo and crocodile safari business, becoming known as the Great White Hunter.

I remember 'Buckley's' for a very personal reason. Readers will have noted, some perhaps with disapproval, that strong drink and pubs are mentioned frequently in this book. But that's the way it was. There was a lot of drinking and it destroyed one or two of our most brilliant writers and journalists. There were occasions when I wondered whether it would destroy me, too. The temptations were many—the nature of the work that had driven many better men to drink, the never-ending free drinks as a columnist, the need for Dutch courage to conquer my nerves to appear on radio or television for publicity and promotion sessions. I was saved, I think, mainly because the older I got, the worse the hangovers became.

The greatest shock I got was while suffering a terrible hangover from some publicity party the night before. Too ill to face work, I sought out Jim Buckley and asked for a room to sleep it off for an hour or two. He gave me Alan Stewart's upstairs room and I fell into a deep sleep. I awoke some hours later and stared straight into the eyes and open jaws of an enormous crocodile. I don't know whether I screamed or not, but I shook like a leaf until I realised it was a stuffed crocodile belonging to the Great White Hunter. It was a comic story to tell afterwards but it gave me a shock and I realised it could have been real. I had been warned and I took heed of it.

A Sydney pub crisis is looming later this year when the large Fairfax staff move from their Alcatraz in Broadway to leased premises in the IBM building in Darling Harbour. There will be much moaning at the Broadway hotel bars and much joy for publicans in the city and nearby watering holes.

A DEATHLY SILENCE: One Friday during the Spring Racing Carnival a lift in the Golden Ball building was taking a full load of *Sun* employees back to work after the luncheon break. Among them was Sir Hugh Denison, chairman of Associated Newspapers Ltd. Sir Hugh was a proper little man, a pillar of the Establishment and a keen racing man, whose horse, Poseidon, had won the Melbourne Cup in 1906. The respectful silence in the presence of the great man was suddenly broken between the third and fourth floors when old Joe Williams, the veteran liftman, asked, 'Excuse me, Sir Hugh, but will the little horse be trying tomorrow?'

There was deathly silence.

9
A Militant Pacifist

Whenever I think of war I think of Jack Rescorl. Jack was a young executive with a Sydney bank in his early twenties with a university degree in economics. The future looked good for him and his adored and adoring fiancee, Becky (not her real name). But it was July 1940 and World War II was at a critical stage. The German blitzkrieg had overrun Holland, Belgium and France. The British Expeditionary Force escaped during the miracle of Dunkirk but was ripe for Hitler's picking. It was obvious, except to head-in-sand isolationists, that if Britain fell, Australia fell with it. That was why enlistments in the Australian armed forces rose from 8,000 in May to 48,000 in June, 21,000 in July and 32,000 in August. The rush to the colours was so great that there were not enough uniforms to clothe all the recruits, arms and ammunition were scarce and few camps existed to train them. The Australian government was forced to temporarily limit enlistments.

That was when Jack Rescorl and I first met as members of the Intelligence Section of the newly formed 2/19th Battalion, 8th Division, AIF. I was 38 years old so there was a difference of about fifteen years in our ages but an instinctive friendship developed between us. Jack was a burly, amiable but thoughtful young man with a big future ahead of him in the bank. We certainly had a physical affinity. Between us we had fallen arches, hammer toes, flat feet and metatarsal troubles. This would not have been so bad if our 'I' section had not included Gordon Smith, a N.S.W. champion walker, and Stan McAlister, a champion marathon runner. With Gordon and Stan in the lead of cross-country training exercises in the Bathurst hills, Jack and I always came staggering in exhausted lasts. But our friendship went much deeper than our feet and I'm sure it would have endured after the war.

The 2/19th Battalion was fairly representative of the enlistments of the Dunkirk era that formed the 8th Division AIF. It had its share of the unemployed, young bloods in search of excitement, pure adventurers and old soldiers from World War I. But the bulk of them were countrymen from the Riverina districts of N.S.W. A relatively large proportion of them were married men with young children. It's not natural for Anglo-Saxons to run around waving flags and uttering patriotic platitudes and these men would have been most reticent and embarrassed if asked why they had enlisted. But you would be sure that if you had suggested that they were there to fight for King and Empire, you would have been laughed out of court. They had gone into the army of their own free will to fight for their families and their farms and other interests in places like Wagga, Cootamundra, Gundagai, Griffith, Leeton and Narrandera. The thought of laying down their lives for the White Cliffs of Dover, the highlands of Scotland, the green hills of Ireland or some remote outpost of Empire in Africa or India was not in their minds. You could sense the general fear in the ranks that if Britain fell, Australia would fall, too. It was clear that there was not a hope in hell of defending it ourselves. Japan was not in the war, so there was no contemplation of America coming to our rescue. Our wives and children would be at the mercy of Hitler's hoons as it was widely known that Australia and New Zealand were high on the list of the Fuehrer's *Lebensraum* ambitions for a German Empire. Simplistic? The truth is always simplistic. The Motherland to these men was Australia and, in particular, the gum trees, the magpies, the old pubs and the bush ways of the Riverina. They knew all about the international arms dealers, the war profiteers, the crooked politicians and financiers—these animals were unimportant in face of the deadly danger at hand. They also believed firmly that it was better to fight it out on foreign soil rather than wait for the enemy to make a battlefield of Australia.

The 8th Division met with an ill-deserved fate. It was sent to Malaya and the so-called 'impregnable fortress' of Singapore as a token of support and strength against a possible Japanese attack. There it remained as a garrison force for more than nine months, the men cursing their fate. Jack and I cursed with the rest of them. We often talked about our homes and what we would do when the war was over. I had a wife and two young children and would go back to my job with Reuters. Jack would marry Becky and have children and I would godfather one of them. The only time Jack expressed real bitterness about our fate was one night when we lay on groundsheets in a tapioca paddock with the rain pounding down on us during a field exercise. Jack spoke about some of his young contemporaries still leading the good life in the fleshpots of Australia. He could not understand, and neither could I, why they had turned a deaf ear to 'the bugle'.

Then Reuters in London reckoned I was wasting my time as a private soldier in a garrison force when I was badly needed for important information work in Australia. They put the screws on me and my family and I was manpowered out of the army in September 1941. I was compelled to agree in writing to the discharge. That led to an agonising dilemma and left me with a permanent chip on my shoulder. My 'I' section mates urged me to get out of the place and half my bloody luck. With their help, I concocted a sort of apologia: 'Although reluctant to leave my army comrades, I agree to the Military Board considering Reuters application for my discharge. I do this on the assumption that the Board will consider the application from the viewpint of whether I would be of greater use to the national war effort as Australian News Editor of Reuters than as a soldier in the AIF.' It did not fool the battalion adjutant, to whom I had to present the message. 'The words are meaningless,' he said curtly. 'You're getting yourself out; it's as simple as that.' I suppose he was right but the words cut at my heart like a knife.

I said goodbye to Jack, perhaps for the last time, I wondered. I had known him for only about eighteen months but the friendship would endure, I knew it would. But it wasn't the last time. The Japanese struck on 7 December 1941, and less than two weeks later I was back in Singapore as a Reuter war correspondent. A reunion in early January 1942 with the 'I' section in their foxholes at Jemalaung on the east coast of Malaya was emotional. 'You *bloody* fool, Gil!' said Jack (to come back, he meant). Then, 'Gee, it's nice to see you again!' There was Vern Benjamin, Bill Tozer, Stan McAlister, Gordon Smith and the others and they soon demolished bottles of Scotch and gin I had smuggled in. This time, it was a last farewell to some of them. I clasped Jack's hand and we looked into each other's eyes. 'Give my love to Becky if you get back,' he said and that was the last time I saw him.

The 2/19th with other small Australian units were soon engaged in the epic Battle of Muar on the other side of Malaya, when for four days and nights they held up the victorious Japanese advance towards Singapore. Perhaps 1,800 strong at the beginning, they fought the crack Japanese 1st Guards Division, probably 15,000 strong, to a standstill. The Australian losses were crippling and Jack Rescorl was among them. He was last seen leading a small group of survivors of the battle through the jungle towards the British lines. The war for Jack was over but you could say in a sense that he won it.

The survivors of Muar and the Battle of Singapore Island soon to come spent the next three and a half years in Japanese prison camps under the most unspeakable conditions of brutality and cruelty, as has been fully documented. They were saved by the atomic bombs on Hiroshima and Nagasaki in August 1945, at a time when many of them had been ordered to dig their own graves in preparation for their execution.

I ask myself: Why Jack Rescorl? Like me, he was a pacifist at heart; he did not want to kill anyone. We thought war was wrong, futile and obscene. But how could you practise pacifism in the face of the imminent military threat to your country and family? You had to become a militant pacifist for the time being. When the dirty mess was cleaned up, then we could begin again and learn from our mistakes of two world wars and try to convert the whole world to pacifism.

There were thousands of Jack Rescorls in the two world wars and the historians have not done justice to them. They are not even mentioned in most history books. Writers such as Manning Clark, Donald Horne, John Pilger and others lure contemporary Australians into the belief that Australia was led by the nose against its will into two world wars to fight for the British Empire. It is undeniable that the volunteer Australian armed forces of both wars contained large numbers of people who weren't fighting for any particular cause—the unemployed, young men seeking excitement, pure adventurers, old soldiers who had forgotten how beastly it could be, and bloodythirsty men who just liked killing other people.

No mention is ever made about the men who were true patriots all, fighting for their country and their families. The omission is a distortion of history and must be rectified. Precious little Australian history appears to be taught in our schools and virtually none at all about our participation in world wars. When the education authorities get around to doing something about it, it is certain that somebody will write, 'Australians flocked to the colours to fight for King and Empire. . .' I beg them to set the record straight by adding, 'though a large number of them felt that they were fighting for Australia and preferred to fight for it on foreign soil'. Just an honourable mention is all I ask to keep faith with the Jack Rescorls of the AIF and our other volunteer armed services.

There was something special about the AIF. I believe it was the only major volunteer army in the two world wars. To have belonged to the AIF, if only for a brief period, is a matter of great pride to me. At the same time, I have always advocated military conscription in a war for survival, if only for the dreadful unfairness of the voluntary system. It seemed to me a shocking waste that the cream of the country's youth should be sacrificed while others, from selfishness or lack of official direction, were able to stay behind for reasons best known only to themselves.

It is only human for historians to have prejudices and strong self-opinions which influence their judgments. Manning Clark, for instance, was a marvellous writer but, as the years pass, many of his conclusions in his monumental *A History of Australia* are becoming open to serious questioning. His interpretations of World Wars I and II are unsatisfactory to me. He readily adopted the 'King and Empire' myth and the 'fighting other people's wars' myth. He did not seem to be aware that many ordinary Australians had gone to war for entirely different reasons; he seemed more caught up in the 'class warfare' aspect of it.

Nevertheless, there was some justification for the 'King and Empire' theory in World War I, as 20 per cent of the AIF were said to have been born in the United Kingdom. There were also strong blood ties with Britain as more than 98 per cent of Australia's population at the time were of British stock. But most of the soldiers were so fiercely Australian in looks and speech and habits that they were looked upon as barbarians by some of the more genteel English.

Not all of them thought much about the British Empire. Take Gunner John Duffell, whose remarkable letters home I edited for publication in 1992 (*Soldier Boy*, Kangaroo Press). Duffell was an ordinary Australian, the son of Hurstville boarding-house keepers. He enlisted at the age of seventeen, impatient for the 'fun' to begin. The frightful Battles of the Somme in 1916, where he was badly gassed, disillusioned him about the 'fun' of it but he made it clear in his letters home that he was fighting for Hurstville and Australia, not some mythical Empire. 'At present I am here for the benefit of Australia and my family,' he wrote. 'Nobody else. I would not give a hang if Fritz took the whole of France and Belgium.'

Hindsight is supposed to shed new light on historical events but sometimes it tends to distort them, depending on how far you look back. Past Australian hindsight books, films and television mini-series may have given a distorted picture of our troops being sent to their deaths by the stupid and wicked English for the glory of Empire. Only now are we learning that it was not quite like that.

One of my teenaged grand-daughters had an abiding distrust of the English after she fell madly in love with Mel Gibson and saw what the English did to him in the Peter Weir–David Williamson film, *Gallipoli*. More than 70 years later, it is now revealed that Australian officers made tragic blunders, too. The public have also become aware that whereas Australian casualties at Gallipoli totalled 27,000, British and Indian casualties were 119,696 and French, 47,000. This should not disturb the Anzac tradition but it puts it in better perspective. The Anzacs I spoke to mostly thought they were fighting for Australia, as I suppose the French troops thought they were fighting for La Belle France.

The Australian population at the outbreak of World War II on 3 September 1939, was still of 98 per cent British stock. This time most of the AIF and the other volunteer armed services were Australian-born and committed to the defence of Australia wherever the field of battle happened to be. Yet the 'fighting other people's wars' distortion is still being put forward by writers. Donald Horne, in his *Ideas for a Nation*, questions why the Rats of Tobruk take precedence as a national legend over the heroic fighters of the Kokoda Trail. He argues that the Rats were fighting for Empire, whereas the Australian troops in New Guinea were directly defending Australia. This would not have been new to the Rats as they listened and laughed in their dugouts in North Africa to Lord Haw Haw making the same gibes that they were fighting other people's wars. The Rats deserve their legend status just as much as the men of Kokoda. They were both fighting for the same cause. The 'fighting England's wars' myth became a favourite propaganda weapon aimed at Australian troops everywhere by the Germans and the Japanese. It did not meet with much success.

It is both fascinating and frightening to speculate what would have happened to us if we had lost both the wars by staying at home and waiting for them to come to us. My guess is that our future would not have been too bad if Kaiser

Wilhelm had won World War I. Our Saxon blood would have conditioned us to intermarriage with our conquerors. We would have been regimented and made to work much harder and listen to never-ending German band music in the weekends and eat large quantities of German sausages.

Our fate in World War II would have depended on who got to Australia first—the Germans or the Japanese. What price multiculturalism under Hitler? There would have been gas ovens for Australian Jews and probably for the Aborigines, too. And the Gestapo forever watching over the rest of us. As for Tojo's Japanese, life would have been for us a brutal and unending nightmare of slaves of the Son of Heaven. Please, somebody, set the record straight and give proper recognition to the tens of thousands of Australian young men and women who died fighting what they thought were our wars and for our survival. We will become a much happier and united nation if our ethnic history and inheritance can be properly explained to the many new ethnic groups now dominating our society.

Another thing not properly understood by our new racial mix is the significance to the older generation of the present Australian flag. They don't care two hoots about the flag, especially that wicked Union Jack, and why should they? But to most of the fighting men and women of Australia that flag, Union Jack and all, was the symbol of their cause, to some it was as sacred as the Cross to a Christian. That is why I hope that the last of the old soldiers (symbol of all the services) will be allowed to fade away peacefully before the revolution comes and the flag is changed. It won't be too long to go. There are only a handful of World War I survivors and the World War II diggers are in their seventies, eighties and nineties.

This may sound painfully like schmalzy flag-waving but I'd like to tell a few flag stories from World War II. Dick Fair was a member of 2/19th Battalion AIF who was taken into cruel captivity by the Japanese after the fall of Singapore in February 1942. Somehow he souvenired a Union Jack as he was being taken away on a train to endure three and a half years of sadistic bashings and unspeakable brutalities by Japanese and Korean guards. He kept that flag in his possession at the risk of his life all that time, managing to secrete it through many searches by his captors. The flag survived the dreadful days of the Burma–Thailand Railway of Death and went with Dick Fair to another prisoner-of-war camp at Ohamma in Japan. There the emaciated prisoners slaved in a coal mine until the war's end.

At first light on 16 August 1945, after Emperor Hirohito's official broadcast of the Japanese surrender, there was an emotional ceremony at Ohamma. The Japanese flag was hauled down at the prison camp and Dick Fair's Union Jack went up in its place. It was joined later by home-made Australian and American flags. Survivors of that camp tell me it was a moving and triumphant occasion.

Dick Fair brought the flag back to Australia and it hangs today on the northern wall of St Andrews Anglican Cathedral in Sydney, with a plaque. Dick presented the flag to the cathedral with the proviso that it should be placed on his coffin at his death and then returned to its resting place. This duly occurred in July 1978.

Don Isles, another member of 2/19th Battalion, recalled returning from prison slave work in a motor convoy to a camp in Thailand on the afternoon of the Japanese surrender. 'We heard a shout from the leading truck "the war's over—the Union Jack is flying in the camp!" I got a shock—I dared not look for fear that someone was playing a poor sort of joke. Then came a shout from someone in our truck, "It's true! It's true!" Then I looked and sure enough there were the two flags flying—the Union Jack and the Australian flag.'

Tom Kane was a prisoner in Sumatra. He and his mates, though weak, starved and sick, had been flogged into building a 60-mile-long railway line to a coal mine in the mountains of the island. It was a month before they learnt of the Japanese surrender. They continued to slave away until the news reached them. Then they did what many people would regard as incomprehensible. 'Our first reaction was to gather together and sing "God Save the King",' Tom Kane recalled.

Flags and the King meant a great deal to these men in their times of travail as a symbol of Home and Australia. The 'Empire' moved them not at all. So please let them fade away quietly before the Union Jack is removed from the flag to make way for a kangaroo or a banana or something. One of the current suggestions for a new flag even has on it a ludicrous red blob supposed to be Ayers Rock or perhaps a Central Australian ant hill. Some people are upset that the present Australian flag is too much like the New Zealand flag. There's a simple way to rectify that: Put the screws on the New Zealanders, tell them their flag is too much like the Australian flag and make them adopt a new flag with a kiwi on it.

FOOTNOTE: My active war service ended as inauspiciously as it had begun. As a Reuter war correspondent I retreated down the Malayan peninsula with the British troops to the last bastion of Singapore, which was not to be so impregnable, after all. The Japanese had advanced 550 miles in 55 days. I was as much a failure as a war correspondent as I had been as a soldier, though there were mitigating circumstances. The military censorship was so stringent that it was virtually impossible to get a worthwhile story out of the country. As for telling the truth about the situation, that was strictly taboo. War correspondents are not expendable, so I escaped with other correspondents a few days before the Japanese swarmed over the Causeway from Johore on to Singapore Island. There followed a few hair-raising days in a British destroyer, HMS *Encounter*, in Banka Strait towing another disabled destroyer and dodging Japanese bombs from the air. And so to Batavia and finally a ship back to Australia.

10
Truth, the First Casualty

After the Malayan debacle, I rejoined my wife and two young children in Melbourne, where they were staying with my sister-in-law. Melbourne was full of American soldiers and there were panic stories of an imminent Japanese invasion of Australia. So I dug a deep slit trench in the back garden of our Mentone home and prepared for the worst. The Japanese never came, the trench got full of water, and it took a team of men some days to drain and refill it with soil. I was summoned, with fellow war correspondent Henry Keys, to an audience with Sir Keith (Rupert's father) Murdoch, boss of the *Herald* and *Weekly Times*. A noted war correspondent in the Gallipoli days, Sir Keith cross-examined us expertly about the Battle of Muar.

Then I reported back to Reuters in Sydney and was ordered from London to move to Canberra and report the war from there. This surprised me as we had two very competent 'stringers' there, Alan Reid and Otto Olsen. I took up residence in the Wellington Hotel and became a member of the Canberra Parliamentary Press Gallery. Being the Reuters Australian news editor gave me considerable clout and I attended Prime Minister John Curtin's frequent press conferences with a small select band of journalists. A former journalist himself, Curtin knew how to handle us. He was totally frank about the progress of the war and much of what he told us was strictly 'off the record'. He wanted us to know the truth and his trust was never betrayed.

Curtin was a Jekyll and Hyde sort of chap. He was a tall, dark man with a rasping Australian speaking accent though capable of passionate oratory. A reformed alcoholic, he sought solace in chain cigarette-smoking. There was a melancholy look about him at times, reflecting perhaps the gradual renunciation of his youthful zeal as a devout Roman Catholic, a rationalist, pacifist and socialist. The idealist had become the realist and he seemed somehow to lament it. He was friendly and approachable enough, but there was a diffidence and introspection about him that served as a barrier against closer acquaintance. John Curtin was not a politician of charisma but there has never been any doubt in my mind that he was the saviour of Australia in World War II. He had tight control over his Labor Party colleagues, even to the extent of making them agree to a limited form of military conscription for overseas service, against all the most sacred principles of Labor policy. Apart from a few brilliant minds, he had a mediocre team of ministers and he needed all his political skills to control them. There was also the need to keep on side, without surrendering any principles, with the great egotistical extrovert, General Douglas MacArthur, Commander-in-Chief of the South-West Pacific Area.

Those were momentous and perilous days in early 1942: Curtin's impassioned speech in the House of Representatives while the Battle of the Coral Sea was in progress. The Japanese midget submarine attack on Sydney Harbour. Curtin's celebrated confrontation with Winston Churchill, insisting on the recall of our AIF divisions from the Middle East to defend Australia and New Guinea. (Churchill never forgot or forgave the colonial upstart who defied him and never visited Australia, despite numerous invitations.) Then there was the famous message by Curtin that Australia now looked to America for assistance rather than to Britain. Actually, it was a few throw-away lines written by Don Rodgers, the PM's able press secretary, in a routine foreword to a Melbourne publication. It created international headlines as a landmark pronouncement.

Yes, those were critical days for Australia, but the world's press had bigger things to headline as the Japanese swept through other parts of South-East Asia and the Germans mauled the Russian armies in Europe. Reuters did not want long messages from me and I realised my presence in Canberra was scarcely justified. But I wasn't prepared for a cable early in July from Christopher Chancellor, general manager of Reuters in London, giving me three months notice of my cancellation of my contract. It was a sudden devastating shock. There was no explanation and no word of thanks for past services. I could scarcely believe it—redundancy (or the sack) after thirteen years of loyal service in various parts of the world. Reuters had become my life, I lived for its traditions and the fascination of its news gathering. I've never discovered what prompted my virtual dismissal. Was it because of my inadequacies as a war correspondent? Or was it engineered from Sydney where I was regarded as an interloper in a closed shop? Or was it simply an economic cost-cutting exercise?

I was so angry and hurt and bitter that I wasted no time in quitting an organisation that had treated me so shabbily. But I still wanted war work of some kind; I owed that to the boys in Malaya. The army would not have me back, that was for sure, but there had to be something else that could use any talents of mine. I took counsel with my colleagues of the press gallery and Alan Reid said, 'Go and see Bonney'.

'Who's Bonney?'

'The Chief Publicity Censor.'

'What!' I cried. 'Me a censor? You must be out of your mind!' I told him about the troubles I'd had with military censors in Singapore and how I'd never be able to look another war correspondent in the face if I became one myself.

'Go and see Bonney,' Alan persisted, explaining that publicity censors were not military censors but civilian watchdogs to see that nothing of a national wartime security risk got into newspapers or was broadcast over wireless stations.

So I went to see Bonney in his office at Parliament House and, to my surprise, he welcomed me as if I was an answer to his prayers. It appeared that he badly wanted staff with my qualifications and my having been a war correspondent was an added bonus. Edmund Garnet Bonney was 57 at the time, a tall man with a commanding personality and intelligence. He had progressed from being a young reporter to top newspaper editorial and executive positions in Melbourne and Adelaide. He had strong Labor Party affiliations and was said to 'have the ear' of Prime Minister Curtin. Bonney was a man of high ambition and, as such, somewhat autocratic, yet his staff were said to be fiercely loyal to him. On the other hand, he was intensely disliked and distrusted by the Australian newspaper proprietors and it was to lead to bitter confrontations as the war progressed. 'Bon,' as he was called, won them all except the last one.

We had a long talk, and with some misgivings, I agreed to discuss the matter with my wife. Subject to a security clearance, he offered me the post of State Publicity Censor for South Australia at a salary far in excess of my Reuter salary and he would move my family and belongings to Adelaide without delay. I explained my aversion to censors. He told me about the censorship and that I would be serving my country well by taking such a job at such a critical period of the war. At no time, he said, would I be asked to deal with matters of censorship other than those affecting the security of the nation. I extracted a promise from him that if at any time I wished to return to journalism, he would release me. I discussed it with my wife and accepted the offer. I cabled Chancellor for an immediate release from my Reuter contract and received an immediate reply. Chancellor could hardly wait to get rid of me and I was sad to be pushed out of a job I had enjoyed for so long and given so much. I've never lost my affection for Reuters itself and am happy to have been made an honorary member of the Reuter Society, a body of retired Reuterians in England.

Times were urgent and a few weeks later I was in Adelaide with Bonney on a round of introductions. The Premier of South Australia, Thomas Playford, service chiefs and departmental heads and the two men with whom I would be most closely associated. Lloyd (afterwards Sir Lloyd) Dumas, editor-in-chief of the (morning) *Adelaide Advertiser*, was a stoutish impassive man, who when sitting at his desk with folded arms, looked like a self-satisfied Adelaidian Buddha. He was to become a powerful figure in the Australian newspaper world. Archer Thomas, editor of the (evening) *Adelaide News* was much younger, tall and good-looking. He was very friendly and was to invite us to his home. I assured them both that I would be using my censorship powers solely in the interests of national security but to bear with me during a settling-in period of an unfamiliar job, when I might make misjudgments. I like to think that I kept my promise, though censors are never popular. Two other men with whom I would have censorship dealings were Charles Wicks of the Australian Broadcasting Commission, and Keith MacDonald of commercial radio channel 5AD. There was no television in those days.

I was no stranger to Adelaide. Nine years before I was there as a Reuter war correspondent with the English forces under General Douglas Jardine during the Bodyline Cricket War of 1932–33. I was able to renew acquaintanceships, including that with Don Bradman. He was now operating as a stockbroker, having been discharged from the Australian armed services as medically unfit. It was a different sort of war this time. We talked of how strange it was that the worst public violence of the bodyline affair had taken place in Adelaide, the 'city of churches' where people were said to be 'more English than the English'. The American presence was strong in the city for this new war. It was a major staging camp for troops and supplies en route along the Stuart Highway and by air to Darwin and the islands. The city was full of Yankee soldiers and many pretty Adelaide girls were falling over backwards to accommodate them.

But some things are sacrosanct. The Adelaide Club was undisturbed as the bastion of the Adelaide Establishment. The Bonythons, Downers, Duttons, Angases, McLachlans, Hawkers and Elders were among the ruling families. A little lower on the Establishment scale was the Naval and Military Club. I was invited to join it but there was a difficulty. The club was an officers-only club and my military rank had been private, with one dizzy spell as an acting-corporal. I had a 'thing' about officers-only clubs. My brother, John, was an active member of the Imperial Services Club in Sydney. He had served in World War I as a lieutenant and, as a colonel, became Chief Legal Officer of Easter Command (Sydney) in World War II. I lunched with him frequently at the Imperial Services Club between the wars, but as soon as I donned an AIF private's uniform in World War II I was not permitted inside the club. Now, I can understand that the club did not want its premises overrun by 'other ranks' any more than a privates-only club would want to be infested by officers. But it seemed to me to be an insult to the King's uniform to bar me. Surely no member would wish to entertain an undesirable person in his club? I resented it deeply then and it still rankles me. What really upset me at the time was that young men much my junior in civilian clothes were welcome guests at the club whereas a private's uniform was taboo. I pointed out to the Adelaide Naval and Military Club my position and, while appreciating their invitation, said there was no way I was going to be ashamed of being a private soldier. Under the heading of 'Rank' I would be compelled to write 'Private'. They are downy birds, these Adelaidian chaps, and they quickly came up with a face-saving compromise. Wasn't a war correspondent regarded as having officer status and privileges? That was perfectly correct and so I was duly accepted on an officer–private basis. I wanted to be a member, anyway, not only because it was an excellent club but its members included top service personnel with whom I was to have censorship dealings.

My powers as a censor were considerable and awed me somewhat. Technically, I could put a radio station off the air and shut down a newspaper or other publication for breaches of censorship (that is, after reference to Canberra). Nobody could talk or write publicly about certain aspects of the war without my permission. And, if you wanted to complain about my censorship, I could stop you doing that, too. Nobody argued about the necessity of censorship; the enemy were doing exactly the same thing. There were German and Japanese spies in Australia and fifth-columnists with short-wave radio and other means of getting information out of the country, and quick to pounce on written or spoken security leaks. The trouble was where to draw the fine line between information useful to the enemy and information suppressed to hide mistakes by soldiers and politicians. In hindsight, I believe we became far too prone to keep bad news from the Australian public for reasons of civilian morale rather than for strict defence security. But maybe that is the repressed war correspondent speaking.

The system was this: The media had a comprehensive set of general guidelines governing the things likely to breach security and give information to the enemy. Any stories dealing with the war would be sent to my office in proof or other form for passing, amending or prohibiting. Radio stations would submit scripts of broadcasts dealing with war matters. I recall that station 5AD submitted every episode of a dramatic serial about submarine warfare. I passed the buck on that one to the naval authorities, who must have had a perplexing time trying to determine whether there was anything of technical benefit to the enemy in the exploits of the underwater hero.

In addition to this voluntary sort of censorship, I would receive daily notifications of specific matters to be censored or submitted to censorship. These directions would come to me by telephone from Canberra (censorship had No. 2 national priority with telephones) and would be relayed to the media. The 'scrambler' would be used for top-secret messages, which I would deliver by hand to newspapers and radio stations. John Hilvert calculated that there were 915 censorship instructions issued from May 1942 to May 1944, or 1.22 per day.

Two such instructions, quoted from memory, spring to mind:

August 1942—*No reference to sinking of HMAS Canberra by Japanese at Guadalcanal*. The reason for this ban was obvious. The Japanese were not sure of the fate of *Canberra* and three U.S. cruisers at the time. The loss of these ships was not announced until some time later when, as Deputy-Director of the Department of Information, it was my sad duty to release the heavy Australian casualty list.

August 1944—*No reference to breakout by Japanese prisoners of war from Cowra camp in N.S.W.* This story was banned until the end of the war because it was thought its publication would result in the Japanese taking reprisals against Australian troops in their camps. Stories filtering out about the horror conditions in these Japanese camps were banned from publication for the same reason. The Sydney *Daily Telegraph* defied the censorship ban on the Cowra breakout by reporting the story in one day's issue but later, at Prime Minister Curtin's personal urging, fell in line with its contemporaries. The brief defiance was a foretaste of a much bigger confrontation to come.

The press continued to berate the government about what it viewed as political censorship. For example, reports of street fights between soldiers on leave were suppressed or only allowed to be published if they were together with an official statement by the military or civilian police. Curtin believed that such matters could have a disastrous effect on morale, especially if the brawls involved white Australian soldiers and black American soldiers.

One of my most important jobs was to censor all media messages coming out of Darwin before their distribution to Australian and overseas newspapers and radio stations. Although I had arrived in Adelaide four months after the big raid on Darwin on 19 February 1942, the bombing was still continuing and there was a strong contingent of press correspondents in the town. Censorship was strict and, indeed, the government had at first denied Japanese reports that the first big raid had even taken place. It used censorship to hide from the Australian people the news of the bombing because it feared the public could not stand such bad news. Dr H.V. Evatt, Attorney-General and Minister for External Affairs, asserted that the release of detailed stories about the raid might strike 'terror and alarm into the hearts of all'.

The government's hand was forced, however, and an official announcement was made on 20 February, truth being the first casualty. The announcement was low-key, stating that total casualties were 17 killed and 24 wounded, several ships had been hit and damage done to wharves and buildings and some of our aircraft damaged on the ground. Efforts have been made in recent years to whitewash what happened that day and afterwards in Darwin. I draw on the conclusions 28 years later by Paul Hasluck in his official war history volume, *The Government and the People, 1942–45*, with all the evidence at his disposal.

The real figures for that day in Darwin were 243 killed and approximately 443 wounded, according to Hasluck's account. Ten ships had been sunk and others damaged. Six Australian aircraft had been destroyed on the ground at the RAAF station and eight American Kittyhawk fighters and three transport planes in the air. The post office, police station, the barracks, cable office and government buildings destroyed. Worst of all was the panic that seized Darwin after the raid. The townspeople stood up remarkably well to the ordeal of the first raid but after the second raid, about one and a half hours later, a rush out of town started. This raid by 54 land-based Japanese bombers was directed chiefly against the RAAF station. Servicemen deserted the station in great numbers. The townspeople joined in the exodus to the south, leaving their meals unfinished, as they ran towards the rail town of Adelaide River with their portable goods. The town of Darwin was looted at night, attributed to servicemen. It was to be years before the truth of that black day was revealed.

Hasluck wrote that it was reasonably clear that the Japanese attack on Darwin was not directed primarily against Australian defences but was necessitated by the fact that the Japanese were about to attack Timor. They saw the need, first, to attack the harbour and the aerodrome in Darwin from where reinforcements might be sailed or flown or a counter-attack mounted. 'The thought of evacuation which had been going on throughout Australia for months, was probably a more direct cause of the panic that seized Darwin after the raids than any defects peculiar to that one day or that group of people,' he wrote. This first big cover-up perhaps set censorship on a course that diverted it from foiling direct security threats to Australia to the doctoring of news likely to injure 'public morale'; apparently Australians could not take bad news. Censorship was to become obsessed with 'prohibiting false impressions abroad' and 'protecting the good name of Australia' as a worthy ally to overseas audiences, particularly in America. It was to lead to Australia's most notorious censorship incident—the day that guns were flourished and newspapers suppressed in April 1944, a day that pushed me to the brink of resignation.

The Japanese air attacks on Darwin continued. There were 64 raids between 19 February 1942 and 12 November 1943, with casualties and damage. The Darwin messages I had to censor came down via the overland telegraph line to Adelaide GPO. I would be advised at any hour of the day or night to vet them before they could be dispatched to their address in Australia and overseas. Off I'd go to the GPO on what, to a former war correspondent myself, was a distasteful task. My orders from Canberra were clear—all messages must conform to the daily official communique of General Douglas MacArthur, from his headquarters. I was sent a copy of the communique each day and was distressed at times at the contradictions between the bombing stories of the correspondents and the MacArthur communiques. The correspondents might report that the Japanese shot down seven of our planes for the loss of two of theirs, whereas the MacArthur version was exactly the opposite—the Japs lost seven, we lost two. This often happened but I'd have no option but to change the figures and perhaps delete or alter other details of casualties and damage to the town.

The same censorship code, of course, was operating in other theatres of the war. Brian Penton, in his *Censored!* book, mentions a day at Port Moresby in New Guinea when Allied fighters lost ten or eleven planes to the enemy's three or four. The MacArthur communique said, 'our interception was successful' and did not mention losses. Eight Allied bombers raided Lae and five were shot down. The communique said, 'A strong interception was encountered. Two of the enemy fighters were shot down. We lost one plane in combat.' The MacArthur theory seemed to be that the admission of such losses might cause panic or unease among the Australian public. It seemed to me that by telling the truth we would not have told the Japanese anything they did not already know, but it was not for me to reason why.

I knew exactly what the Darwin correspondents would be saying when they discovered how their stories had been doctored. I remembered how some idiot of a British military censor in Singapore had once altered the word 'poignant' into 'sad' in one of my dispatches to Reuters in London, probably thinking that it was a code word of some sort. Frank Legg, a soldier turned war correspondent, came to see me in Adelaide in protest. I told him of my position and how it hurt me and I suggested I should resign. 'No, don't do that,' he said. 'It's better to have you than some dumbcluck of a military censor. At least you know how we feel.' English-born Frank was one of our best war correspondents. He had been a sergeant, and later a lieutenant, with 9th Division in the Middle East before being seconded as a war correspondent.

So, my life as a censor went on for the next eighteen months or so without any great drama. It was hard and worrying work, with long hours, but it gave me a feeling that my pen was mightier than my sword. Sometimes the line was hard to draw between legitimate criticism in the press of our war effort with statements and reporting which might be of use to the enemy. My relations with press and radio were cordial. I made errors of judgment at times but they forgave me because they knew I was interested only in national security. The Premier, Thomas Playford, insisted on bringing in his radio scripts personally to my office, though I offered to go to his office. I can't recall ever having to alter or delete anything. Playford had been a private and an officer in the 18th AIF Battalion and he knew all about security. Dame Enid Lyons, MP, turned up one weekend with a radio broadcast script and insisted on coming out to our house for its vetting. I had met her before in London when her husband, Joe, had been Prime Minister of Australia. It was just as well Dame Enid had submitted her script; in it she referred by name to a march through Melbourne of a brigade of the

9th Division which had just returned to Australia from the Middle East, headed for the critical battles in New Guinea. I cut out all references to the identification of the brigade and the division, changing it into merely a 'military parade'. Dame Enid understood at once when I explained that it was vital that the Japanese be kept in ignorance for as long as possible of the return of these troops. She stayed for afternoon tea, a delightful and accomplished person and the first woman ever elected to the House of Representatives.

While things remained fairly quiet in Adelaide on the censorship front, relations between Censorship and the Sydney press were unhappy. It was to become worse after the Labor Party's landslide election victory in August 1943. Arthur Augustus Calwell was appointed Minister for Information in September and immediately appointed Bonney as Director-General of Information, also retaining him as Chief Censor. The Calwell–Bonney axis was to lead to a long period of confrontation with the newspaper proprietors. It even appeared to shake the 'fierce loyalty' of some Bonney admirers, as a parody circulated around the corridors of Parliament House in Canberra:

> My Bonney lies over the ocean,
> My Bonney lies over the sea,
> And sometimes I have a notion,
> My Bonney is lying to me.

If Bonney was unpopular with the press barons, Calwell was their raging bull. Brian Penton, the volatile editor of the Sydney *Daily Telegraph*, described him as 'Irish, irascible, with lots of ambition and ability—especially in hot-headed mudslinging debate—he was one of the leaders of Labor's isolationalist, red-bogey-hunted, book-burning, church-ridden, anti-intellectual, anti-libertarian wing'. Calwell's comments on Penton, Sir Keith Murdoch and other proprietors were equally vitriolic.

It was not long before there was a clash. Two months after Calwell's appointment, the *Daily Telegraph* published some critical comments on coal strikes in N.S.W. in defiance of censorship instructions. The Censorship view, apparently, was that Japan or the world must not be given the impression that Australian workers were sabotaging war production. Calwell hit back, authorising Bonney to place the *Telegraph* under the first order-to-submit since 1940. This meant that the paper had to submit for censorship copies or proofs of everything meant for publication. It was a form of punishment rather like a schoolboy being given 100 lines. This clash made me uneasy about the direction Censorship was taking, as by November 1943 the Japanese threat was in decline. I could not see why Japan would worry much about how Australia's coal production was being reduced by strikes. The order-to-submit operated from 30 November 1943 to 1 February 1944. Penton wanted to challenge the legality of the order but eventually the matter was settled out of court. It was a full dress rehearsal of a major confrontation.

The issue was too complicated to explain in full here. Briefly, the flashpoint came when Calwell attacked the Sydney papers for suggesting that his department had misled the American people about the withdrawal of some Australian troops from the front line to carry out war work in Australia. The chairman of the Australian Newspaper Proprietors Association, R.A.G. Henderson, hit back by quoting examples of 'political censorship'. 'Calwell was in his element and the punches were flying,' John Hilvert wrote.

On Friday, 14 April 1944, the Sydney censor deleted Henderson's references to specific acts of censorship and the fight was on. The Saturday issue of the *Daily Telegraph* left blanks on page 3 identical with the censorship cuts. When the *Sunday Telegraph* (circulation 300,000) attempted to publish with blanks, Commonwealth peace officers confiscated all editions.

The proprietors of all Sydney newspapers decided to fight the issue collectively by publishing all the banned statements attacking the censorship. Calwell authorised Bonney to suppress all the defiant publications. Commonwealth peace officers prevented the bulk of the Monday morning newspapers from being distributed. One officer was photographed brandishing a pistol. There was further high melodrama and scuffles during the seizures of the afternoon *Daily Mirror* and *Sun* and reports of another gun being waved.

In Adelaide, I was shocked by the events in Sydney and supposed it would be my turn next. What had all this to do with the security of Australia? I telephoned Canberra for guidance. They said if Adelaide papers insisted on publishing the censored material, I would have to seize them. They reminded me that I was under oath to do so. I expressed my feelings about it all, saying that I could not be depended upon to cut the banned material if it were resubmitted to me. If they wanted to censor non-security matter, they could get somebody else to do it. They calmed me down and persuaded me to 'hold your horses'.

Then I rang Tom Hoey, Victorian Publicity Censor. I had never met him but knew he was a distinguished journalist and a good bloke who enjoyed the same cordial relationship with the Melbourne press as I did in Adelaide. Tom was sympathetic. 'I'm as horrified as you are,' he said. When I mentioned something about resigning in protest, he said, 'Hang on in there for a while; I think there will be an armistice. If you resign now as a senior Publicity Censor, the press will be on to you in a flash and you'll bring the whole thing down.'

'We can censor it all,' I said cynically.

'Just stay put for a while,' Tom said. 'It's a private Sydney gang war. Let them fight it out there.'

Blake Brownrigg, Chief of Staff of the *Adelaide News*, telephoned: 'Gilbert, we're going to print the forbidden matter. What are you going to do?'

'I'm going to do what I have to do. I'm sorry, Blake, but I'll have to seize you. I don't like it any more than you do, but I'm bound to uphold the law as it is.'

We arranged a time for the seizure and I went off to see the Commonwealth Solicitor in Adelaide. He prepared the necessary official seizure papers and insisted on a Commonwealth peace officer accompanying me to the *News* office. This man had a pistol and I sensed that he was trigger-happy, being aware of the troubles in Sydney. I guess he was disappointed at the peaceful nature of the seizure. I felt a proper dill turning up with an armed escort.

I served Blake with the appropriate seizure papers and 12,000 copies of the *Adelaide News* were put into a room somewhere and the door padlocked (at least, that is how I remember it). I've often wondered what happened to those thousands of newspapers. Were they recycled or are they still there waiting for someone to unlock the door? After the seizure, I adjourned to Blake's office where we had a round or two of Scotch whiskies to show there was no personal ill-feeling. Even my armed escort put away his gun and joined in. (Tom Hoey was to do the same thing in Melbourne; having seized a few copies of the *Herald*, all adjourned to the pub for drinks.)

When I returned to my office, there was a telephone message to call Mr Lloyd Dumas, of the *Advertiser*. I confirmed to him that I would have to seize the *Advertiser*, too, if he flouted the Censorship. Which was exactly what he intended to do, he said. But Mr Dumas was another Adelaide downy bird: he would print one copy of the *Advertiser*, which I could seize, then he would comply with Censorship for the remainder of the morning edition. Would I care to come to his office at midnight for the seizure? Having already heard that I had enjoyed drinks at the *News*, perhaps I would care to join them in beer and sandwiches afterwards?

As it turned out, I did not have to keep my midnight assignment with Mr Dumas. As Tom Hoey had predicted, feverish negotiations were taking place in Sydney to get the matter under control. Public reaction to the incidents and gun-flourishing had culminated with some 2,000 university students marching through the streets in protest. On the afternoon of 17 April the newspapers applied to the High Court and were granted an interim interlocutory injunction restricting the Censor from forbidding publication of the material at issue. In the course of the hearing, Justice Sir Dudley Williams asked the question that was bothering me most: 'What have the articles to do with the safety of the Commonwealth?' The later substantive hearing continued until May 1944, when a negotiated 'code of censorship principles' was added to the Press and Broadcasting Censorship Order. This laid down that censorship should be imposed exclusively for reasons of defence security. It said censorship should not be imposed merely for the maintenance of morale or the prevention of despondency or alarm. Censorship should not prevent the reporting of industrial disputes or stoppages. Both sides claimed victory but, in my view, a draw would be a more accurate assessment. The newspapers obtained a certain amount of latitude but Censorship maintained its powers.

(I met Tom Hoey for the first time more than 30 years later, shortly before his death, when he and his wife, Eileen, called on us at Port Macquarie. He was a lovely bloke with a dry sense of humour, and we nattered for a long time about those momentous days in 1944. We have a visitors' book with a 'Remarks' column in it. It contains 25 years of trite remarks such as 'Like your house', 'Thanks for having us', 'So nice to see you again'. Tom wrote one word, no capital letters, no exclamation mark, just 'censored').

The whole affair had disillusioned me but I stayed on until nearly the end of the war in August 1945. As the Japanese threat receded further, censorship was liberalised and there were no more serious crises. I had one big scare when I was advised that Minister Calwell was to visit Adelaide for two days and I would show him all courtesies. Here's trouble, I thought; what will I do if he tells me to censor things right and left? Raging bull Calwell could not have been nicer. He called me 'Mr Mant' throughout and refused to use my private office room. All he wanted was a desk, a chair and a telephone in the outer office and the services of a typist. 'Just go on with your work as if I am not here,' he said. So far as I could tell he spent two days on the telephone on political matters. At the time, he was having a feud with Albert Dunstan, conservative Premier of Victoria. Bushfires were raging up and down the state and one day Calwell jumped up and down with glee in my office. 'I've just given some press interviews and called Dunstan "Bushfire Bertie"!' he chortled. 'That will go all over Australia! "Bushfire Bertie"—he'll never live it down!' There's another well-known cliche: You take people as you find them. It's a principle I've always followed. I found Arthur Calwell an agreeable fellow and I took him that way. On occasional meetings in the street and at official functions years afterwards, he always gave me a wave and a smile, and I always smiled back.

In July 1945, I reminded Bonney of his promise to release me if I wanted to return to journalism. For some reason, he wanted to retain me and dangled before me the post of Press Attache to the Australian Embassy in Paris after the war ended. This was very tempting but I wanted to get back into newspapers and the family went along with it (although my grown-up daughter and son still chide me for denying them the delights of Paris). The truth is that I felt myself acquiring a sense of petty power, capable of corrupting me, and a bureaucratic mind. I could not bear the thought of becoming a cosy and complacent public servant in peacetime. I wanted to get back into a competitive and chancy world with the excitement and satisfaction of newspaper work. No doubt there are plenty of estimable public servants, content with nine-to-five (or is it four?) jobs, but I did not want to become one of them, even in Paris.

I wanted to write a daily or weekly newspaper column of some sort, not a sensational Walter Winchell type of American column, but a mixture of gossip, stories of people, contemporary comment and some humour. Archer Thomas sponsored me in an approach to Sir Keith Murdoch, of the *Melbourne Herald* and *Sun-Pictorial*. I sent him a sample but he was unimpressed (though politely). Then I wrote to my old colleague, Tom Gurr, now editor of the Sydney *Sunday Sun*. Luck was with me. It so happened that Tom had a weekly column in mind and was looking for someone suitable to launch it. Tom took a big gamble when he engaged me. I had been out of the print media as a cable agency man for thirteen years. I did not know whether I would be able to adjust back to ordinary reporting and other newspaper work. I worried about it and wondered whether I would be better off as a bureaucrat in Paris. I wanted to call the column 'Now and Then' but Tom opted for 'The Way I See It'; Tom's gamble must have come off because the column appeared for the next thirteen years of Sundays. We left Adelaide with some regret. We had made many friends there; among them being Judge George Ligertwood and his wife, Edith.

11
The 'Grand Old'

A love of the Australian bush never left me during my years as a journalist and then, suddenly and unexpectedly, I was back in the rural world at the age of 54. You can take the boy out of the bush, they say, but you can't take the bush out of the boy.

Wherever I had been—in Britain, in Canada, in Malayan jungles in wartime—the images of the bush haunted me. I smelled the smell of burning gum leaves and heard the songs of the magpies; I rode with the musterers at Gigoomgan, remembering wild scrub gallops after runaways; I re-lived my jackeroo days and general knock-about work in Cooma and other parts of the Monaro; I winced at the memory of the blisters on my hands as I felled trees for a living at Blackfellows Lake, near Tathra on the N.S.W. South Coast; and more hard work lumping wheat for my oldest friend Ted Connor at Ootha, near Condoblin. That was a black summer to remember with fear. The fires raged throughout the wheat country, annihilating the tinder-dry ripe crops in a few furious minutes and taking a toll of human lives. Once, four of us drove from a fire at top speed for our lives in a utility. The fire, fanned by a westerly gale, was too fast for us and we abandoned the utility and dived headlong into a tank (a small dam) as the flames swept over us like a red rain squall. For a few terrifying moments we thought we would be burnt to cinders. It was the ability and courage of the farmers to survive these natural disasters and come back for more that gained my admiration. Their faith, especially that of the bush women, in the better times to come was an inspiration. So I pined for the solitary quiet of the bush and the companionship of bush people. Maybe I glamorised it all in my nostalgic mind but it was there all the time. Maybe the 'strong, silent bushmen' were just a myth like those 'handsome bronzed surf lifesavers of Bondi'.

My life suddenly took a U-turn in 1955 when the Sydney branch of the Printing and Kindred Industries Union went on strike over some dispute or other. The newspaper proprietors countered with one composite newspaper, produced by non-union executive staff. Now, strike-breaking composite newspapers are like red rags to many bull journalists. In this case, it so happened that the Australian Journalists' Association 'owed' the PKIU for support in a previous AJA dispute.

So the decision was taken to go on strike. It was by no means a unanimous vote but, except for a few, we abided by the decision. Journalists are (or were then) an odd mixture of militancy and romanticism, idealism and pragmatism. Many of us were reluctant and uneasy about going on strike, for the first time in our lives. The editorial staff of all newspapers were called in individually and asked to work on the composite paper. Those refusing were either dismissed or stood down. My editor of the *Sun-Herald*, Ken Hackett, was almost in tears as his friends, one after another, refused to comply and he was obliged to fire them. It was strange for me to start receiving strike pay for my wife and two children and I thought, 'Ben Chifley, we're in the same league now'. I seem to recall that the few who stayed at work were promised jobs for life but, alas, were all out of work a year or so later.

Then we produced our own daily paper, *The Clarion*, with editorial headquarters at the Journalists' Club in Phillip Street. The editor was Jack Paton, a talented journalist, editor of the popular *FACT* supplement of the *Sun-Herald*. All the principal Sydney columnists, except one, contributed to *The Clarion*. We wrote under the pseudonym of various Sydney streets. I was Phillip Street, easily identifiable for future punishment as I was silly enough to include Dr Balsam items. We had enormous public support. *The Worker* and the *Catholic Weekly* gave production assistance, the police, taxi drivers and others joined in. There were distribution problems as the newspaper proprietors controlled all Sydney newsagents and forbade them to handle copies of the renegade newspaper. Volunteer newspaper employees, including many women, sold the papers on street corners throughout Sydney; volunteer lorry drivers delivered copies to outer Sydney suburbs. By the third issue *The Clarion* was selling more than 180,000 copies a day. It was not a strike propaganda affair but a first-class paper of hard news, with financial, sports and women's sections. On its editorial page, the paper maintained that journalists were not on strike but were defending a principle. I'm not too clear now what the principle was but we won the case. *The Clarion* was about to produce a Sunday edition when the dispute was settled.

Retribution was swift and stern for some of us. When the next staff gradings were announced, Jack Paton found himself downgraded from a top Super A to an A (a big drop in salary) and I from A to B, becoming the only non-A journalist on the *Sun-Herald*. Jack Paton made a quick and indignant move. The editorship of the *ABC Weekly* was vacant and Jack got it, going on to found Australia's first television magazine.

If Jack, both of us 54, could do it, so could I, but I was not editor material. I scanned the Positions Vacant columns of the *Sydney Morning Herald* each day and there it was. The Royal Agricultural Society of New South Wales, presenters of the world-famous Sydney Royal Easter Show, was advertising for a public relations officer. Rural background essential, it said. Well, I argued to myself, I had Gigoomgan and Eenaweena, and the less said about the rabbit-trapping, the wood-chopping and the wheat-lumping the better. I went to see Harry Hauptmann, Jnr, the presiding PRO, a former *Sun* journalist who had accepted a post as PRO for the Victorian Railways. He gave me the run-down on the job, saying there had already been about 25 applications and wasn't I a bit long in the tooth for it? With my mind on the highly paid public relations people I had dealings with as a columnist, I asked him what was offering as an expenses account. 'There's no expenses account,' he said. 'We don't buy goodwill through a bottle here.'

Well, that's that, I thought as I left the RAS offices in Macquarie Place. But it wasn't that. Just for the fun of it, I put in an application for the job, expecting to hear nothing more of it. To my great surprise, a week or two later I was summoned to an interview with the recently appointed director of the RAS, Lieutenant-General Sir Frank Berryman. In some ways, the General, as he was to be called, was as much in the same boat as I was. A professional soldier all his life, he had little knowledge of rural or show affairs, except as a keen horticulturalist. In fact, he was known as Frank the Florist by putting gardens and trees at Victoria Barracks when he was GOC Eastern Command, the top Army job in N.S.W. His military record in World Wars I and II was impressive. He served in the Middle East, Java and New Guinea and became Chief of Staff to Field Marshal Blamey. He was an official Australian Army observer on USS *Missouri* in Tokyo Bay at the surrender of Japan in 1945.

I felt very much the private soldier again at our first meeting. He was a short, thick-set and formidable-looking man; when he spoke, it was a command. The only other general I had known was Lieutenant-General Gordon Bennett and he and Berryman were at daggers drawn, the professional soldier versus the civilian soldier. But I was to discover a warm heart beneath his gruff exterior and develop a friendly working relationship with him. The General was well aware of my miserable army service record, but did not embarrass me by referring to it; he seemed content with the knowledge that I had at least 'heard the bugle'. By then, although I did not know it at the time, they had already decided to appoint me and he wanted to look me over face-to-face. We discussed terms and when I asked about an expenses account, he confirmed Harry Hauptmann's statement that the RAS did not go in for that kind of thing. Any out-of-pocket expenses incurred in the line of duty would, of course, be reimbursed after filling in an expenses form. The dream of a big expenses account evaporated.

At any rate, I joined the RAS with a salary in excess of my previous A grade at the *Sun-Herald* and apparently had the last laugh. There was another odd sequel. After my resignation, the editor of the *Sun-Herald* travelled to Macquarie Place to ask General Berryman whether I would be allowed to continue my weekly column, 'The Way I See It', as it was a very popular feature of his paper. This made me laugh more sardonically than ever. Reluctantly, the General agreed. I certainly welcomed the extra income but it was an impractical arrangement, greatly restricting my ability to comment on public events. This column continued for a further two years when the new editor discontinued it in an abrupt and curt letter. No thanks or good wishes or other comment, but I was used to that. 'The Way I See It' had appeared for thirteen years and it was to be reincarnated in *The Land* fifteen years later, with an older but still reprobate Dr Friar Balsam in tow.

I was to stay with the RAS for the next thirteen years, carrying out the Society's advertising, promotion and public relations work from 1956 to 1969. During those years I travelled more than 50,000 miles to every corner of the state as manager of the pre-show journalistic tours and as the Society's representative with the judges of RAS field, wheat and other crop competitions. The bush and its people did not disappoint me; I made lasting friendships and confirmed my opinion that the country and its people are the real heart and backbone of Australia.

I learnt that annual shows were part of the way of life in the country, culminating in the 'The Royal' in Sydney. The history of these shows is the history of Australia itself. Descendants of the original members of show committees serve on many of today's committees. As well as attracting agricultural and livestock exhibitions from the surrounding districts, the show is a recognised social meeting place for country families. It is an occasion for the exchange of ideas of all kinds. It brings business into the local town and generates press, radio and television publicity. As the Oscar Hammerstein, Jnr, song put it, 'There's no business like show business . . . There's no people like show people'.

Agricultural shows are not as old as one would imagine. According to the *Encyclopaedia Britannica*, properly organised shows did not evolve in Europe until the latter part of the eighteenth century and early part of the nineteenth century. One of the earliest agricultural and livestock shows was the National Show held in 1821 in Aldridge's Repository, London, only a year before the first agricultural show in Australia. Specialised shows had been held much earlier, such as the beef cattle industry show at Smithfield (London) in 1799.

The first agricultural society in Australia was the Van Diemen's Land Agricultural Society (now the Royal Agricultural Society of Tasmania), formed at Hobart on 8 December 1821. This was just short of 34 years after the arrival of Captain Phillip's First Fleet at Sydney Cove. It is surprising that such a society was formed so quickly, as there was only one farmer, a housebreaker named James Ruse, among about 1,500 people aboard Phillip's ships and no ploughs. This was a strange oversight in view of the fact that among Phillip's instructions was one ordering him, immediately upon landing, to proceed to the cultivation of the land. So Ruse became Australia's first farmer and pioneered his way to successful farming. He was the first to use compost and build a primitive plough with his own hands out of a forked ironbark tree (the plough is on display in the Museum of Applied Arts and Sciences in Sydney). A model convict, Ruse was pardoned and granted land at Rose Hill, Parramatta, in 1789.

As well as the general encouragement of production from the soil, one of the Van Diemen's Land Agricultural Society's objectives was the 'protection of stock'. This was necessary as the free settlers of Tasmania were being subjected to a reign of terror by bushrangers and escaped convicts. Some of the worst convicts from New South Wales and Norfolk Island had been transported to Tasmania. Some were on the verge of starvation because of lack of food on the mainland and had to be freed. Others escaped. Gangs of convicts ran wild over the countryside, terrorising settlers and plundering their flocks and herds. The new society staged Australia's first official agricultural show in January 1822, in the Old Market Place, Hobart, immediately in front of Parliament House. Prizes in the form of medals were given for sheep, cattle and boar, the best acre of wheat, barley, artificial grasses, largest crop of potatoes taken from three acres of land and for a collection of vegetables. Awards were also given for the 'best conducted convict', male and female. The promoters of the show also hoped to 'inculcate improved moral habits among the population', presumably among the convicts and thieves who were harassing their lands.

Six months after the formation of the Van Diemen's Land Agricultural Society, the first effective step to form a similar body on the mainland was taken at the house of Mr J. Robertson, jeweller and watchmaker, 96 George Street, Sydney, on 5 July 1822. The Agricultural Society of New South Wales (forerunner of the Royal Agricultural Society of New South Wales) was formed, with Sir John Jamison, KGV, pastoralist, banker and former Royal Navy surgeon, as its first president. The list of the foundation honorary office-bearers includes the names of some of Australia's great pioneers whose families are settled in N.S.W. to this day. Vice-presidents were Hon. Mr Justice Barron Field, Judge of the Supreme Court and author of the first book of verse ever published in Australia; Rev. Samuel Marsden, clergyman, farmer and magistrate; Captain William Cox, who had built the first road across the Blue Mountains in 1814–15; and Dr Robert Townson, LLD, scholar, scientist, settler and one of the ringleaders of the 'mutiny' against Governor Bligh in 1808. Joint secretaries were George Thomas Palmer and Alexander Berry. Palmer was a former army officer said to have fought against Napoleon and owned extensive lands and stock near Parramatta. Berry was an influential merchant and landholder. The official *Sydney Gazette* reported that 'His Excellency the Governor (Sir Thomas Brisbane) has very condescendingly accepted the patronage of the Institution'.

The KGV after the name of the first president, Sir John Jamison, has caused historians some research. The letters stood for Knight of the Order of Gustavus Vasa and there are at least two versions of how Jamison was awarded it. According to Percival Serle's *Dictionary of Australian Biography*, Jamison treated an outbreak of cholera in the Swedish Army and was made a KGV by the King of Sweden. Another version asserts that while in port in Sweden with the Royal Navy, Jamison was asked to attend the Queen of Sweden who was suffering from a poisoned breast. He succeeded in curing her and, in recognition of his services, the King of Sweden conferred the order on him. He also advised the King of England of his action and the Prince Regent, in the absence of the King from the throne, later confirmed the order.

The first show of the new Agricultural Society of New South Wales was held at Westmead, near Parramatta, on 9 October 1824, but was restricted to cattle and sheep. The first properly arranged agricultural show, called the Parramatta Fair, was held in October the following year. There were classes for Australian Merino sheep, colonial-bred bulls, stallions, boars, sows, teams of horses and bullocks, and prizes for the best colonial cheese, tobacco and beer. The exhibits for the best beer section were apparently sampled by the crowds and a newspaper published the following morning moving descriptions of the consequences: 'Reason was dethroned and folly reigned in its stead'. Annual 'medal' shows were held for some years and then the society went into a decline and ceased to exist after 1836. Other agricultural and kindred organisations came into being and, after a hiatus of 23 years, the old Sydney-born Agricultural Society of New South Wales was resurrected in 1859 and has functioned continuously ever since.

The first show society to be formed outside the Sydney area was the Hunter River Society at Maitland on 6 October 1842. Other pioneering societies founded in the 1840s and 1850s included the Cumberland Agricultural Society and the Penrith Agricultural Association, both in 1843, Illawarra Agricultural Society at Wollongong in 1844, Hawkesbury (1845), Mudgee (1846), Kiama (1848), Bathurst (1855), Dapto (1856) and Albury (1857). The explorers conquered the mountains and rivers and opened up vast new areas of country. The establishment of show societies was a natural development in the wake of a flood of new settlers. Today, there are nearly 600 such societies in Australia, including more than 200 in N.S.W. The N.S.W. societies are bound together with the Agricultural Societies Council of New South Wales, formed in 1929.

The first Sydney show of the revived Agricultural Society of New South Wales was held in Prince Alfred Park in 1869, extending over four days. The ground had not been improved for the purpose and livestock and machinery were shown mainly in the open. Cleveland Street School buildings were used for the produce and other interior displays. The City Corporation's rental charge of £1,850 sterling for the ground and Exhibition Hall at Prince Alfred Park proving burdensome, the Society acquired 40 acres—'a desert of rocks and swamp'—from the common at Moore Park for £10 sterling per annum rental. With stout hearts and only £71 sterling in the coffers, the Council of the Society tackled the problem of converting the area into a Showground. The first Show was held in 1882 and ran for seven days. This appears to have been the first Show at Easter.

During the next few years, thousands of loads of rubbish and street sweepings were dumped by the city council in the Showground depressions, some of them fourteen feet deep. From those small beginnings, the 'desert of rocks and swamps' was transformed into the magnificent Showground of today.

The 1994 Royal Easter Show was the 106th annual show staged at Moore Park since 1882. It is now ranked as one of the Big Three of such shows in the world with the Canadian National Exhibition in Toronto and the Texas State Fair in Dallas. It has been called the Shop Window of Australia for the extent of its primary and secondary exhibitions. Kings, queens, presidents, prelates and prime ministers have graced it with their presence and great national and international pageants have been staged within its grounds. A grand total of nearly 50 million people have attended the shows since 1947.

The Showground was a military camp for four years during World War I, free of rent, upkeep and compensation, but shows and society business continued without interruption. Hundreds of thousands of Australian troops passed through, large numbers of horses were stabled and handled there for the army or broken in on nearby Moore Park. The Showground and its big buildings was turned into a giant public hospital during the deadly influenza pandemic after World War I in 1919. The Society made the grounds available to the health authorities free of charge and there was no show that year. Some 40 buildings were occupied by staff and patients and the emergency hospital held nearly 500 patients at the height of the epidemic. The Royal Hall of Industries, home of commercial displays, became the morgue with coffins as its exhibits.

The Showground was taken over again in 1941 during World War II, the army being in possession for seven years. The staggering number of 700,000 soldiers passed through the ground. The troops at the Showground slept on straw palliasses in the pens of the pig and other pavilions. They trained on the Showground's 30 miles of sealed roads and paraded on the five-acre main arena. They went AWL over the prison-like stone walls along the perimeter of the Showground but there was surprisingly little trouble and nobody shed any tears, least of all the RAS, when the war was over.

There were no Royal Easter Shows between 1941 and 1946 and then came the 1947 bonanza. The first day's record of 93,461 was a portent of what was to come. The public were war-weary and eager for distraction and entertainment.

Tens of thousands of children had never seen a Royal Easter Show in their lives. The city children had never before seen such large numbers of cattle, horses, pigs, goats and other livestock. There were the added delights of Sideshow Alley, there was Ajax, the tallest horse in the world, the fattest brother and sister in the world, and an Irish giant. In contrast, there was Chang, only 36 inches high and weighing a mere 36 pounds. There was a Cobra Woman in a snake pit, wearing about her body an eighteen-foot rock python. Ram Chandra a 26-year-old Indian described as the 'Cobra Boy', was in another pit with 50 snakes (early in the Show, the Cobra Boy was bitten by a venomous tiger snake and taken to hospital in a serious condition, but he recovered).

An astonishing total of 200,376 crowded the Show on Good Friday but this was nothing to the chaos on Easter Saturday when 259,829 poured through the gates; by noon a queue of 40,000 people were waiting in the street for admission. More than 50 ambulance men and 30 nurses attended to 370 men, women and children suffering from collapse and other injuries. In addition, more than 300 lost children were eventually found again. During peak periods, the huge crowds prevented the expeditious movement of cash wagons conveying turnstile money to and from the banking chamber at the Showground. It was found impracticable to keep the turnstiles supplied with empty money boxes to receive the large sums of money paid by the crowds. An SOS went out to the Colonial Sugar Refining Company for empty sugar bags. Hundreds of these were crammed with silver coins and taken away for counting. On occasions, the bags were carried upside-down, the end pieces broke under the weight and silver coins spilt in all directions. When the exhausted RAS staff gave up counting the money and the people, the total atendance for the ten days of the 1947 Show was 1,232,413 and the total amount of cash (mostly silver) handled was £208,593. The total attendance was amazing when it is realised that Sydney's population in that year was officially given at 1,549,590.

The Royal Easter Show has been praised for its national importance, condemned for its noise and brashness. But it goes on, bigger and better each year (so they say), important, noisy, brash but somehow part of the Australian way of life. It can capture the hearts of its regular exhibitors and spectators, as two examples will show. A Mrs Pelloc rode more than 600 miles from Mildura to Sydney on a grey horse to attend the 1916 Show. Mr George Lynn Gibson and his wife, Mavis Edna Gibson, of the Sydney suburb of Ashfield, attended the Show together as members of the Society for more than 20 years. Mr Gibson especially liked to watch the trotting events in the main arena from a seat in the Members Grandstand. As he and his wife watched the 1969 Show, he expressed a wish that when he died his ashes should be scattered over the Showground he loved so well. Mr Gibson did not live to see the 1970 Show but, in accordance with his request, his ashes were scattered on to the main arena during the Show from the Members Stand enclosure by a nephew.

The same sort of tradition was born and still lives on in the 1,000 or more country shows throughout Australia. The most common origin of these early shows were regular ploughing matches held in paddocks near country towns. This led to challenges by horsemen and others and gradually some kind of local organisation was formed. Display areas were rough contraptions made of saplings and hessian screens. Many such societies had a brief life but were resuscitated and consolidated in later years as Australia's population increased and economic conditions improved.

The shows have changed since then and yet they haven't changed. Axemen no longer wear bowler hats in the woodchipping arena; they are still popular at the shows but chain saws have taken over in the bush. Women ride horses astride instead of sidesaddle. But there are still the horses, the cattle, the dogs, the chooks, the big pumpkins, the rodeo, the show jumping, the lamingtons, the CWA lunch rooms and everything that goes to make a country show. And giggling town girls still follow the swaggering young roughriders around the showgrounds. Sideshow Alley has changed only in some of its content. The spruikers use microphones instead of megaphones. Jimmy Sharman's boxing troupe disappeared, punch-drunk, a long time ago. But there are still the big dippers, the ferris wheels, the dodgem cars, the shooting galleries, the hooplas, the merry-go-rounds, the fair floss and a whole new program of video and computerised attractions. In compiling potted histories of 207 country show societies for my book, *Show People*, for the Agricultural Societies' Council of New South Wales, I dug up some unusual happenings at Australian pioneer shows.

Torrential rain during the 1893 Walgett Show compelled many exhibitors to take their stock home via the Barwon River in the steamer *Brewarrina*.

The first Junee Showground was on a railway line one and a half miles from Junee station. Patrons had to jump from the running boards of carriages as the train went by the grounds.

The billiards table of a local hotel was used for exhibits at the first Grafton Show in 1867.

Queensland cattle were judged on the Queensland side of the Barwon River and N.S.W. cattle on the N.S.W. side at the first Mungindi Show in 1898. The reason was an interstate quarantine restriction caused by a pleura outbreak.

An exhibit of three tons of butter excited interest at the Kiama Show in 1856.

The first Walbundrie Show in 1911 was inspired after the local publican and the storekeeper raced their trotters over a five-mile course from the cemetery to the school for a £5 wager.

The first secretary of the Coonamble society was a German-born stock and station agent, Baron Von Barthold, Bernard Wilhelm Heinrich Titus Barnar Streglin (known locally as Barney Streglin).

Officials at the 1857 Albury Show blundered when they advertised 'free admission'. It was not long before very fine strawberries exhibited by the local police magistrate, choice cherries, green peas and other raw vegetables had all been gobbled up by the crowd.

The Nimbin Agricultural and Industrial Society claimed to be the only show society to have struck a gold medal for a show event. Such a medal was awarded in the 1930s to a chestnut horse named Aviator who jumped seven feet six inches, a record at the time.

At an early Inverell Show in the 1870s, so the story goes, a famous footrace took place between a young lad and lass, who dead-heated for the prize. The crowd urged them to 'fight it out'. They did and the girl won.

The Cumnock Show Society lost all details of its early history when its secretary died of tuberculosis near the turn of the century. All the records in his possession were ordered to be destroyed for fear of infection.

A word or two about the lamington, an icon of all country shows, might not be amiss. The lamington, for those ignorami who have never tasted the delicacy, is a square or oblong piece of sponge cake, coated with a soft chocolate icing and rolled in desiccated coconut. It is often cruelly lampooned by Dame Edna Everage. For some unaccountable reasons, the origin of the lamington in Australia has been cloaked in mystery and is still the subject of much argument and speculative stories.

The most popular theory is to link the cake with Baron Lamington, Governor of Queensland from 1895 to 1901, but my research suggests otherwise. There is no disputing that Baron Lamington is immortalised with a town and plateau named after him in Queensland and by a volcanic mountain in Papua New Guinea. Although known as a bit of a 'tooth man' with a particular partiality for sweets, there is little evidence, if any, that he gave his name to a cake. One writer wrote, 'Did Lamington enjoy eating it so that the coconut-coated sponge was identified with him? Or was the name chosen actually after the Governor had left because people felt that he should not be forgotten and ought to be remembered by something that was really sweet?'

The answer to both questions was 'No', according to a statement given to me by the Master Pastry Cooks' Association of New South Wales some years ago. A spokesman suggested that the Australian lamington was an adaptation of a delicacy from the English market town of Leamington (famous for its spa) in Warwickshire. 'Leamington sponges was the name given to small cakes made from a rich sponge mixture in oblong moulds rounded at the ends,' he said. 'The moulds were dressed in the same manner as sponge frames and two small pieces of citron peel were placed along the bottom of each. When the cakes were baked they were turned upside down upon a wire tray and lightly brushed with warm syrup. Leamington sponges are now practically obsolete. A similar sponge cake was made in the nearby village of Kenilworth, but this was baked in a paper hoop and the batter heavily sugared before baking. In Australia in the early 1930s the single-deck pastry cook's oven was introduced which brought about the innovation of sponge kitchens. Home-style sponge kitchens sprang up everywhere and pastry cooks, looking for a way to make use of 'stales', hit on the Australian version of the leamington. This consisted of similarly shaped sponge oblongs dipped in chocolate and rolled on desiccated coconut.'

So the truth seems to be that lamingtons are no more Australian than Dame Edna Everage's beloved gladioli.

The Royal Agricultural Society of New South Wales reeked with tradition and was a benevolent oligarchy in an old-fashioned world when I joined it in 1956. It was referred to satirically by some as the 'Grand Old Society', sometimes just as the 'Grand Old'. Much of that was about to change, chiefly because of the coming of television to Australia.

12
An Abominable Showman

Generally speaking, I had a miserable time of it as work went during my first two years as an abominable showman with the Grand Old. I began to pine for newspapers and the free and easy ways of newspapermen. The work was unfamiliar and complicated and sometimes I envied whoever got my promised job as Press Attache to the Australian Embassy in the fleshpots of Paris. But as the years went by, I grew to be part of the Grand Old, despite its infuriatingly old-fashioned ways and petty feuds and jealousies. When I left, thirteen years later, there were handshakes all round and the warm satisfaction of having made enduring friendships.

I got off to a bad start at the first monthly Council dinner I attended, a black-tie affair. Instead of wearing the usual black jacket, I bought the very latest fashionable cream coloured jacket to show them they had a new up-to-date promotions man. The attendant vetting people at the door of the Council Stand of the Showground took one look at me and said, 'Entertainer?' 'No,' I said sharply. 'I'm not an entertainer; I'm the new public relations officer.' He looked surprised but admitted me. I knew then that I had made a ghastly mistake. This was confirmed when I went into a room of 50 disapproving black coats. Only Clive Ogilvy, who would have liked to have worn a cream one himself, showed any understanding. I thereafter conformed and regained respectability.

I had imagined that my job as public relations officer was to promote and publicise the Royal Easter Show, but I had not read the fine print closely enough. In addition to this work, the public relations section issued up to twenty news bulletins each week to the press on behalf of animal breed societies, for whom the RAS did secretarial work. That was easy enough but I was confounded to find that I was also in charge of the financial sponsorship for the Show. These amounted to about £17,000 ($34,000 at today's rates). This chiefly meant writing letters to firms sponsoring main arena events such as trotting and rodeo, woodchopping and other competitions. In return for their money, the events were given the firms' names, advertising plugs over the loudspeaker and acknowledgment in the various RAS Show publications.

What I did not expect was to be asked (or instructed) to seek sponsorship in person. So I was shocked when asked to go and see if a Mr Brockoff, of Brockoff's Biscuits, would sponsor a prize for the cookery section at the Show. As I recall, the biscuit factory was out in the suburban sticks somewhere and Mr Brockoff was a very large man who kept me waiting for half an hour. He was polite enough when I eventually gained admittance to his office and, in response to my hopeless salesmanship, agreed to sponsor the home-made damper class with a first prize of two guineas (about four dollars) and a second prize of one guinea. I thought to myself: 'What the hell am I doing at my time of life, a fairly influential newspaper columnist, seeking prizes for home-made dampers?' I jacked up next time I was asked to go on a similar mission. I tried to get rid of the sponsorship responsibility to the accounts department, but without success. I despaired, too, of ever mastering the intricacies of the Show's schedules of prizes for horses, cattle, pigs, goats, dogs, cats, arts and crafts, horticulture, agriculture, fruit and vegetables, poultry, wine and God knows what else. These things were way out of my orbit but I persevered.

Behind the stone walls of the Showground lay a 71½ acre feudal kingdom, benevolently ruled by a Council of 55 members, including a president, 15 vice-presidents and a treasurer. The councillors fairly evenly represented the city Establishment and the country Squattocracy. All councillors gave their services in an honorary capacity. Some of them journeyed many hundreds of miles to Sydney for the regular monthly Council meetings but did not receive a travel allowance or expenses of any kind. The family service given voluntarily to the Society for more than a century was surely unique. Many second, third, fourth and fifth generations served on the Council. Show business gets in the blood and is handed down from grandfather to father, to son. Many gave the Society 20, 30, 40 and even 50 years of devoted service. Since its beginnings, the lists of office bearers have borne the names of prominent and respected Australian families in public life, the professions and the rural community; names such as Angus, Badgery, Barnes, Downes, Fairfax, Hordern, Playfair, White, Vickery, Darling, Ross and so many others.

The Council was a tightly closed shop. Councillors were elected by vote of the general RAS members (about 10,000 today) for a term of three years. They retired in groups, in rotation, usually offering themselves for re-election. Under the rules, the Council itself could elect new councillors to fill casual vacancies caused by death, retirement or resignation. This made it virtually impossible for an 'outsider' to break through the stone walls. As the names of the retiring members were marked with an asterisk on the ballot papers, a maverick candidate had practically no chance of getting in. Only one unendorsed man to my knowledge ever succeeded in scaling the walls of the Showground and that was because one of the asterisked candidates died after the printing of the ballot papers and the outsider was the only other name. What's more, he turned out to be one of the best councillors the Society ever had. It was the most thoroughly undemocratic system one could imagine yet, to confound the critics, it worked. It was a non-profit organisation dedicated to the 'development of the agricultural, pastoral, viticultural, horticultural, mineral and industrial resources of the nation'.

I joined the RAS at a time of great change. Television came six months later and this involved many conferences with the various television stations as to how the Royal Easter Show should be covered. The Show made marvellous television but would wholesale televising of it keep the paying customers away? A system of rationing was worked out but neither side was entirely satisfied with the arrangements. This was a new crisis for the Show. For more than 100 years the Show had been a way of life for country and city people alike. Going to the Show was an annual habit. People just went with their children each year and when the children grew up, they took their children. Each year they marvelled at the livestock, the exciting day and night main arena events, the industrial exhibits, the sideshows, the arts and crafts. Each year they complained about the price of Show sample bags, and each year they came back for more. There was no need to advertise the Show—it sold itself and people came in their hundreds of thousands without any urging. The advertising budget for the giant 1956 Royal Easter Show was a paltry £2,749 2s. 3d. (about $5,500). But things were changing and other counter-attractions, as well as television, were challenging the popularity of the Show. The advertising budgets were to rise spectacularly in coming years. The public relations section was heavily involved in operations to keep up with the times and I was kept busy.

Efforts also had to be made to improve relations with the working press, which were at an all-time low. Councillors had little time or respect for journalists and the feeling was heartily reciprocated. It was clear that there was little chance of getting publicity or cooperation until the ordinary journalist was brought on side. The Journalists' Club was cajoled into sponsoring an annual prize for the best sherry at our Wine Show, which still continues. Club president, Kenneth Slessor, OBE, spoke brilliantly at a pre-show press luncheon. Titles and decorations were revered by the older and more conservative councillors—they were surprised and impressed to discover that a working journalist was not only a famous poet but the recipient of a high imperial honour. The RAS-Shell Journalists' Tours, began in 1958, also created much goodwill. These tours were sponsored by the Shell Company of Australia Limited and Shell Chemicals (Australia) Pty Ltd. The four-day pre-Show tours took 30 press, radio and television journalists and cameramen to country properties and enterprises that would be represented at the forthcoming Show. Everyone was happy. Civic receptions were put on to welcome the visitors in local towns. The Show got invaluable publicity and Shell, who paid the bills, got a lot of kudos for their products in the country. The media sent their top men and women journalists and cameramen on the early tours and the RAS councillors who led the parties were surprised to find that working journalists were not only human but extremely intelligent and companionable.

Another very successful promotion was the Royal Show Girl Contest, first held in 1962. Today, Show Girl contests are a regular and popular feature of most country shows in N.S.W., all competing for the grand final at the Royal Easter Show. There were some slightly raised eyebrows among the more conservative members of the RAS when the Society launched itself into the 'beauty contest' business. The first contest was a modest affair with about 20 entrants but it grew into one of the Society's biggest promotions with national sponsors providing around-the-world trips for two, spending money and other prizes. Chief sponsors of the early contest were the Murdoch-owned *Daily Mirror* and Qantas. When the *Mirror* withdrew their sponsorship, it was taken over by the *Australian Women's Weekly, Daily* and *Sunday Telegraph*, whose proprietor, Sir Frank Packer, was an RAS councillor and, naturally enough, member of the publicity committee and also sponsor of the polo. He was treated with great respect at all times.

The first Show Girl Contest gave me a massive promotional nightmare. The winner was the daughter of the Show's ringmaster and a councillor and afterwards I heard outside whispers of a 'fix'. That was ridiculous and unjust because she had won it by a mile for beauty, charm, poise and intelligence. But I saw the potential damage to the Society's reputation in future contests and urged the publicity committee to ban councillors' daughters from entering the quest. The councillors did not see it that way, however. Some of them had attractive daughters and grand-daughters with ambitious mothers coveting the honour and glory and a free overseas trip as a chaperone.

I did succeed, later, in getting them to approve a ban on councillors' wives acting as judges in the zone and grand finals to avoid any charge of nepotism. This was to lead to a dramatic scene during a meeting of the publicity committee at the Showground a year or so later. The meeting was discussing the appointment of judges for the grand final at the forthcoming Show. Sir Frank Packer, a big burly man who could look fearsome at times, said pleasantly, 'Florence [Lady Packer] will be glad to be one.'

There was a awkward silence and the councillors looked at one and other in dismay and uncertainty. It was left to me to muster enough courage to break the quiet.

'With due respect, Sir Frank,' I said, 'that won't be possible.'

Sir Frank swung around in my direction. 'Why not?' he demanded.

'The publicity committee had decided that councillors' wives be banned from judging the final,' I replied.

Sir Frank blew his top. 'Is that so?' he shouted, getting red in the face. 'Then you can ____ your bloody contest as far as I'm concerned! I withdraw my sponsorship!'

If there had been a hush in the close tonight, there was a deadly silence now. The stunned councillors looked at me accusingly as if I was the Devil incarnate, there was anger in their combined glare at the loss of the Show's biggest publicity sponsor. And then, as quickly as the volcano had erupted it subsided. A few seconds later, Sir Frank said, 'I'm sorry for that outburst, gentlemen. Of course the sponsorship will continue. I'll explain it to Florence.'

You could actually feel the relaxation of tension in the room; the councillors were all smiles; 'dear old Gilbert', you could see it in their faces. As I was leaving the room, Sir Frank came across and put his hand on my shoulder. 'I'm sorry about that, Mr Mant. If you're going back to the city office, I'll get my man to drive you there.' So I returned to the city in the back seat of the huge stretch Packer limousine and its American driver, with a new and healthy respect for this legendary newspaper tycoon. It seemed that Sir Frank, on his part, respected somebody who would stand up to him.

I recall two other major crises with the Show Girls. One year a mother alleged that another contestant was over the age limit of 25. There was a frantic search for a birth certificate. The story was false and the girl went on to win the grand final. In the 1960s a winner asked to take away her boyfriend as a chaperone instead of her mother on the prize-winning air trip. Everyone was horror-stricken by such an outrageous and improper suggestion and it was rejected out of hand. How things have changed!

I looked after the Show Girl finalists during their Sydney sojourns for the next eight years. The girls were lovely and no trouble but the mothers had to be handled diplomatically. They were like hens fussing over their chickens and jockeying for positions in the poultry section of the Show.

It took a full year to make a Royal Easter Show. When the gates closed on one Show, work began immediately on another. The end result was something to be proud of and a few vital statistics show the magnitude of it. In those days entries exceeded 30,000. There were more than 14,000 pure-bred livestock on show, the dog show was the largest in the Southern Hemisphere. The daily Grand Parade, a triumph of intricate organisation, is still the most colourful livestock spectacle on Earth. More than 800 livestock prize-winners—horses, cattle and goats—slowly circle the main arena in their brightly coloured ribbons—all this in the centre of one of the world's greatest cities. Their movements are like a slow-motion ballet and form an ever-changing kaleidoscope of colour and form.

The main area program includes trotting races, polo and polocrosse, rodeo and fireworks. The Show's woodchopping competitions are uniquely Australian and crowds go wild with excitement during world championship events. Axemen come from many parts of Australia and New Zealand and sometimes America. The six main general exhibition buildings were jammed with crowds admiring secondary industry displays of everything from a needle to an anchor.

One of the most exciting main arena events, the equestrian high-jumping, was eliminated in 1959 because the contests were taking three hours to conduct and jumping had become part of the Equestrian Federation of Australia's new Olympic events. The high-jumping and water jumping had been great crowd-pleasers. When the high jump was discontinued, the Royal Easter Show record of seven feet six inches was held jointly by R. Chittick's Dungog (1929) and A.L. Payne's All Fours (1939). Some wonderful horses had contested the events over the years. The Radiums had included Mark Radium and Dark Radium. Among many other great jumpers were Victory, Hereford, Desmond, Silverwood, Young Bill, Gray Hawk, Musician and Sundown. The last-named was killed while jumping at Albany (Western Australia) in 1925. I wrote some lines about it for *Country Life* newspaper:

> Old horse, you have gone to your kingdom, the kingdom where good horses go,
> The grass will be over your fetlocks, the days will be sunny and slow,
> The rails that you jump will be matchwood, the jockey who rides you will sit
> As light as the wind on your saddle, as free as the touch of your bit.
>
> Old horse, you will still know the canter, the vivid desire of your feet
> To rise and rise clean at the timber—the feeling, old man, that was sweet;
> Aye, sweet as the set of your shoulders, the joy of the jump as you veered,
> The crowd on their feet in the grandstand, the roar of applause as you cleared.
>
> Old horse, as you lived for your jumping, 'twas proper and fit that you died
> The bit in your teeth on the Showground, the plunge for the rails in your stride—
> And so you have gone to your kingdom, the paddocks marked out on your plan;
> 'Good jumping, Sundown, by Ben Buckler, you've earned it twice over, old man.'

I remember odd episodes and crises during my stay at the Grand Old. A big day each year was the official opening of the show by the Governor-General of Australia and the Governor of New South Wales, in rotation, and sometimes by the Queen. The ceremony took place on a dais in the centre of the main arena and strict dress rules were enforced on people in the arena after television arrived. Members of the media had to obtain special passes for the arena and the wearing of coats and neckties was compulsory. There was much muttering and grumbling about this, especially among the photographers, but the Society was determined to present a dignified ceremony to the world. Entry to the arena was through a special gate on the grandstand side and protected by me and a security man.

One year a Russian journalist from the Tass agency based in Canberra tricked us all by vaulting over a fence on the opposite side of the arena without a coat or a necktie. I was ordered to intercept him before he reached the dais but he was too quick for me. The television cameras had started rolling by the time I reached him and I dared not grapple with him in front of them. A stiff letter of complaint was written to the Soviet authorities of Tass about the incident.

All RAS press releases and breed society news items were issued under the name of the director Lieutenant-General Sir Frank Berryman. On my trips around the bush as the Society's representative, property owners and show presidents continually asked me, 'why do you have to have a military general to run the RAS?—the war has been over for years'. Something would have to be done about it but the General, a professional soldier, was very prickly about such matters. So I quietly canvassed the matter among his closest friends and colleagues in and out of the Society, suggesting to them that it would be to the great advantage of the RAS to drop the 'Lieutenant-General' part of his title. 'Sir Frank Berryman', on its own, was far more appropriate for the times and had a distinguished ring to it. It took a while but about three months later the General summonsed me to his presence. 'I've been thinking that it might be a good idea if I dropped the Lieutenant-General from my name for press statements. You know, the war has been over for some years now and we don't want people to get the impression that the Society is a military establishment. You're the public relations officer, what do you think about it?' I pretended to think about it for about five minutes and then said I thought it was an excellent idea. 'Well, attend to it,' he said. 'Yes, General,' I said in the manner of Sir Humphrey Appleby.

You will think that my actions were very devious but that's what I thought public relations officers were for. The General was succeeded as director by the popular W.N. (Bill) Parry-Okeden, secretary of the Australian Jockey Club. He, too, was an ex-army officer but as a civilian soldier, an AIF lieutenant-colonel, but dropped his rank to 'Mr' on joining the RAS. (My crusade was in vain, however. The next two directors were major-generals and both used the title.)

The two men I most liked working for were two RAS presidents, Sam Hordern and Sir Philip Charley.

Samuel Hordern III had been elected president in 1954 at the age of 45. He thus became a third-generation president of the Society, following in the footsteps of his father, Sir Samuel Hordern, and his maternal grandfather, Sir John See. In addition, his uncle, Anthony Hordern, Snr, was a vice-president and his cousin, Anthony Hordern, Jnr, was a councillor. 'Young Sam,' as he was known, was steeped in the tradition of the RAS and had exhibited in the horse, cattle, dog and agriculture sections of the Show and served as Ringmaster for five years. So tall (six feet five inches) that he stooped as he walked, he had a smile as wide as a saucer and was once described as being 'more like a cheerful Texas cowpoke than a fifth-generation financial mogul'. A man of restless energy and charm, Young Sam was also popularly known to the general public as a keen racing man (an AJC committeeman), a fast car driver and a pilot with his own aeroplane. During World War II he served in the Middle East and New Guinea, where he commanded a squadron of tanks, being awarded a military OBE.

Young Sam was a marvellous boss, not only to me but to the other 150 or so Showground permanent employees. He knew most of them by name—the office staff, plumbers, carpenters, electricians, engineers and gardeners—and also their wives and children. He was the perfect ruler of the feudal kingdom of the Showground and might have made it into a Camelot had he lived.

He was in great demand for opening country shows, usually travelling in his plane with his personal pilot. Sometimes he flew it himself and I recall the alarm of the Tenterfield (or was it Glen Innes?) show officials when he announced he intended to follow the railway line as a map and land at a little-used airstrip near a meatworks. On another occasion he was just stopped in time from planning to land at Adaminaby, which was by then under water as part of the Snowy Mountains Scheme lake. On those occasions he would ask me to prepare notes about the show he was scheduled to open. I went to great trouble with these, though knowing that he would never use them, as he spoke spontaneously. Tuesday was a traditional Children's Day at the Royal Easter Show and it was the custom of the President to address them over the loudspeaker system in the main arena. He asked me for notes and I used the word 'children' a few times. He *never* used them, of course, but I noted afterwards that he had crossed out 'children' and replaced it with 'boys and girls'. He would have said 'kids' today—he was that sort of man.

Young Sam was a wonderful, warm and understanding man and a convivial one, too. On 25 July 1960, he was due to fly to Sydney from his country estate at Bowral for the regular monthly Council meeting at the Showground. There was a thick fog and he was obliged to take a taxi. There was a collision on a bridge near Warwick Farm Racecourse and Young Sam was killed instantly. He was only 51 and there would never be a Camelot.

Sir Philip Charley, my other presidential boss, did not need a public relations officer either. At 71 when he was elected president in 1965, he was his own PR man. I wrote notes for him for special occasions but he never used them. All he had to do was stand up in front of a crowd of country show people and say, 'I'm just a cow cocky from Richmond...' and he had them in the hollows of his hands. A strong traditionalist and a Queen's man, he was nevertheless in some ways the most unconventional president the Old Grand ever had. He was a son of Major Philip Charley, a former RAS vice-president who, as a young jackeroo, had been one of the syndicate of seven who discovered what was to become the silver city of Broken Hill. Sir Philip had been in 'show business' for more than 60 years when elected president. He liked nothing better than an informal yarn with people in the bush and had a happy knack of getting on with people in all walks of life. It was Phil and Gil when we travelled together on Shell journalists' tours and field crop judging competitions and we had some grand times.

After thirteen Royal Easter Shows, I reckoned I'd had enough and announced my intention to retire. I was 67 years of age and wanted to do some private writing before it was too late. Besides, my assistant and good friend, Doug Denham, was waiting in the wings to take over. (Doug turned out to be a far better salesman than I—by the time he retired in 1989, the sponsorships had risen to more than $600,000.) They wanted me to stay, but I would not change my mind. There were some anxious moments when it was discovered that through an accountancy mistake in 1956, I was not entitled to any superannuation. But I need not have worried—the Grand Old Society did not let me down. I was given a golden handshake far beyond my expectations, with which I paid off a War Service Homes loan and bought a block of land at Port Macquarie for $5,000. 'You're mad,' Brian Russell said to me. Not so mad, Brian, seeing that if that block were available today it would cost you more than $200,000. I was commissioned to write a short history of the Society *(The Big Show)* and after a few years with *The Land* newspaper, I retired to the Mid-North Coast, bought a camera, and learnt to photograph best uddered cows.

From a distance I have followed with interest the controversy about the future of Sydney Showground. Even when another 'final decision' is announced, I will greet it with some scepticism and believe it only when the removal vans move in.

It all began when plans were made for the redevelopment by the N.S.W. government of Homebush Bay, a derelict area off Parramatta River in north-west Sydney. One of the major projects was a proposal to move the Showground and the RAS from Moore Park to Homebush. This caused immediate controversy which heightened when Sydney won the 2000 Olympic Games. The government estimated that the sale of the Showground might raise $74 million to help finance and provide sporting facilities for the Games. The government envisaged that the Showground's 28-hectare site could be developed into units and townhouses. Another plan was to convert part of the land into a major film-making complex. The RAS was agreeable to the move as the new Homebush site would be closer to the demographic centre of Sydney, with easy rail, road and water transport facilities for people and livestock. Moreover, the showground area would increase to 35 hectares, the main arena would be larger with eventual seating capacity for 90,000 people, and parking for up to 20,000 cars would be available.

Opposition for the move was led by Ms Clover Moore, MP for the local Moore Park area, who maintained that the Showground was needed for essential open space in a densely populated inner-city area. She succeeded in having state legislation passed in 1992, ensuring that the land remained in public ownership. The N.S.W. parliamentary opposition and South Sydney Council joined forces with Ms Moore to pressure the government to abandon its plan for the move, the cost of which had spiralled to $230 million by 1994. Meanwhile, the old Showground was deteriorating through government indecision and an estimated cost of $80 million was named to restore its ageing buildings and bring it up to an acceptable standard of safety. It was a no-win sort of situation.

1994 was to have been the year of the last Easter Show staged at Moore Park, but once again its life has been extended. The shabby old Showground and its century-old traditions for bushies and city slickers alike is going out in style, with 1994 Show attendances the best for years. As a clear sign of the times, it was not the big bulls that drew the crowds but a 40-foot high mechanical monster from America named Robosaurus. Higher than a five-storey building, it breathed 10-metre fingers of fire, ate motorcars, bit and ripped roofs and doors with its stainless-steel teeth, to the great edification and excitement of the crowds.

13
Last of the Bohemians

One Sunday, maybe in the late 1940s, Dr Erasmus Bligh, a fashionable Sydney surgeon stood up in his North Sydney home to carve the family roast. The doctor always took such a grave professional interest in this operation that observers felt it should be preceded by a swift stab of a hypodermic needle in the side of the joint. The carving knife became a scalpel in his hand. The carver was somewhat astonished, therefore, when suddenly a tall, handsome man with greying hair swept into the dining-room, snatched the steaming roast from the dish and ran from the room with a cry of triumph.

The interloper was Hugh McCrae, an Australian poet who wrote what were regarded in his day as some of the loveliest poems in the English language. Poet, writer, artist and actor, he was the last of the bohemians, a man of infinite zest, wit and whimsicality.

The poet's snatching of the Sunday roast from under the surgeon's scalpel was not as preposterous as it sounds. The doctor's wife happened to be his sister and Hugh and family were occupying a wing of the house. Some visitors had dropped in unexpectedly, and as is well-known, poets' larders are usually empty. What was more natural than that Hugh should stage a lightning and perfectly timed raid on the good neighbour's pantry?

McCrae, the poet, is forgotten now but someday someone will write a full-length biography of this full-length man of wit and whimsy and rare literary talent, whose laugh, as described by Kenneth Slessor, was like an active volcano. When lyrical poetry stages a revival the poems of Hugh McCrae will be in the forefront. The work of his young disciple, Slessor, is still being read, which is a good sign. Meantime, the old bush balladists—Paterson, Lawson & Co.—are enjoying a huge boom, under clever promotion. The Man from Snowy River is an Australian industry of its own with books, films, television and other exposure.

The prevailing vogue in academic poetry is based on what used to be known as 'blank verse'; to rhyme is a sin. I try very hard to understand many of the poems of today. I love the words and images but become annoyed to see them set out in poetic form. To me, they are 'poetic prose' and should be presented as such. Some of them seem to me to be utter, unintelligible rubbish. I wonder whether they have been composed by pressing a button on a word processor, without any real human feeling or emotion. I suppose I will be called an old diehard or an 'old square' for this heresy. It would be more accurate to call me an 'old oblong', with more room to move my thoughts and opinions. I move with the times but it's a free country and I don't have to agree with them. I don't read much poetry these days but of the living Australian poets I like and admire Judith Wright, Les Murray and Bruce Dawe; they all write ancient and modern, not afraid of a rhyme or two.

If John Keats were alive today and submitted poems to a poetry magazine he would quickly be shown the door. So would Hugh McCrae, whose magical words and images were about satyrs, nymphs, knights, medieval ladies, unicorns and centaurs rather than sick stockmen, sheep, horses, drovers, drought and bushfire. This lack of specifically Australian images in his poems was acknowledged by Douglas Stewart, one of McCrae's greatest admirers. But Stewart pointed out that McCrae was not trying to write ballads any more than Paterson was trying to write lyrics. It would be absurd to change McCrae's 'nymphs' into 'sheep' or to change the 'Columbine' in one of his most exquisite poems into 'lubra'. McCrae lived in the past but Mary Gilmore wrote after he died: 'He walked with today and the past walked with him. I would have given the world for him to have re-written Chaucer in today's English in his own way. Had he done so we would all be looking out the window to see what cavalcade was passing by—Chaucer would be living now.'

Listen to McCrae's 'I Blow My Pipes':

>I blow my pipes, the glad birds sing,
>The fat young nymphs about me spring,
>The sweaty centaur leaps the trees
>And bites his splendid dryad's knees;
>The sky, the water and the earth
>Repeat aloud our noisy mirth...
>Anon tight-bellied bacchanals,
>With ivy from the vineyard walls,
>Lead out and crown with shining glass
>The wine's red baby on the grass.
>...
>I blow my pipes, the glad birds sing,
>The fat young nymphs about me spring,
>I am the lord,
>I am the lord,
>I am the lord of everything!

And other unforgettable first stanzas and fragments:

> My unicorn ... my unicorn is dead;
> He with the swift long flanks and kingly head,
> The great tall spring horn ... the yellow-eyed
> Fierce bearded husband of the forest side...
>
> ('Lament')

> Exit the ribald clown—
> Enter like bubbling wine,
> Lighter than thistledown
> Sweet little Columbine...
>
> ('Columbine')

> I saw the stoop,
> One long lean arm set taut upon his bow
> The other crook'd, and in his finger's loop
> The straining cord where crouched the shaft of woe...
>
> ('The Archer')

And the magical

> I watch her fingers while they prance
> Like naked women, tango-mad,
> Along the keys...

Hugh Raymond McCrae was born in Hawthorn, Melbourne, in 1876, a son of George Gordon McCrae, known as the 'father of Australian poetry'. The boy grew up in a cultural atmosphere of art and letters and a mild form of bohemianism. His father was a gifted poet, writer and artist. He was the leader of a coterie of writers and artists in the fledgling colony of Victoria in the 1860s and 1870s. He, Orion Horne, Henry Kendall, Marcus Clarke, Adam Lindsay Gordon and others founded the Yorick Club. McCrae befriended the wayward Gordon and also took the weak and temperamental Kendall under his wing. When a despairing Gordon shot himself in 1870, Kendall was so distraught as to write a note to Gordon, care of McCrae, apologising for not being able to attend the funeral: 'Dear Gordon, At 4 p.m. this afternoon, I haven't the money to spare, or I would attend. Indeed, I am penniless. Yours truly, Henry Kendall.' The letter is still in existence, a letter to the dead.

Hugh McCrae grew into a tall, handsome youth with high spirits, and when he was seventeen his mother decided that he should make the church his career. So he dutifully became an unpaid curate and put on a surplice. He was soon taking mid-week services unassisted and once christened an elderly woman who was seeking salvation in later life. Some of his boisterous young friends were appalled by Hughie being taken from them in this way. One day, a few months later, a bunch of them kidnapped him, surplice and all, outside the church and made him a not unwilling prisoner in a Collingwood pub. They plied him with drink for three and a half days and persuaded him to 'change his ways'.

His mother surrendered and had him articled to a Melbourne architect and thereafter Hugh's life was a mixed grill. He is said to have learnt nothing but how to make tea in the architect's office but became interested to find out more about a young man with a tarboosh on his head who spent hours sketching on a roof of a building across the street. The young man was Norman Lindsay and soon Hugh was a joyous member of Lindsay & Co.'s bohemians, a much wilder mob than those of his father's bohemia a decade or two earlier. Hugh and Norman were to have a long love–hate relationship but, sadly, drifted apart in their older life. Two mercurial personalities having blazing rows and emotional reconciliations, theirs was a relationship not destined to survive.

Under the Lindsay influence, he took art lessons and soon found a market for his black-and-white drawings and cartoons. He visited England and America just before World War I. In New York he met Pat O'Sullivan, the Australian creator of the *Felix the Cat* cartoons, who wanted him to do the drawings on a 50/50 basis. Hugh declined, thus losing his only chance of ever making a fortune. In New York he carried a spear in a biblical stage production of Granville Barker. He returned to Australia and for the rest of his life wrote poetry and prose of the highest quality but to little financial advantage. He married Anne Geraldine Adams, daughter of a well-to-do Victorian grazier, known to the family as 'Nancy'. She looked after him like a wife and mother until her death in 1942. In their early married days, they shared a house with Norman Lindsay in Lavender Bay, Sydney. There were three daughters, Huntly ('Honey'), Marjory ('Mahdi') and Rose ('Smee'). As a child, Rose would knock on a door and in answer to 'Who's there?' would reply, ' 'S'mee'. The girls grew up into beautiful women and all three were talented artists, selling their work commercially. It could not have been very easy for Nancy. Despite his endearing qualities and impish humour, Hugh was possessed of an unmanageable 'artistic temperament'. His son-in-law Sir Norman Cowper, who married Huntly, described him as a 'hypersensitive and tempestuous person . . . He was capable of moods of black depression, titanic rage and then leaping exultation'. Nevertheless the family adored one another and the girls called him Mac. Norman Lindsay once wrote about the Jekyll and Hyde aspects of Hugh's character: 'I don't wonder that Hugh McCrae has made laughter and humour his surface defence against the black depression and disgusts which must be the other side of any vision of life based on lyricism, passion and an enduring love for beauty and offered to a generation as morally inert as so many mudfish. We all wear a mask.'

Stories abound (whato for another cliche!) about the other side of Hugh McCrae's mask. A vintage story concerns the day he and Mick Paul, a one-eyed *Bulletin* black-and-white artist, went into a Sydney cafe for a feed of meat pies without a penny in their pockets. Mick became very agitated when the time came to pay but Hugh said not to worry. He whispered in Mick's ear and the artist removed his glass eye from its socket and placed it inside a pie Hugh had left on his plate. 'There's an eye in my pie!' Hugh cried out in great indignation, summoning the cafe proprietor. While the proprietor was gazing in horror at the eye in the gravy, the two conspirators vanished into the street.

This was a refinement of Mick's other dodges to evade payment in restaurants, according to Jack (Norman's son) Lindsay in his autobiography, *The Roaring Twenties*. Mick, he wrote, would catch mice and put them on an almost empty plate under the potato, so that he could haughtily summon the waitress and shout, 'Take this to the manager, look what you feed to your customers!' In his cups, Mick sometimes slept in the Domain (a Sydney public park) among the dossers and derelicts. There he learnt to wear under his coat pepper, salt and vinegar bottles and containers to hold pilfered food from eating houses. He became disenchanted with the Domain, Lindsay relates, when sleeping a drunken sleep among the derelicts who covered themselves with newspaper shreds. Someone stole his trousers while he snorted and failed to wake up. In the early dawn he discovered that he had cold legs, scratched himself and then started off to run through the streets in a newspaper kilt for the nearest studio. Good-natured as he was, he felt that someone had gone too far in pinching trousers from a harmless drunk.

Another classic story centres around McCrae's brief period as a censor in Melbourne during World War I when he was in his forties. It was never discovered that it was he who frequently drove his fellow censors into a frenzy of spy-detection. On one occasion he telephoned them in a guttural German accent with a request to send an allegedly 'quite innocent' package out of the country uncensored. On another occasion he sent a group of spy-catchers slinking out at midnight to Princes Bridge to an assignment, made by telephone, with a mysterious lady who would be identified as wearing a red rose in her hair and carrying an arum lily in her left hand.

Which reminds me that my friend, Dr F. ('Call me Friar') Balsam, once told me that his aunt, the fifth Lady Balsam, was involved in an espionage drama during the war.

'For some time, you know, she was a member of the British Secret Service,' said the doctor, taking a puff at his meerschaum pipe. 'On one occasion she was carrying top-secret despatches written on special paper that dissolved when put into water.

'Her arch-enemy, the Baron von Stinkwurt, who had a duelling scar on his left cheek, tracked her down to Balsam Castle and cornered her in the dining-room.

'"Hand over the secret, your ladyship!" the baron demanded in guttural tones, covering her with a sawn-off shotgun.

'Without hesitation, my aunt flung the secret paper into a glass of gin and swallowed it in one gulp. The baron was foiled again.'

The doctor coughed and added: 'Of course it was child's play to my aunt. She had been a secret drinker all her life.'

The McCraes lived at Camden for some years and Hugh was happy in his rural retreat. He made friends with the local magpies and wrote poems about them. He called his garden spade Rochester and the household broom Van Tromp. Occasionally he invited people to visit him there and on one occasion Alec Chisholm, ornithologist, author and editor, had some difficulty finding the place. The invitation had been addressed from River Road, Camden, but he searched vainly for it. Then he inquired at the local Poets' Pub. 'Know Mac?' cried the hotelkeeper. 'Of course I know where Mac lives. There isn't any River Road in this town but Mac calls it that because his house is beside a river. And, faith, why shouldn' he if he wants to? The postman's a pal of his, anyway, and sees that he gets his mail all right.'

There was a small room in Hugh's house which he called the Book Robbers' Library. In it he kept a collection of second-rate books he had no further use for, his real literary treasures were under lock and key elsewhere. Visitors bereft of book-conscience were ushered into the Book Robbers' Library and left there to do their worst, with Hugh rocking with laughter in the background. One day he overheard another poet complaining bitterly to a friend: 'I can't think what's come over poor Hughie—he reads a lot of absolute trash now. There's not a book worth pinching in the whole place!'

Hugh was a compulsive letter-writer. He wrote literally thousands of letters to hundreds of people for more than 50 years. Most of them were written in Indian ink and illustrated by little drawings and decorations. The penmanship was unique and looked a bit Chinese as each letter was carefully drawn, the g's having a squiggle tail. After the death of Nancy, he lived on and off with his daughters and the addresses on his letters bore evidence of this—'Honey's Place, Wahroonga' or 'Mahdi's Place, Vaucluse' were likely to puzzle the Dead Letter Office if ever lost. Some of the letters bore the warning, 'Be sure to burn this before reading it'. *The Letters of Hugh McCrae*, selected and edited by the poet Robert D. Fitzgerald, was published by Angus and Robertson in 1970. Fitzgerald culled 261 letters out of the 3,000 sent to him by the public.

It's time now for me to disclose that Hugh McCrae was my cousin. He and my mother were double first cousins, their brother fathers having married sisters.

Hugh and Francie were the closest of friends all their lives and he frequently dropped into her Double Bay flat when he was staying at Mahdi's Place. They wrote hundreds of letters to each other, some of which are in Fitzgerald's book. He wrote dozens of letters to me, too, addressing me as 'Dear Gilly', or 'Gilly-O'. Once I sent him some jokes I had manufactured which I thought he might use for his *Bulletin* cartoons. Back came a drawing of an editor's office with a caricature of Hugh as the editor at a desk, with a swarm of flies around his head, and me as a contributor. 'The flies are bad today!' I am saying. 'Not as bad as the jokes!' says the editor.

One long McCrae letter in Fitzgerald's book was to poet-novelist Kenneth Mackenzie, a wild invention describing the loss of his false teeth:

> Just as young girls lose their virtue through drink, so do old men lose their teeth— through drink (but also through the railway carriage window). When I arrived home I had to explain becos (once more like the young girl) it was impossible to conceal my condition; so I said Lennie Lower did it. 'We changed teeth,' I said to Nancy, 'and he wouldn't give me mine back!' 'Do you mean to say,' she exclaimed, 'that that little beast is wearing the teeth your Aunt Nelly gave you?!!!!! They'll be stretched to bits and you'll never be able to get them into your mouth again! You must threaten him with the police. If you don't I'll go to the Telegraph office with a tin-opener and drag them from him myself!' So Yoicks, Tally-Ho and Gawd 'elp Lower! altho it's the Upper she's after...

Another letter is a sidelight on the ever-impecunious Henry Lawson and the old *Bulletin* days. The wooden stairs of that ramshackle building in Lower George Street should have been preserved. Up and down them, especially on pay days, trudged the poets and writers and artists of the golden days of Australian early literature. Victor Daley, Louis Becke, David Low, 'Hop' Livingstone, Phil May, the Lindsays and so many others. The casual contributors took their cheques to a nearby pub to drink some or all of it out. In a letter, McCrae recalls one such occasion: '. . . and Henry Lawson collared my shilling laid down for a sixpenny shout: "D'you mind if I take this into the tripenny bar where we'll get TWICE as much beer!"' (Which reminds me that Mary Gilmore gave me a two shillings IOU signed on a piece of paper by Lawson. I presented it to the Grenfell Lawson Museum many years ago and I suppose it's still there.)

I also had a correspondence with Hugh's father, George Gordon McCrae, my grand-uncle, when I was very young and writing awful bush verses. He gave me sound advice and some comments on the English language which are even more apt today. In August 1921, when I was nineteen, he wrote:

> I would see that my descriptions continued always to reach out in plain clear English, steering completely clear of the corruptions of our language that encompass us on every side. Avoid as you would the Devil 'boss', 'Britisher', 'do-

nate', 'con-clude', 'figure' and most obnoxious of all, 'disgruntle'. They are dumping down this rubbish into our well of English, hitherto pure and undefiled, every day and it will be a far more arduous essay (the Hercules provided) to clear out our well than to have cleansed the Augean Stable. There is perhaps no language (take it all round) so beautiful or so flexible as ours. No purer. Let us do all in our power to keep it pure, as purity makes always for dignity as well as beauty.

I wonder what George Gordon McCrae would think of the Americanisation of our language today? Cookies, crackers, guys, buddy, skedule (schedule), jump-rope (skipping) ad nauseam.

Hugh McCrae lived until he was 81. His death in 1958 released a flood of eulogies from the literary world, but his poems languished in public taste. In his book, *Six Australian Poets*, T. Inglis Moore had written: 'In his multiple personality he mingles the romantic troubadour of glorified love with the Rabelaisian realist of sex, the swashbuckling bravo with the moon-haunted dreamer; he is as much at home with Puck as with Pan; he can sing as truly of a Camden magpie or a gardener's pipe outside his domestic windows as of a tantalised unicorn'. Alas, there's no place today for troubadors or unicorns, only the pop musicians and dinosaurs are in fashion.

Hugh McCrae's published work included *Satyrs and Sunlight, Poems, Forests of Pan, Voice of the Forest, My Father and My Father's Friends, The Du Poissey Anecdotes, Story-Book Only, Georgiana's Diary* and *The Ship of Heaven*, a play produced in Sydney in the 1950s.

Ronald McKie, a fine writer himself, wrote a wonderful profile of the poet in 1949 when McCrae was 73. Harking back to the youth in the surplice, he told McKie that although he had no truck with religion, he believed in God.

> 'I believe in God,' he said, 'but not in the God you read about, not the Almighty with a trumpet. I believe in God because there is so much that can't be explained in real life—like the seasons, the construction of our own bodies, the urge to reproduce. Let's say I believe in continuity. I'm alive today to a certain extent and I'm positive of the continuity of life after death, probably in some different form. I believe I'll be alive after death and I'll be more alive than I am today. I feel that death will be like the unwrapping of a parcel.'

McKie commented wryly: 'If what he says is true then I'm game to take a bet that when his parcel opens there'll be much story-telling and deep belly-laughs in Heaven—unless, of course, Hughie McCrae has gone to the wrong address'. If Ron were alive today, he would probably add that Hughie had gone to the right address and was now writing letters from God's Place.

Hugh always said that he had inherited his literary and artistic talent from his father and his grandmother, Georgiana Huntly McCrae. Georgiana! She demands a chapter to herself.

Gilbert Mant, age 12 or thereabouts.

Off to war.

Georgiana McCrae, the author's great grandmother, was the illegitimate daughter of the 5th (and last) Duke of Gordon. Brought up at Gordon Castle in Scotland, she became a noted painter, diarist and pioneer woman of Melbourne in the 1840s.

Left to right: Former Australian captain, Ian Craig, Lieut.-General Sir Reginald Pollard, G.O.C. Eastern Command, Lieut.-General Mohammed Yousef, Pakistan High Commissioner in Australia, Australian captain Richie Benaud and Gilbert Mant. A memorable match between Pakistan and the Sydney Journalists' Club.

Gilbert Mant and the Grand Parade.

Gilbert Mant today.

14
Georgiana

There was a rabbit plague when I went out from Sydney as a seventeen year old jackaroo to Eenaweena Station, a stud merino sheep property between Warren and Nyngan in western N.S.W. The rabbits were everywhere despite a severe drought, eating what little grass remained. We jackaroos were armed with .22 rifles and part of our work was to shoot every rabbit in sight. I reckoned I shot 25,000 rabbits during my first year. It was mostly a painless, sudden-death, sitting-shot operation as hundreds of the animals took shelter from the blazing western sun under individual clumps of bindiis (bindy-eyes), a spiky native weed shaped into round balls by the wind. One bindii, one rabbit; you could bet on it. You just aimed at the bindii and pulled the trigger.

It was pre-myxomatosis days and the main eradication campaign against the pests was directed at destroying their warrens (burrowed underground settlements with large populations). This required gangs of men armed with shovels and pick-axes. Some of the warrens were small underground cities with a maze of interconnecting burrows. The warrens were dug up completely by hand and the rabbits killed on the spot or poisoned. Gangs of between ten and twenty men worked on the properties. Another one of my jobs was to look after the station store at times and take out stores to the rabbiters in a one-horse cart. The gangs ordered a variety of goods—flour, sugar, tea, etc.—and I was puzzled at first by the large number of requests for bottles of 'pain-killer', a medicant advertised for the alleviation of pain. I supposed they were subject to accident and injury in their work. That is, until I was laughingly told that the pain-killer formula contained a generous proportion of alcohol. The men drank it neat and, in the end, we had to ration it.

The make-up of the gangs was a fascinating study of humanity. They were mostly middle-aged, with some older and younger men, of various nationalities and backgrounds. You'd strike such assortments wherever you went in the bush in those days. There were 'remittance men', exiled from their country for their country's good to Australia, with a regular money allowance. There were others fleeing from their own battles against grog and women and the responsibilities of life. Many of them were willing to talk about their pasts, as a form of confessional.

After delivery of the goods, I used to linger on yarning with them. One bearded fellow (who said he was a Cambridge graduate) was an agnostic, quoting Huxley and Kant. I had never heard of agnosticism or atheism before, blindly accepting what I had been told about God and the hereafter at home and at church. This man's arguments were compelling and I became an instant unbeliever. (I began to question this conversation later on and ended up a 50/50 doubter.)

The men were human derelicts really, and when they were paid once a month most of them went in a group to the pubs in Warren or Nyngan, handed the publicans their cheques and drank them out. It was better than pain-killer. The publicans were honourable men and did not cheat them, but sent them packing back to the rabbit warrens as soon as their money was gone. The most common story among the English exiles was one of being robbed of great inheritances or hereditary titles. One old chap, when primed with pain-killer, would tell me how he was the bastard child of Prince Albert, Queen Victoria's Consort, and had been exiled to avoid a royal scandal. Another said he had had to renounce an earldom because he had put the pantrymaid in the family way; he was really the Earl of Nottingham and could he please have an extra bottle of pain-killer with my next delivery?

Hilaire Belloc wrote a satirical 'cautionary tale' about it. A peer's son had brought his family name into repeated disrepute through drink, gambling and girls. Finally the father pronounced the ultimate punishment:

> 'But, as it is, my language fails,
> Go out and govern New South Wales!'

My friend, Dr F. ('Call me Friar') Balsam, once told me about his ne'er-do-well nephew, the Honorable Freddie Balsam, who was exiled from England to South America:

> 'He was the black sheep of the Balsam family and was expelled from Eton because of an affair with the school's French mistress. His fatal weakness was women,' said Dr Balsam, taking a swig of pure (for medicinal purposes only) alcohol.
> 'To cut a long story short,' went on the doctor, 'the Honorable Freddie managed to stay out of gaol until he went to Buenos Aires. He got pinched there for a traffic offence, and they gave him twenty years.'
> 'That's pretty steep for an offence like that,' I remarked.
> 'Not at all,' said the doctor, with a bit of a leer. 'It was the white slave traffic.'

It was about this time that I became aware of a skeleton in the Mant (or rather McCrae) family cupboard. My mother spoke in hushed and conspiratorial tones about her grandmother, Georgiana Huntly McCrae, being the only child of the Fifth Duke of Gordon in Scotland. But there was a bar sinister, the supposed sign of bastardy on a family escutcheon, and nobody spoke about it. There had been a Gretna Green marriage but proof of it had never been found. The Duke had died 'without male issue' and the title had passed to his nephew, the Duke of Richmond. My grand-uncle, George Gordon McCrae, of course, was really the sixth Duke of Gordon but it could not be substantiated. There was also a Wicked Duchess to add spice to the story. This was a marvellous yarn for someone of my romantic disposition and I revelled in it. But I bracketed it with the stories of the rabbiters and did not really believe a word of it.

I did not tell anybody about it, not even my two children, in fear of being jeered at for boasting about aristocratic connections with a concocted story. Those were the days when Australians with convict connections also kept jolly quiet about it. How things have changed! Today, a convict connection is of great social advantage. The impression is growing that the 700 or so convicts who landed with Phillip at Sydney Cove in 1788 were all innocent, snow-white victims of a cruel English Establishment, transported for life for stealing a loaf of bread, or a reel of cotton or some other minor misdemeanour. I fear it was not so. The bar sinister has changed, too, though I suppose it still operates for hereditary titles. Couples live together openly and legally today, without marriage, and their children suffer no stigma of illegitimacy. On the other hand, any claims to a ducal descent in these republican days is a matter of shame and disgrace in some people's eyes. There is some comfort, however, in the illegitimacy side of it; to call anyone a bastard these days is, as it always has been in Australia, a term of endearment.

So for the next fifteen years or so I kept the family skeleton securely locked up in its cupboard until suddenly Georgiana was in the news. In 1934, Angus & Robertson published *Georgiana's Journal*, edited by Hugh McCrae, her grandson. This was the day-to-day diary of a Scottish woman who arrived in Port Phillip by sailing ship in March 1841, with her four sons. It was only six years after the foundation of Melbourne; Collins Street was a goat track; and the population numbered only a thousand or so. The journal covered a period from 1838 to 1852 and is one of the most treasured Australian historical documents in existence. The book has since run into four editions. The suburb of McCrae on the Mornington Peninsula is a permanent memorial to this remarkable woman and her family.

The publication of the diary was warmly received by critics and the public and soon the spotlight was turned on to the diarist herself. And what a story it turned out to be, far exceeding some of those told to me by the Eenaweena rabbiters. The unlocking of the skeleton cupboard still took some years to complete, with the subsequent knowledge that Georgiana was indeed the only child of the Fifth (and last) Duke of Gordon, Marquis of Huntly. The public reticence of the family is strange, perhaps the suggestion of illegitimacy was a restraining influence. Hugh McCrae makes no reference to the Duke in the introduction to his book, merely stating that the keeper of the diary was 'born in London at the beginning of the last century'. The diary itself makes mention of 'Her Grace' and 'Madame' (obviously the Duchess of Gordon) and the book has a photograph of the Duchess without saying what she has to do with the story. Thirty-two years later, in 1961, Georgiana's great-grandson, the second George Gordon McCrae, bluntly refers to his great-grandmother as the daughter of the Duke's first wife, Jane Graham, Marchioness of Huntly. In an introduction to the third edition of the *Journal*, as late as 1978, Norman Cowper (a lawyer) is more cautious. He simply describes Georgiana as the 'natural daughter' of the Duke.

Before we dip into the diary, let me set out the story as I know it. Vital information is still missing, though several writers have taken up research on it. One was Susanna De Vries-Evans, who featured Georgiana in her *Pioneer Women, Pioneer Land* (Angus & Robertson) published in 1987. A full-length definitive story has now been completed by noted Melbourne academic, Dr Brenda Niall, whose biography of the novelist Martin Boyd was widely acclaimed. She has been researching the Georgiana story for several years. *Georgiana: A Biography of Georgiana McCrae, Painter, Diarist, Pioneer* will be published by Melbourne University Press in October 1994. I am looking forward keenly to the publication of her book—by far the most thoroughly researched account of an extraordinary life. I imagine that Brenda Niall has fallen for Georgiana, as everybody does, but I am braced for a more mundane, or less romantic portrait than what follows here, which I have written in blissful ignorance of her new research.

I do not know how, when or where George Gordon, Eighth Marquis of Huntly ('The Cock o' the North') and later Fifth (and last) Duke of Gordon first met Jane Graham, the 32-year-old daughter of a Northumberland farmer. It is clear, though, that a daughter resulted. Jane Graham always maintained that she had gone through a marriage ceremony with the Marquis but no evidence of this was ever found. Apparently the Marquis did not think he was committing bigamy when at the age of 43 he married Elizabeth Brodie in 1813, when Georgiana was nine. Miss Brodie, 24 years younger than her husband, was plump and plain but immensely wealthy; the Marquis, on the other hand, was tall and handsome and not very rich. A perfect match.

The Marquis had been born in 1770, son of Alexander, Fourth Duke of Gordon. he entered the army at the age of twenty, and was present at the various actions connected with the Duke of York's expedition to Flanders in 1793. In the following year, on his return home to Scotland, he raised a regiment of the line from his grandfather's tenantry known as the Gordon Highlanders. He was appointed colonel of the regiment and was present with them at the Battle of Bergen and several other engagements. He succeeded to the Gordon title on the death of his father in 1827. He was appointed Keeper of the Great Seal of Scotland and Governor of Edinburgh Castle.

Georgiana Huntly McCrae was born in London in 1804. Her father, Lord Huntly, and Lord Reagh (a Gordon kinsman) were godfathers at her christening. Apparently she and her mother were supported financially for some time by the Gordon family and she was educated privately, including a convent school kept by noble French refugees from the Revolution. She became an accomplished linguist and well grounded in Latin and Hebrew, and showed considerable talent in painting and music. Her music teacher fell violently in love with her when she was fifteen but was sent packing. She was taught painting by the noted British artists, John Varley, John Glover, MD, Serres and Charles Hayer. Some of her paintings as a teenage girl were exhibited in the august Royal Academy in London.

Georgiana grew into a beautiful and vivacious young woman and, after leaving school, lived for about seven years at Gordon Castle at Fochabers on the River Spey in the Scottish highlands. There she was acknowledged and treated as the duke's daughter. One senses, perhaps, that her presence at the castle aroused feelings of resentment and jealousy within the Duchess of Gordon's ample bosom. For a while she used Georgiana as an unpaid social secretary but the duke intervened and gave his daughter a special room in the castle as a studio. A bigoted Protestant, the duchess thwarted an intense love affair between Georgiana and 'Perico' (Peter Charles Gordon of Wardhouse, a 'Spanish' Gordon and a Roman Catholic).

When she was 24, Georgiana left Gordon Castle to live in Edinburgh, where she hoped to earn a good living from her portrait and miniature painting. There she re-met Andrew McCrae, a lawyer and distant cousin of the Gordons.

The McCraes (formerly Macrae) were also a distinguished Scottish family. Andrew's grandfather, Alexander Macrae (1748–96) was known as the 'Nabob', a term used then to describe men who made their fortune abroad, usually in India. Alexander made his from sugar plantations in Jamaica. His son, William (1769–1829) became a close friend of William Wilberforce and joined him in working to abolish the slave trade, the basis of his father's wealth. Alexander promptly disinherited him and William retaliated by changing the spelling of his name to McCrae. Because of his work for the emancipation of slaves, William is known as the 'Liberator'. Five of his children migrated to Australia.

One gathers that Georgiana was not greatly enamoured by her serious but handsome suitor, but Andrew, aided by the duchess, wore her down. The duchess, obviously anxious to get her husband's illegitimate daughter off her hands, promised the couple a handsome dowry, which was never forthcoming. So Andrew and Georgiana were married in the Chapel at Gordon Castle on 25 September 1830. She was given away by her father. There were great celebrations and a grand bonfire in honour of the event. Andrew became a Writer to the Signet (a senior legal rank in Scotland) and for nine years they lived in Scotland and England, four sons being born to them.

Georgiana's father, the duke, died in 1836. His will containing a generous bequest to her was unsigned but she received a small annuity from the duchess. (As he left no male issue, the title of the Duke of Gordon became extinct and the marquisate of Huntly developed on the Aboyne branch of the family. The Duke of Richmond, a nephew of the Fifth Duke of Gordon, was created Duke of Gordon in 1876, adopting the title of Duke of Richmond and Gordon.)

The disappointment over the unsigned will and the high cost of living in London caused the McCraes to look to a future elsewhere. Andrew, a born loser, decided to seek his fortune in Australia by establishing a legal practice in Melbourne. His brother Dr Farquhar McCrae had preceded him there and become the first to use chloroform in surgical cases at the settlement. (He later became a magistrate.) Andrew sailed off in 1839, Georgiana and her four children following him a year later in the sailing ship, *Argyle*. The duchess, after some arm-twisting, agreed to contribute just enough money for the passage—one-way only. Georgiana took with her two Scottish maid-servants and 71 packages, including a bath, a four-poster bed, and nine square bottles of water from the pump in the Tower of London.

1. Case containing bedstead.
2. Dining-table and bedding.
3. Sofa and pillow.
4. Case of chairs.
5. Cellarette, brushes, etc.
6. Side-table and smaller ones.
7. Pictures.
8. Chest-of-drawers full of clothing.
9. Cabinet-drawers, pictures.
10. Books and dressing-table.
11. Pedestal. Tartan and plaiding.
12. Baby-linen. Box of books.
13. Book shelves. Kitchenware.
14. Copying press.
15. Two easy-chairs. Pillows.
16. Glassware.
17. Hogshead of chinaware.
18. Chest of earthenware.
19. Bedroom chairs, carpets.
20. Four-post bedstead.
21. Fender, pots, kettles, etc.
22. Small case, folio books.
23. Hardware.
24. Bath tub.
25. Tinned case of dresses.
26. Saddle, habit, etc.
27. Bed and table linen.
28. Jane Shanks's chest.
29. Books, work-box, etc.
30. Jane Sutherland's chest.
31. Black trunk (M), clothing.
32. Tin box of dresses (cabin).
33. Leather bonnet-box.
34. Hair trunk. A.M. clothing.
35. Bonnet-box (cabin).
36. Jane's box (in her cabin).
37. Jane's trunk (do.).
38. Letters, papers, pencils, etc.
39. Trunk, G.M.C. Children's clothes.

40. Chest-of-drawers (do.), these placed side by side in my cabin to form a bed for Willie and Sandy.
41. Chest-of-drawers. Clothing.
42. Box of Elgin oatmeal (cabin).
43. Books and toys (cabin).
44. Preserved fruits, and jams, (do.).
45. Soap and candles (Jane's cabin).
46. Shoes, boots, etc.
47. Nine square bottles of water from the pump in the Tower of London.
48. Box with rope handles containing my box of plate.
49. Flat bath and hand shower.
50. Table for my cabin, with folding leaf and borders.
51. Children's chairs.
52. Portable folding-chair; this useful walking-stick was broken to bits on our voyage from Arthur's Seat to Melbourne in 1851.
53. Roll of oilcloth.
54. Two mahogany chairs.
55. Clothes-bag (cabin).
56.   do.   do.
57. Books (cabin).
58. 'Aunt Martha's Bag.'
59. Cabin lamp.
60. Case of maps. Not tinned. Destroyed by sea-water during a gale.
61. Basket containing bottles of drugs.
62. Large carpet bag. } cabin.
     Smaller do.
65. My writing-desk.
66. My dressing-case, damaged by sea-water.
67. Medicine-chest.
68. Tin case of medicines.
69. Work-basket.
70. Hamper.

The 71st package was a large one—a cow she had purchased in England so that her boys could have fresh milk on the voyage. She sold it for a handsome profit when they arrived in Australia.

Georgiana kept a daily diary through the four-months voyage but it differs little from many similar accounts of such journeys. The historical importance of her diary begins with their arrival at Port Phillip on 1 March 1841. Such a fastidious and cultured woman, still only 37, could scarcely have been prepared for the 'house' Andrew had rented for them in the still primitive settlement of Melbourne. It was little more than a wooden shell in Bourke Street, unlined and raised on stumps above a sea of sticky mud and animal dung. There was one large room and several box-like bedrooms. The kitchen was a tiny hut at the rear with a smoky fire-hole where the maids managed to cook for a family of six and the privy was outside in the muddy yard. Georgiana noted eight days later, 'Perambulated the town with Agnes [her daughter] that is to say, we went up the north side of Collins Street, without any signs of a pavement; only a rough road, with crooked gutters—the shops, built of wood, and raised on stumps.'

Georgiana spent 49 of her 87 years in Melbourne. Brought up in an England that saw comfort amongst the well-to-do at its highest pitch, she endured with courage, humour and ability the harsh years of early Australia. Women in particular had to cope with the crudest makeshift conditions. Slush lamps provided light of a kind, strips of calico were used on the window frames in place of glass, floors were earthen, snakes and other 'nasties' abounded. She charmed all who made her acquaintance in those difficult years. She was described by a contemporary as a 'handsome woman with brown hair, dark eyes and a red-lipped face whose sweetness of expression in no way detracts from the intelligence of the eyes that gaze so calmly at us'. In May 1843, Georgiana wrote to the duchess suggesting she might purchase a house in Melbourne as a permanent home for the family. 'Madame' replied: 'In the present bad prospects of the colony the purchase of a house is not considered a wise investment'. No help there.

The McCraes lived in rented houses until 1843 when Andrew took up a stock run of 12,800 acres at Arthur's Seat near Dromana on the Mornington Peninsula between Port Phillip Bay and Western Port Bay. Georgiana, her sons and Scottish servants moved into an unfurnished slab homestead in 1845. At first Georgiana had to live in the kitchen set apart from the house. A gale raged the night they moved in and she recalled: 'I had no bedstead, only a mattress on the mud floor and found it impossible to be still'. It was an isolated place 53 miles from Melbourne and six miles from the nearest neighbour. The homestead was at the foot of Arthur's Seat, named in 1802 by the first man to map Port Phillip Bay, Lieutenant John Murray. He named the 1,000-foot-high mountain after a hill near Edinburgh. The family lived on a diet of salted beef, supplemented by wild duck, roasted kangaroo meat and fish and drew their water from a spring. Monthly shopping trips to Melbourne had to be made in a dray drawn by four oxen.

Conditions continued to be rough but Georgiana, the elegant and cultured artist, gradually accustomed herself to a pioneer Australian way of life. She ran the house, helped with the cattle and horses, made friends with the local Aborigines and bore Andrew four more children. Her diary chronicles how a sort of social life began in Melbourne. Ladies began the practice of tea drinking, they attended evening parties, walking through the mud in their husbands' Wellington top boots over their dress shoes. Returning home, they were guided by lanterns and candles. She became close friends with Charles La Trobe, soon to be lieutenant-governor of the new colony of Victoria, and his Swiss wife.

Andrew was no more successful in raising cattle than raising mortgages as a lawyer. The Arthur's Seat run did not pay its way, so Andrew sold it in 1851 for £1,000 and the family returned to Melbourne. Georgiana and Andrew gradually drifted apart and there was a final separation after La Trobe (at Georgiana's request) appointed Andrew as a magistrate on the Victorian goldfields.

In May 1864, news arrived of the death of the Duchess of Gordon in January of that year; with it came a bitter blow to Georgiana. The duchess had never re-married. She travelled frequently to the Continent and became fatter, more imperious and more obsessed by religion. Georgiana was furious to learn that the duchess had deceived her totally and left the whole of her vast fortune to the Church (shades of Grandfather Mant and the Lost Tribes of Israel!) with no bequests whatsoever to her step-daughter or her husband's grandchildren. She had failed to honour the promise she had made to Georgiana that on her death she would be recompensed for the loss of the bequest by the duke in his unsigned will.

After the separation from Andrew, Georgiana moved into a small house where she held court in a sort of cultural salon, a meeting place for the leading literary and artistic figures of the day. She resumed her art career, producing more than 80 miniatures and pencil portraits in Australia.

On her deathbed on a cold May day in 1890, Georgiana summoned her grandchildren to distribute farewell gifts. To Hugh, her favourite, she gave a gold coin. To her eldest son, George, she gave her original diary, which she had never shown to anyone, containing her deepest emotions. It is thought to have contained the full story of her separation from the wayward Andrew and also hints of a closer relationship with Charles La Trobe than mere friendship. The diary was burnt by George to avoid hurt to the descendants of important people in Victoria. A series of intimate letters were also burnt later by a spinster female descendant.

Hugh McCrae, in a beautifully written piece of prose, described his last visit to his grandmother at the age of twelve:

> She sat in a room upstairs, with her face towards the sunset; and, to reach her, I had to pass a bed made mysterious by curtains and gathering darkness. When my grandmother put her arms around me I felt uncomfortable in the embrace, because it was Death's strength that held me. Her mouth, pressed against my own, seemed to be trying to take my life away; so that, after she let me go, I stopped frightened and exhausted...
>
> The old lady pressed into my hand something hard, wrapped in tissue-paper. 'Get a book,' she said, 'to remember me by.'
>
> That night she died and on the next day, with the guinea she had given me, I bought a child's tricycle. A week later, the plaything being broken, I said to myself in a spirit of bravado, 'I have lost a tricycle—and a grandmother. How important I am!' Then suddenly I realised I had bought the tricycle to remember the old lady by, and wondered whether in the absence of this memorial, she would become forgotten.
>
> At once my grandmother kissed me again. That unsquanderable kiss: richer than the guinea. I began to study her portrait in our drawing-room. I read her diaries and looked at her water-colour sketches; learned to love them; to adore her.

Soon she gave me her first book. I mean, I saved up five shillings and bought a copy of *Paul and Virginia*. After I had made sure of this possession, I wrote across the fly-leaf 'For dear little H. from his affectionate grandmama. 4 October 1891'.

Since that time the old lady has methodically filled my shelves; and, at odd intervals, she still subscribes herself in handwriting singularly like my own.

Though many of the entries in the journal Georgiana left behind are family trivia, the diaries as a whole painted a priceless picture of the life and people of early Melbourne and Victoria. The following extracts illustrate the style and character of the journal (she called her husband 'Mr McCrae' throughout, as was the custom of the day).

5th Mr John and Mr Edward Cotton, and the two Misses Cotton to early dinner; wet up to their ankles in crossing the bog. Miss Cotton sang: 'O lovely night!' and played for us (The irony of it!)...
3rd Thunder, lightning and enormous hailstones. In the evening, Mr McCrae listened to Bishop Broughton's diatribe against the doctrines of Dr P.S. Geoghegan...
27th Grasshopper plague. Spring-cleaning. Carpets beaten, floors washed, carpets re-laid. Tired out by tea-time...
15th Enter my fortieth year today, like everyone else, the boys have forgotten me...
3rd McCrae and Tuck [an Aborigine] came on horseback from Arthur's Seat bringing several ducks and a kangaroo-tail. At night Captain Reid arrived...
19th The second last bit of beef boiled today. The 'round' still in the cask. George chopping banksia bark to make a dye to colour his pinafore. Ellen made a grand sea-pie for dinner...
10th A white frost, which I knew of before I got up by hearing the crows. Mr McCrae and Mr Jamieson talked loudly on their way to the beach. When they returned they brought thirty flathead between them...
1st Mr La Trobe came to see Nellie and brought with him Judge Jeffcott to see my portrait of her...
22nd Raining again. Cut out five pairs of trowsers, and nearly completed one pair...
7th Dr Myer to dinner. The comet distinctly seen, and most brilliant. Mr McCrae, gazing at it, stumbled over the wheelbarrow and had to hurry inside to doctor his broken shin! A sad outcome to star-gazing.

The McCrae homestead at Arthur's Seat and the people who lived in it gradually faded from public memory for 110 years until, in 1961, Georgiana's great-grandson, George Gordon McCrae II, purchased it. Andrew's 12,800 acres had shrunk to 160 feet by 100 feet and the house was a wreck. George restored it and furnished it with his inherited possessions and other relics. It was opened to public inspection until the death of George in 1968. Then it was acquired by the National

Trust of Australia (Victoria). Further extensive restoration was carried out and McCrae Cottage was officially opened in 1971. It has since became a prime tourist attraction and the area around is known as McCrae.

This, then, is the story of my great-grandmother, Georgiana, as it has been told to me. I wish I had known her; she must have been a woman to remember. I have a copy of her self-portrait on a wall and beside it her father the kilted Duke of Gordon, Eighth Marquis of Huntly, from the Raeburn portrait, and one of her mother, Jane Graham.

I wonder at times whether the wicked marquis did indeed seduce and betray the farmer's daughter? Or was it true love and did Jane sacrifice herself and her daughter for the sake of her beloved marquis so that he could maintain his noble position with the wealth of another woman? Either way it will surely make a ripper of a TV mini-series.

There are many of Georgiana's descendants living in Australia today and we have a Georgiana McCrae Association, founded by Janet Hay, a great-great-granddaughter. Those of us who dabble in writing and drawing are encouraged by the fact that the blood of George Gordon, Lord Byron and Adam Lindsay Gordon is in our veins. We're proud of it and why not?

FOOTNOTE: In 1993, my grand-daughter, Jennifer Brown, got herself a job at Glenlivet in Scotland in the heart of Huntly and Gordon country. Having found a Mant Lane in Winchester, she went in search of Gordon Castle, home of her great-great-great grandmother.

Alas, most of the castle was demolished in 1953. A Lady Gordon-Lennox was in residence in the only remaining wing. She was too ill to receive her, but the housekeeper showed her around the large and beautifully kept gardens. The castle was first built in the 1500s; the village of Fochabers was removed holus-bolus to a new location to make way for extensions in the 1800s. The castle was open to the public for many years and used as a military hospital in World War II. It fell into disrepair and became the victim of crippling costs.

The castle has gone and so have the Gordon Highlanders, the pride of the 'Gay Gordons' as they were known when the word gay meant gladsome, blithe, merry and joyful. Mrs Thatcher axed them after more than 170 years of valiant and distinguished service in the British Army. They don't think much of Mrs Thatcher in Scotland, as you can imagine. There was a battalion of Gordons on garrison duties in Malaya when I served there with 2nd AIF in World War II. Sometimes I felt tempted to say to some of them, 'What would you say if I told you my great-great-grandfather raised you lot in 1794?' I know what they would have said: 'You lying Aussie bastard'.

15

Dr Balsam's Pub Crawl

In the late spring of 1982, my friend Dr F. ('Call me Friar') Balsam set off on a momentous pub crawl on the North Coast of N.S.W. Dr Balsam had thought it prudent to close his city surgery after mislaying his forceps in the stomach of a patient during an appendectomy (fortunately the forceps were recovered during the autopsy).

The doctor set off via the Pacific Highway in a fairly dilapidated motor car, carrying in the boot an ample supply of his tipple, pure (for medicinal purposes only) alcohol. Dr Balsam was to visit 22 bush pubs on his crawl, which extended from the Manning Valley in the south to the Nambucca Valley in the north. During the weeks of his journey he breasted hotel bars in Beechwood, Bellbrook, Bellingen, Bowraville, Coppernook, Frederickton, Dorrigo, Harrington, Kempsey, Kew, Krambach, Kundabung, Long Flat, Macksville, Port Macquarie, Taylors Arm, Wauchope and Willawarrin.

By the end of the crawl, he had learnt that the history of the local pubs was the history of the country itself. The pubs and the annual agricultural shows were the focal community meeting places of bush people and there history was made and past history yarned about. Some of the outback pubs were more than a century old and still surviving despite the competition of motels and clubs. Others in the bigger towns, however, had succumbed to the clubs' poker machines, keno, cut-price liquor and other attractions.

The doctor had met many friendly publicans and hotel 'regulars' during his crawl, heard countless yarns of bushmen riding their horses in and out of bars, up and down stairs. He had been intrigued by the number of pubs that had been burnt down in mysterious fires with dark stories of their origin. It was all very fascinating and yet at times Dr Balsam pined for his old city surgery and the drama of the operating table. Alone at night in his hotel room he spent hours sharpening his favourite scalpel with a piece of emery paper. At other times he compiled copious notes about the places he visited during his famous crawl. He recently gave me copies of these notes, from which I have extracted some of the more interesting details. I cannot vouch for the condition of these pubs today.

The first port of call on Dr Balsam's pub crawl was the Exchange Hotel, the oldest surviving hotel in Taree, 335 kilometres north of Sydney. The waters of the wide Manning River were sparkling in the spring sunshine as the doctor drove across the bridge into the town. He thought he had never seen a more inviting approach to a country town than the beautifully kept parks alongside the river, with avenues of stately poplars and jacaranda trees. Although the Exchange was the oldest surviving hotel, it was built by the McMahon family as late as 1914. William Owen McMahon had built a timber mill at Pampoolah on the banks of the Manning River near Taree in 1865. The district was rich in cedar and the Manning River crowded with steam and sailing ships arriving in ballast to take the timber back to Sydney. There was also a big trade in local hardwood. It was so hard that, in earlier days, it was sent to England for the hulls of British warships to repel ramming attacks by enemy vessels. In the 1880s, McMahon's son, William, purchased the Steam Packet Hotel in Taree, then only a village. Near the steamships' wharf, the hotel was highly popular with members of the ships' crews, who called it the 'Sailors' Arms'.

McMahon installed his wife, Hannah, as licensee of the Steam Packet Hotel. There she remained for more than 30 years, attending to the needs of local citizens and a multitude of sailors from all parts of the world. In 1913, the Steam Packet Hotel was destroyed by fire, a sensational day in the history of Taree. Apparently, the flue of the kitchen stove was choked with soot when the cook started the fire for the midday meal and that was the end of the Steam Packet. Instead of another Steam Packet Hotel arising from the ashes on the same site, Hannah McMahon purchased land on the corner of Victoria and Manning Streets, closer to the centre of the growing town. Hannah applied for a licence as the Steam Packet Hotel, then unaccountably changed her mind and the name to the Exchange Hotel. And there it has stayed.

Harrington was a small fishing resort at the entrance to the Manning River when Dr Balsam drove his fairly dilapidated motor car into the car park of the local hotel in 1982. It was a local saying that more fish are caught in the Harrington Hotel bar than from the adjacent breakwall and seawall. The doctor's knowledge of fishing was limited although he once received some notoriety in the *Australian Medical Journal* by removing a fish hook from the stomach of a man without surgery. His method was to lower a live fish via the epiglottis into the patient's stomach, the fish obligingly swallowed the hook and was retrieved by the doctor without resource to the knife. It was a story that left his listeners agape as he told it in the bar of the hotel. The hotel was the noted nerve centre of Harrington, even with non-drinkers. It was the headquarters of the Blue Water Fishing Club, the Lower Manning Rugby League Football Club, the Lions Club, the United Services Club and the Old Bastards Club, not to mention the Harrington Hotel Darts Club.

The hotel began life as a guest house and the first liquor licence was granted to James Hogan in 1902. He named it the Brighton Hotel and after his death in 1925 it was conducted by his widow and son and renamed the Harrington Hotel. The hotel was the watering hole and refuge for deep-sea pilots, ships' captains and fishermen in the old days when the river trade was brisk on the Manning and its tributaries. A breakwater was completed at the entrance to the river in 1904 but the bar remained as treacherous as any on the North Coast. Thirty-one major shipwrecks were recorded there. As the years passed the silting of the river bar grew worse. That, and the coming of the railway, sounded the doom of the river trade.

All that survived of the great days of Harrington at the time of the doctor's visit were the sea wall, a few piles, the remains of wharves and the peaceful little cemetery of Flagstaff Hill where so many deep-sea pilots were buried. But the stories were still being told and re-told in the bar of the Harrington Hotel, where the walls were crowded with pictures of shipwrecks and fish. The most famous fish was a 364-pound Queensland groper, caught in a net in the nearby Lansdowne River by professional fisherman, Russ Maddalena, in 1959. His son, Alan Maddalena, who happened to be in the bar, told Dr Balsam about the incident. 'I was only a kid at the time,' he said, 'and I remember we hit the fish on the head and tied it to the pulling boat behind our launch. On the way back to Harrington, the fish revived and sank the pulling boat but we managed to recover it. It was so big I was able to stand up inside it after I gutted it.' The picture of the upright fish was proof enough; it measured seven feet from nose to tail and towered over tall Russ Maddalena.

The afternoon was wearing on; the stories had turned to shipwrecks and the Harrington Hotel football team had left by bus for a feud match against a Port Macquarie hotel. Dr Balsam decided he, too, had better depart before his name was added to the long list of wrecks.

Dr Balsam decided to get away from the sea for a while and made his way west to the village of Krambach in the Upper Wallamba Valley about five kilometres south of Taree. When he sighted the two-storey Commercial Hotel in the main street, he thought this is the sort of pub where somebody once rode a horse up the stairs. Yes, they told him, somebody *had* ridden up the stairs on a horse in the 1890s and there was still a hoof mark on a stair to prove it (so they said).

The somebody had been one of the district's most noted and popular characters, a crack horseman named Campbell Roy. Crack horsemen are still men of note and popularity in the Wallamba Valley where the Krambach and Nabiac rodeos are high in the Australian calendar. Campbell was a farmer, dairyman, logger, mailman and horse-breaker extraordinary. Not only did he occasionally ride horses into the bar of the hotel but he rode wild bulls bareback and performed other unusual equestrian feats. On one occasion Campbell gave dramatic assistance to an agent with two large travelling bags who had just missed the Cobb & Co. mail coach at Krambach. Campbell quickly pulled the saddle off a horse tethered outside the pub and attached the bemused animal to a sulky in the yard. He bundled the agent and his bags aboard, gave the horse an almighty whack on the back and set off after the mail coach at full gallop. As the horse had never been harnessed in its life, the agent had a hair-raising journey, but he caught the coach.

Quaffing a stimulant or two with the locals at the bar, Dr Balsam learnt that the area around Krambach was part of the huge holdings of land originally granted to the Australian Agricultural Company. The Wallamba River is thought to have been discovered in the 1820s and settlers began arriving in the district in the late 1850s, making long, arduous journeys by bullock dray over rough bush tracks. Descendants of the early settlers are still living in the Lower and Upper Wallamba Valley. These include such names as Deer, Roy, Easton, Lynch, Paff, Shneider, Martin and Gallagher. The Gallaghers outnumbered them all in the old days and one of them established the Commercial Hotel in 1890. The first of the Gallaghers, Lawrence and Honora and family, arrived at Krambach in 1877. By the 1900s there were said to have been about 200 Gallaghers in the district. Strangers entering Krambach for the first time were told it would be pretty safe to say 'Hello, Mr Gallagher' to the first person they met.

The old pub at Krambach played an important part in the history of the district (it has been modernised and added to over the years but some of the original timber and galvanised iron roofs are still intact). In the horse-and-buggy days, Krambach occupied a strategic position on the main road from Raymond Terrace through to the north. It became an important stopping-off point for mail and passengers travelling to and from Tuncurry on the coast. Like all hotels of the day, the Commercial had a special room for the display of samples of travelling salesmen. The 'travellers' have disappeared and so have the hawkers, Afghans, Syrians and Lebanese, who sold everything from needles to anchors to the people of the bush. The coming of the railway in 1913 reduced Krambach's importance and the diversion of the Pacific Highway to the coast road in 1952 turned it into a ghost town. At the time of Dr Balsam's visit in 1982, Krambach was enjoying a mild revival by the arrival of semi-retired city people establishing hobby farms in the rich valleys and hills. Otherwise, apart from rodeos, nothing much disturbed the peace of this more-than-one-horse-and-cattle-town. There was talk of putting down a town swimming pool but few thought it would really eventuate. (It has. G.M.)

Turning the nose of his fairly dilapidated motor car northwards, the doctor pulled up for a heart-starter at the two-storey Hotel Coopernook on the banks of the Lansdowne River on the other side of Taree. He was fully prepared for another horse-on-stairs story but was given a new twist on that kind of thing. The locals still talk about the day during a big flood when a thirsty regular rowed a boat into the hotel, roped it to a railing half way up the stairs and presumably got a drink from the temporary upstairs bar.

The locals thought that the name Coopernook was an Aboriginal word meaning 'elbow in the river' and that seemed plausible as there were plenty of bent elbows in the bar of the hotel when Dr Balsam called. Coopernook was once a thriving river trade township with a timber mill and shipyards that built many wooden coastal vessels. There were two pubs in the town in the 1860s to cater for the timber-cutters, bullockies and crews of the ships (sail and steam) that plied as far as Langley Vale, five miles up the river. The ships brought up general goods and sailed back to Sydney and elsewhere with rich cargoes of cedar and hardwoods from the Manning Valley district, and livestock such as horses, cattle and pigs. The timber bridge over the river had a span which was opened for the passage of ships by ropes wound back on a drum system by a horse.

Time passed and the railway came, the era of the motor car began and as the river trade declined so did the township of Coopernook. The two original pubs had fallen down or become relics when Paddy McCabe built a brand-new two-storey hotel on a 50-acre site beside the river in the 1920s. It was a wonder of the day of massive concrete walls, all hand-mixed, with a private golf course and racecourse on the south side of the river. There was still plenty of activity there in the 1920s and the Coopernook Rugby League team was famed throughout the valley, often winning a special shield presented by Paddy McCabe. One day the shield disappeared from its honoured place in the hotel bar—the story goes that the hotel staff got tired of forever cleaning it. It was not seen again for more than 20 years when it was brought up from the bottom of the river during dredging operations for the building of a new steel bridge over the Lansdowne.

The old part of Coopernook is a ghost town today. Remains of the original sailing and steamship wharf were still there when Dr Balsam called in, but falling to pieces and vandalised. Derelict cottages beside the river were believed to have been built for the river pilots who guided vessels across the dangerous Manning River bar. Regular customers at the Hotel Coopernook were mostly farmers, railway workers and forestry men, with a sizeable passing tourist trade from the adjacent Pacific Highway. The rest of Coopernook slumbers in the sun, overtaken by 'progress' and bypassed, but apparently not very disturbed about it.

The historic old town of Port Macquarie had been the doctor's intended next stop but a puncture in a tyre of his fairly dilapidated motor car caused him to make an enforced stay at the Royal Hotel, Kew. A poor mechanic, Dr Balsam was nevertheless able to diagnose the trouble by examining the tyre with his stethoscope. Being unable to detect any sign of breathing in the tyre, the doctor shrewdly came to the conclusion that there was no air in it. Dr Balsam was lucky that the incident occurred near the intersection of the Pacific Highway with the western road to Kendall and the eastern road to Port Macquarie via the coast. Kew is a hamlet whose only industry is a cluster of smash repair specialists strategically located on both sides of the busy highway. Business was so brisk that the doctor had to wait his turn for puncture repairs. He picked his way through the broken glass and adjourned to the bar of the Royal Hotel on an eastern corner of the intersection.

The Royal, he learnt, was first licensed about 1894 and was originally situated at Ross Glen, a few kilometres south of Kew, to serve thirsty local timber-mill workers and those at Kendall. The pub was moved to its present position at Kew because of flood danger from the Camden Haven River. The timber mills have gone but the Royal still serves the people of Kendall (named after the poet, Henry Kendall, who lived in the Camden Haven district). There were once big stables at the back of the original wooden Royal Hotel for the convenience of horse and bullock teams. Kew was a regular stopping place for the old horse-drawn mail and passenger coaches. The coming of the railway pushed the horses off the road and meant even bigger days for the Royal. There was a camp of more than 300 railway workers of many nationalities near Kew as the North Coast Railway snaked up towards Grafton. The first train reached Kendall from Taree in 1914. There were some wild nights in the old pub in those days and four policemen were stationed at Kew to control the revellers. The Royal was burnt down in 1927 and rebuilt in 1929. Old-timers of the district hint darkly about the circumstances of the fire.

It was time for Dr Balsam to inquire about this puncture. His stethoscope dangling around his neck, he tottered off to examine his tyre. It being satisfactory, he took the coast road to Port Macquarie, which led him through Laurieton, North Haven, Bonny Hills and Lake Cathie. Dr Balsam was both surprised and enchanted by Port Macquarie. He was surprised because it did not appear to have a port, only fishing trawlers and pleasure craft seemed to venture across the sometimes treacherous bar at the entrance to the Hastings River. There was a time (he was told later) when it was a busy port for hundreds of large steam and sailing ships, it being not unusual for 30 or 40 vessels to be in port at the same time.

Port Macquarie had been one of the earliest settlements after Sydney, being established as a convict colony in 1821 by Governor Lachlan Macquarie, after whom it was named. It was, in fact, one of Australia's most historic towns and the doctor's further surprise was caused by the fact that there was precious little to show for it now. Only three major relics of the past remained—St Thomas' Anglican Church, built in 1828 and the fifth oldest church in Australia; the government cemetery where the first burial took place in 1823 with 80 headstones still standing; and the Court House built in 1861 and recently restored. The first Government House, the gaol and female factory and all other historic buildings and monuments had been destroyed or neglected by official vandals and developers. The doctor felt sorry for the local tourist authorities trying to promote Port Macquarie as an 'historic' town. The doctor's enchantment was caused by the natural beauty of the place, the many white sandy beaches, the pine trees, the breathtaking views out to the sea and to the mountains.

But Dr Balsam was not there to admire the beauty of nature but to investigate the beauties of the pub scene. And, alas, only an underground cellar and a few convict bricks remained of the numerous pubs of the early days. No hotel existed in the first years of settlement and access to alcohol to convicts was strictly forbidden. But in the 1830s, when free settlers began to arrive, the first innkeeper's licence was issued for the New Inn to Stephen Partridge, the Superintendent of Convicts from the colony's beginning. Other inns soon followed in its wake. The Hotel Royal is the only one still trading on the same site under the same name, although it is now called the Royal Hotel. The hotel was opened with much fanfare in 1841. Although it was burnt down in 1890 and re-built, some of the original brickwork still remain. It was discovered by accident in recent years when the floor of a lounge room was being pulled up for repairs. Part of it collapsed and a workman, Frank Yeo, fell into an underground room. Adjoining the room was another with walls and a well-preserved fireplace made of marked convict bricks. All the other early hotels have since gone, pubs with such names as the Settlers' Arms, Speed the Plough, Royal Oak Inn, The Case is Altered and the Shamrock Tavern.

The doctor was to have much better luck with other pubs in the Hastings district, finding several with absorbing histories of the old days and ways. The 'timber town' of Wauchope, eighteen kilometres west of Port Macquarie, still had only two hotels, as it did a century or more ago. Not the same hotels, for Wauchope has been a phoenix as far as inns are concerned. The first hotel, the Carrington, was built by Thomas Wallace in 1870 and was burned down the same year. The Star, built in 1888, was burned down twice in its first 50 years.

Rebuilt on the opposite side of the street, the Carrington became the Hastings, a favourite watering hole for cattlemen. Dr Balsam learnt that fires have not been the only hazards in Wauchope's hotels. When Lionel Leonard arrived from Mittagong to take over the Hastings in 1968 he found the waters of the Hastings River had reached their highest level on record and were lapping at the hotel doors. Leonard also became aware, for the first time, that the trapdoor to the cellar was directly inside the Cameron Street entrance door and could represent danger to those a trifle unsteady on their feet. 'One of these days some silly bastard will fall down that hole,' Bubby Hollis, a local identity, told him. A couple of hours later some silly bastard did—Bubby himself. They took him off to hospital but Wauchope boys don't cry and Bubby was soon back at the bar with seven stitches in his head. The Star was popular with bullockies, timber-cutters and other bush workers. The old pub saw some wild nights after the bullock teams wound down from the mountains of the Upper Hastings to unload their logs by the river and the bullockies adjourned to the Star for refreshment. Trade was not all in cash, though, for many of the early settlers had little ready money. So they would bring to town produce such as eggs, fowls and pumpkins and take away a bottle of Star brandy or Star OP rum in exchange.

Nobody was stirring in the village of Beechwood, a short distance from Wauchope, when the doctor parked outside the local hotel. 'I suppose this hotel was burned down some time or other,' he said casually to the man behind the bar. 'Yes, mate,' the man replied without hesitation. 'In 1924. Right down to the ground.' The doctor was slightly taken aback by the prompt reply but tried again. 'And I suppose people have ridden horses up and down the stairs here?' 'No horses allowed in here, mate,' said the man. 'Besides we haven't got any stairs.'

The man went on to explain that the loss of the hotel by fire did not deter the thirsty timber-cutters and teamsters. A temporary structure, known as the Tin Trunk, was put up with galvanised iron from the old pub's roof to serve as an oasis until a new hotel was built. The original Beechwood Hotel was built of red mahogany in 1890, as is the present building. Beechwood was a thriving settlement in the early days, rich in beech, mahogany, rosewood, tallowwood, cedar, blackbutt, ironbark and turpentine forest. It also maintained busy horse and cattle saleyards. Horse and bullock teams took the logs to wharves on the nearby Hastings River. There the logs were taken down the river by drogher or log-punt to the mill at Port Macquarie for subsequent shipment to Sydney and New Zealand. Up to 40 horse and bullock teams drew logs from the forests around Beechwood, including 80-foot long ironbark and turpentine girders.

If it had not been for the Traveller's Rest Hotel, Dr Balsam could easily have passed through Long Flat, 25 kilometres west of Wauchope on the Oxley Highway. The central business district of Long Flat, in the Upper Hastings Valley, consisted mainly of a butcher's shop, small store, post office, hall, church, bush school and garage. But the timber hotel and, in particular, the magnificent century-old fig tree, commanded attention and Dr Balsam was not the first traveller to make an unscheduled 'comfort stop' there. The doctor braked his fairly dilapidated motor car to a halt outside the old pub. It was Saturday afternoon and apart from an old Labrador dog sleeping in the sunshine, Long Flat appeared to be the sort of deserted town seen in a Western movie. Everything was so quiet that Dr Balsam fancied he could hear the waters of the nearby Hastings River as they gurgled and rushed over the stones and pebbles on its bed. It was more animated inside the public bar where Dr Balsam, after being subjected to a few moments of curious scrutiny, received a hearty welcome from the assembled drinkers. He was told that the town was quiet because it was an 'away' day for local cricketers, footballers and other sporting lovers.

The present owner of the Traveller's Rest is Kevin O'Neill and it is one of the few hotels in Australia that has been owned continuously by the same family or a direct descendant for more than 100 years. It all began when Thomas Henry, his wife Elizabeth and their three children came to Australia from Northern Ireland in 1856 and made a home at Long Flat. A settlement began to grow around their vineyard in the valley where they crushed and sold their wine from a grog shanty on the convict-built road between the coast and the New England tablelands. Long Flat was on the route of the explorer John Oxley when he crossed the mountains in 1818 and followed the Hastings River (he named it after the Governor-General of India) to the coast. The Henrys built the Traveller's Rest about 1878 on the site of the grog shanty. Their first official licence, in the name of James Henry, appears to have been issued in September 1875, to sell wine, cider and perry (a fermented drink made from pears). James was the son of Thomas Henry.

The hotel soon became a popular rendezvous for bullockies, teamsters, timber-cutters, mill workers, farmers and other bush characters. Reports of boisterous nights at the old pub indicate that travellers got very little rest at the Traveller's Rest in those days. James Henry died in 1880 and his widow, Sarah, ran the hotel until the 1890s when her son, Robert, took over. Robert (Bob) Henry's daughter, Katherine, married Cyril O'Neill, and was the mother of Kevin, the present owners. He is thus the great-great-grandson of James and Sarah Henry. The only time the hotel looked like leaving the control of the Henry family was about 1930 when Katherine's father was offered a good price for it. Young Katherine protested and her father put £100 in the till and said, 'All right, it's yours and you can run it'. Which she did for many years. The big fig tree which dominated the hotel is said to have been found by Edward Henry, son of James, while on a scrub turkey shoot expedition in 1880, and he planted it outside his father's hotel.

Life has changed somewhat for Long Flat since the Oxley Highway was upgraded and sealed right through to the New England Highway. It has resulted in a spectacular increase in road traffic—a steady stream of cars, tourist coaches, caravans, motor cyclists and even a few semi-trailers. Maybe this was why Long Flat decided to celebrate its 'centenary' in 1980, 24 years late, according to Dr Balsam's reckoning. Perhaps it was really the centenary of the Traveller's Rest fig tree—at any rate, it was a marvellous success with the locals dolled up in period top hat and crinoline costumes for the occasion. Although urged to 'rest' the night at the Traveller's Rest Hotel, Dr Balsam decided that discretion was the better part of valour. He was conscious that later the 'away' cricketers and footballers would be returning to celebrate victories or defeats at the pub. The doctor's fairly dilapidated motor car disappeared into the dusk from the Traveller's Rest to the cheers and raised glasses of all the inhabitants—men, women, children, dogs, a horse and a couple of girl motorbike riders.

If it had not been for the fact that a butcher's picnic coincided with Dr Balsam's arrival in Kempsey, he might not have found himself pulling up at the large two-storey hotel at Willawarrin, 30 kilometres west on the road to Armidale. Nowadays, the doctor found these picnics increasingly tiresome—the same old nattering about post-mortems, scalpels, saws, pliers and other surgical paraphernalia. Besides, he felt that the recent unfortunate mishap with his forceps might have made him *persona non grata* with local practitioners.

So he took the Armidale Road to the west and found himself in Willawarrin, which in some ways reminded him of Long Flat. Apart from a heavily laden timber jinker standing outside the hotel, traffic seemed to have come to a halt for the time being. Life itself seemed to have ceased in Willawarrin and the only people in sight were a couple of youths reclining in what Stanley Holloway used to describe as 'somnolent posture' outside the local bakery. Dr Balsam could have sworn he heard the haunting chords of the *High Noon* theme song echoing down the street. Soon, he thought, Gary Cooper, guns on hip, would come out of the hotel saloon and walk down the Armidale Road to his fateful confrontation with a bad hombre who would emerge from the shadows of the general store.

Maybe, thought the doctor, this epic North Coast pub crawl of mine is beginning to gnaw at my nerves. What I need is a double slug of pure (for medicinal purposes only) alcohol, of which I have an ample supply in the boot of my car. Instead, Dr Balsam zipped up his apprehensions and entered the pub bar prepared to meet Gary Cooper or any bad hombres who were in town. As it happened, the inside of the pub was as quiet as the outside and the doctor was soon in conversation with the licensee. By some lucky chance there was also present that day Jack and Peggy Watts, who had conducted the hotel for thirteen years and were paying a sentimental return visit. The Watts were able to tell the story of the hotel, which was not old, as pubs go. It was built of concrete as late as 1926 next door to the original Willawarrin Hotel, which by then had become a cafe. The first hotel, a small weatherboard building with a gabled roof, had been built more than a century ago.

Willawarrin ('many possums', in Aboriginal language) was once one of the busiest centres on the Upper Macleay. Up to 3,000 head of cattle went through the fortnightly cattle sales and the district had a rich dairying industry. Rodeo events and cricket matches attracted people from far and wide to Willawarrin in the old days, and the district has always been noted for its horsemen and roughriders. The pub did a roaring trade and yes, a Jack Chapman once rode his white horse, Warrigal, up the stairs to the first-floor landing for a bet of a glass of beer. A more macabre story persists of the old days. For years, it is said, there were mysterious bloodstains on the ceiling of the bar, said to have been the result of a murder or a suicide in the bedroom above.

Mrs Peggy Watts recalled to Dr Balsam a startling experience during one of the old rodeo meetings. 'I was pulling beer,' she said, 'and turned around to look straight into the eyes of a wild-looking horse with its head over the bar. The rider told me afterwards it was a stallion, too.' This led to a story that captured Dr Balsam's professional interest as proof of man's spirit, if strong enough, to overcome physical difficulties. It was the story of a local character—Jack Chapman's cousin, Bert—who could walk only with the aid of two sticks, but triumphed over his disabilities with the help of his faithful old white horse. The horse learnt to do many things for Bert and gave him four extra 'legs'. It used to wade deep into the Macleay River so that Bert could fish for perch from its back and Bert and his horse won many fishing competitions.

Willawarrin died the same way as so many other small Australian towns and staging centres. The coming of the motor car, chain stores in the bigger centres and other modern facilities turned it into a ghost town. 'You must go on to Bellbrook,' they urged him, as the doctor prepared to continue his journey. Bellbrook, they said, was one of the loveliest places on the North Coast and thereabouts Slim Dusty was born. So, sometime later, Dr Balsam tottered out to the Armidale Road, waved goodbye to the recumbent figures outside the bakery and headed west.

The village of Bellbrook on the Upper Macleay River was everything claimed for it and the area is now part of Australia's National Estate. It was the setting for the film version of Thomas Keneally's *Chant of Jimmie Blacksmith* and has been featured on television by the ABC and the BBC. According to the old hands, it was named by an early settler, Caroline McMaugh, after a colony of bellbirds on nearby Nulla Nulla Creek, which flows into the Macleay.

The Bellbrook Hotel started life as a timber boarding house and staging post between Armidale on the New England tablelands and the coast. It first became an hotel in 1913 with the transfer of the licence of another historic old hotel, the Merriwa, which had been demolished four miles away. The original red mahogany timber, including the bar, was taken to Bellbrook. Throughout his tour, Dr Balsam had been regaled at every pub by stories of 'wild nights' of the past and the Bellbrook had its share of them. There was the story of a teamster who had spent a convivial weekend there and asked for a reviver before resuming his journey over the mountains on the Monday morning. The publican refused so the teamster harnessed up his horses, backed them into the verandah of the hotel and attached a snig chain around one of the tall wooden posts. 'Listen boss,' he said. 'Do I get a drink or do you lose your verandah?' He got his drink.

Other than the locals, the pub's customers consisted of out-of-town cattlemen and timber-cutters, itinerant DMR, telephone and postal workers and a few tourists braving the rugged road between the tablelands and the coast. For many years the politicians have promised to upgrade the road into a modern highway. The locals still dream about the boom town it would create as they lazily catch perch, mullet and catfish in the river at the back of the hotel. The old-timers reckon the opening of such a highway would be the biggest gala occasion since the first electric light pole was set in position at Bellbrook in 1912. On that famous day, a Union Jack flew from the side of the pole and a local celebrity climbed up to break a 'bottle of plonk' on the summit. Bellbrook is Slim Dusty–Shorty Ranger country. As Gordon Kirkpatrick and Edwin Haberfield, the two bush troubadours and songwriters grew up at nearby Nulla Nulla Creek. Dr Balsam said farewell to Bellbrook with genuine regret and promised to make a return visit someday, perhaps (if he lived long enough) to celebrate the opening of a new highway to Armidale.

Among Dr Balsam's notes I found brief mention of the Macleay River Hotel at Frederickton, six kilometres north of Kempsey, where the doctor apparently called for an emergency comfort stop. 'Freddo', as it is known locally, was one of the earliest settlements on the Macleay River. It was established as a private town by Frederick Chapman in 1857 when he subdivided his 170 acres of land at the junction of the Macleay River and Christmas Creek. The first pub was a wooden shanty-type affair, erected about 1878 as the Post Office Hotel (it was re-named in 1970).

These notes are valuable because it was there that Dr Balsam heard the story to end all stories about horses being ridden upstairs. One day, way back, a drinker took a bet of a bottle of rum that he could not ride his horse up the stairs and on to the hotel balcony. He got there all right but then the trouble started—he could not get the horse down the stairs again. Frederickton was in an uproar as the indignant horse was finally lowered into the street from the balcony by block and tackle.

It was at Freddo that an elderly sunburnt stockman handed Dr Balsam a copy of what must be a classic bush poem entitled 'Bloody'. I have searched in vain for the author's name to acknowledge:

> A sunburnt bloody stockman stood,
> And in a dismal bloody mood
> Apostrophised his bloody cuddy:

'This bloody moke's no bloody good,
He doesn't earn his bloody food.'
Bloody! Bloody! Bloody!

He leapt upon his bloody horse,
And galloped off, of bloody course,
The road was wet and bloody muddy,
It led him to the bloody creek,
The bloody horse was bloody weak.
Bloody! Bloody! Bloody!

He said, 'This bloody steed must swim,
The same for me as bloody him!'
The creek was deep and bloody floody,
So, 'ere they reached the bloody bank,
The bloody steed beneath him sank,
The stockman's face a bloody study.
Bloody! Bloody! Bloody!

Nobody was quite sure how many illicit stills there were in the hills and gullies of the Nambucca Valley in the old cedar-cutting days—but there were certainly a number of illegal operators, including a few women. One sly-grogger was known as 'Gussie the Frenchman' who ran a whisky still a Bowraville. The Frenchman served local residents and outlaying hotels at Taylors Arm and possibly Congarinni with what the authors of a Bowraville centenary booklet, published in 1975, described as 'high octane liquor'. The booklet also noted that Gussie the Frenchman was the bane of the life of Senior Constable John Reynolds, custodian of law and order in the district in the 1890s. Apparently, Constable Reynolds pursued the Frenchman with the same sort of intensity as Inspector Javert pursued Jean Valjean in *Les Misérables*.

The pubs of the Nambucca Valley provided Dr Balsam with some of the most fascinating stories of all. There were two hotels worthy of note in the Verandah Post Town of Bowraville, often immortalised on film and television. It lived up to its name with a surprising number of original buildings and verandah posts still standing. The main street was accepted by the National Trust for its historical interest and the Bowra Hotel was declared a Recorded Historical Hotel. Once a rich timber and dairying centre, Bowraville went through some bad times but began to enjoy a minor boom period in the 1980s. Tourists flocked to see the Verandah Post Town and retired people from the rat-race of Sydney and Melbourne purchased or built homes there with small areas of land.

The first white settlers in the Nambucca River district were timber-getters in 1842. The cedar was cut out by the 1870s and settlers came in to farm the bush land. The first hotel in Bowraville was apparently the Bull and Bush, built sometime in the 1870s. It was succeeded by the Bowra Hotel, built on a new site in 1912. This handsome two-storey hotel had, and still has, wonderfully decorative iron lacework along the wide verandahs and enough tall verandah posts to satisfy the most ardent admirer. The two-storey Royal Hotel up the main street was built in 1900. Although the Royal has been extended and renovated over the years, much of the original timberwork is still intact. Both the hotels had extensive stables for up to 30 horses in the horse-and-buggy days. A groom was always in attendance and he would be sent out for 'six-pennorth of feed'.

Without doubt, the two-storey Nambucca Hotel at Macksville was the biggest pub Dr Balsam encountered on his travels. It was built of reinforced concrete, with local cedar and mahogany, with 48 bedrooms, and opened on 7 August 1915. A promotional booklet at the time described it as 'an ornate edifice...the modern and spacious characteristics of the building are distinctly in its favour; and they are a delightful revelation after putting up at some of the old-fashioned and dilapidated hotels in other centres...and there is only one bed in each room—a great desideration to guests who are strangers to each other'.

The moment he entered the vestibule of the hotel Dr Balsam's attention was riveted on a magnificent cedar staircase. Doug and Gwenda Bonser, the proprietors of the hotel at the time, were only too pleased to tell him about the staircase, of which they were justifiably proud. When the Bonsers bought the freehold of the Nambucca in 1968, it was in a very run-down condition. One of the first things they did was to see what was under the hideous orange paint on the stately staircase which led to the upstairs bedrooms. In fact, they were obliged to take off five or six coats of various coloured paint before revealing the original cedar, hewn in the Macksville district. Later, they learnt that the staircase, the bar counter and fittings had been cut out of one cedar log when the hotel was built. Alas, the bar counter is no more—it was hacked up into wood plugs by some earlier, less aesthetic licensee.

In the early days of the hotel, ships berthed at the wharf on the Nambucca River near the present Star Hotel. Passengers and ships' crews drank, ate and slept at the Star and the Nambucca under strict class distinction. First-class passengers were ushered up the cedar staircase at the Nambucca to their bed and dining room, the second-class passengers were segregated downstairs. Even drinkers in the main bar downstairs were separated by a partition. The wharf on the Nambucca River has long since gone and the ships don't come up there any more. But the Star and now Cavanagh's Nambucca Hotel are still there, dreaming of the old upstairs-downstairs days.

'Shangri-la!' exclaimed Dr Balsam as he drove his fairly dilapidated motor car over Marx Hill and down into the beautiful Bellinger Valley. Marx Hill, named after an early German wine-grower named John Marx whose wine won prizes in London, seemed to separate the valley and the township of Bellingen from the rest of the world. The doctor thought that this was the most peaceful and enchanting valley he had encountered during his epic pub crawl. He was not surprised to learn later that the valley of the Bellinger River, and especially its upper reaches, had become a haven and escape for followers of the 'alternative lifestyle', who no longer liked being called 'hippies'.

The doctor was considerably confused by the spelling variations of the district. The town was BellinGEN, the river was BellinGER and local organisations took their pick. There was the Bellingen Shire Council, the Bellinger River RSL Club, the Bellingen Welfare Centre and the *Bellinger Courier-Sun* newspaper. It was thought that the handwritten 'n's' and 'r's' of Government Surveyor, Clement Hodgkinson, were misinterpreted when he surveyed the district in 1841.

Bellingen's first pub was the Exchange, a single-storey hotel built about the 1880s, with a second storey added in the 1890s. It was joined by the Federal in 1901, noted for its wide verandahs and delicate 'Paddington lacework'. The Exchange gradually deteriorated and was condemned by the Bellingen Shire Council in 1967 and demolished, despite local controversy and protests to the historical society. The Federal is still there, nearing its century.

In the 1970s the 'alternates' started to move into the district and the Federal Hotel saw a different style of drinker. The alternates acquired old farms at the top of the north and south arms of the Bellinger River, built their houses, grew their own crops and multiplied so exceedingly that they were able to establish a school for their children. They were mostly young people from Melbourne, Sydney and other centres; poets, artists, university students, academics, atheists, idealists—all seeking a nonconformist alternative lifestyle, though not averse to drawing conformist dole cheques and pooling their resources to acquire more land and farms. They came to town in outlandish garb in the eyes of the conservative burghers of Bellingen, the men with beards, the women without bras. Their clothes were shapeless, though some wore wild-looking hats with feathers stuck in them. But largely, Dr Balsam was told, they lived by themselves, kept to themselves and caused few incidents in the town. 'The Bellingen Shire Council causes us far more trouble than the alternates,' a drinker informed the doctor, as he quaffed a medicinal-purposes-only alcohol in the public bar.

The man went on to say that there was at that time a minor exodus of alternates taking place in the Bellinger Valley. 'It was the helicopters, you see,' he explained.

'The helicopters?' Dr Balsam repeated. 'What helicopters?'

It appeared that the helicopters had been manned by members of the police drug squad during a surprise raid on the upper Bellinger, after which numbers of alternates left the district. Local gossip said that they had gone to join another big commune on the coast on land valued at between $250,000 and $500,000.

'Where does the money come from?' the doctor asked.

'It was the helicopters,' muttered the man mysteriously, dodging the question.

There are still alternates in Bellingen but the valley has changed since Dr Balsam's visit. The Shangri-la on the other side of Marx Hill is now a haven to city refugees of a different kind in pleasant homes on five-acre blocks of land. They include such celebrities as television star George Negus, comedian Jimmy Hannan and other people of note happy in the anonymity of their bush hideaway. Dr Balsam's notes reveal his state of mind as he drove back over Marx Hill to the reality of the Pacific Highway: 'Bellingen was the twenty-first centre I had visited during my tour. I was beginning to feel jaded but, at the same time, anxious to get back to my surgery and resume practice. But there was one more hostelry that I simply had to visit—the Pub With No Beer at Taylors Arm. I thus turned my car southwards in its direction.'

Taylors Arm is a village on the Taylors Arm River in the Nambucca Valley about 30 kilometres west of Macksville. Its pub, which has become world-famous, began as a timber boarding house in 1896 and was licensed as an hotel in 1903. Whoever named it the Cosmopolitan must have had enormous faith in the future as Taylors Arm consisted only of the pub, a blacksmith's shop, a general store and a few other buildings. The publican turned out to be right, as the woman who wrote the following letter in 1904, turned out to be wrong:

> . . . tell Lizzie not to write to Hugh Sheridan. He was drunk again on Saturday last. He was not able to get up and Ben Cot was on the spree and nearly went mad. Mr Crick, the Police, fired 3 shots at him, put one through his hat. And Joe Brazel put the house on fire and there was a job to get it out. So I will let you know more later. That pub is the ruin of Taylors Arm.

The rise of the Cosmopolitan Hotel into a legend began in 1956 when the late Gordon Parsons—country music singer, writer and recording artist—was working with Joe Cooper at Sheet-O'-Bark Creek on the Upper Nambucca. Someone handed him some pencilled verses on a scrap of paper about a pub without beer and suggested it might be made into a good song. Parsons (as he said later) assumed it was another of those anonymous bush ballads that circulated around the country. He rewrote parts of the poem and added verses about four characters he knew at the old Taylors Arm pub. He called it 'The Pub With No Beer' and showed the song to his old mate, Slim Dusty, who recorded it in 1957. To everyone's surprise, it took off, instantly, like a rocket.

'The Pub changed my professional life,' Slim Dusty says in his autobiography, *Walk a Country Mile*. It sold in tens of thousands in Australia, Britain, Europe and the U.S.A. Total sales soon exceeded half a million including 250,000 in the U.K. Suddenly everybody had heard of the Pub With No Beer and everybody had heard of Slim Dusty. And everybody had heard of a remote little village in Australia named Taylors Arm. Although the hotel is licensed as the Cosmopolitan, the Pub With No Beer had become immortalised.

Then arose a controversy that agitated country music circles for years. It was not until 1979 that Slim Dusty revealed the full facts of the matter in his autobiography. His troupe were performing at Ingham in North Queensland when he was informed that a local sugarcane farmer, Dan Sheahan, had written a poem, 'The Pub Without Beer', which appeared in the *North Queensland Register* in 1944. A comparison of the first stanza of the Sheahan and Parsons poems clearly showed that Parsons had been influenced by the Sheahan version, but had added four new characters in four-line stanzas instead of Sheahan's six lines. Slim Dusty strongly rejected the suggestion that Parsons had deliberately stolen the poem for a song and Parsons himself was extremely hurt by the accusation. In his book, Slim Dusty says that no formal claim on the rights of the song was ever made by the Sheahan family; in fact, he and Dan Sheahan became friends. The first stanzas of the Sheahan and Parsons versions are reproduced in Slim Dusty's book:

> It is lonely away from your kindred and all
> In the bushland at night when the warrigals call—
> It is sad by the sea where the wild breakers boom
> Or to look on a grave and contemplate doom.
> But there's nothing on earth half as lonely or drear
> As to stand in the bar of a pub without beer.
>
> (Sheahan)
>
> It is lonesome away from your kindred and all,
> By the camp fire at night where the wild dingoes call,
> But there's nothing so lonesome, morbid or drear
> Than to stand in the bar of a pub with no beer.
>
> (Parsons)

The Pub With No Beer is truly cosmopolitan these days as a top Australian tourist attraction. The permanent population of Taylors Arm remains steady at about 100 but the floating population seems limitless as tourists from all parts of Australia and the world float into the old pub. And all because of a song! Tony Brown, the present licensee, and his wife, Sophie, have refurbished the hotel but it still retains its old charm and character, with a small museum of bush artefacts. The annual Pub With No Beer Country Festival and Fair has drawn crowds in excess of 8,000. The annual Charity Day Walkathon from Macksville to Taylors Arm is another crowd-pleaser. The program includes the World

Twosome Egg-Throwing Championship—a raw egg is thrown over the pub by one contestant and caught (perhaps) on the other side by his partner. Some finish up with egg on their faces.

Dr Balsam's notes about his visit to the Pub With No Beer in October 1982 are disturbing. He seems to have been more worried about his own physical condition than the charms of Taylors Arm. The notes are rather disjointed and in one part he reports informing the licensee that he once amputated the left arm of a man named Taylor and was there any connection? 'I think it will be prudent of me to end my pilgrimage at this stage,' he wrote. 'I seem to be developing symptoms of some kind of hallucinary syndrome, dreaming of pink elephants and snakes. I think it might be caused by something I ate.'

Shortly after that, the doctor collapsed and was taken to Macksville Hospital for observation. He was later flown to Sydney where, in due course, he recovered. I have given it a lot of thought and I really believe that it was not something he ate that led to Dr Balsam's breakdown, but something he drank. The official diagnosis was that he had been stricken by an obscure Italian disease, *delirium tremens*. It was not the fault of the Cosmopolitan Hotel but, rather, the cumulative effect of the overwhelming hospitality offered him at the 22 hostelries he had visited. There is also evidence that he had regularly dipped into the boot of his fairly dilapidated motor car for a slug or two of pure (for medicinal purposes only) alcohol. Perhaps some day a plaque will be erected at Taylors Arm with the simple inscription: 'Dr Friar Balsam broke down here in October 1982'.

16
Bodyline and All That

The game of cricket has been very good to me. Although not much chop at it as a player, cricket changed the course of my life on several occasions and I'm grateful to it. Apart from that, I love the game. I set out for England in 1930 in search of journalistic fame and fortune. After starving in the traditional garret for a while, I was engaged, out of the blue, by the Sydney *Daily Guardian* to cover the highlights of the Australian Test tour which set Don Bradman on the road to legendry. I knew nothing whatever about cricket reporting but all that was needed was a thesaurus of idolizing adjectives describing young Don's amazing exploits. To illustrate the euphoria that surrounded Bradman's triumphant tour in England, *The Guardian* published the following hundred tributes to him:

BRADMAN'S CENTURY

1. Marvellous. 2. Wonderful. 3. Magnificent. 4. Brilliant. 5. Tophole. 6. Phenomenal. 7. Excellent. 8. Bosker. 9. Remarkable. 10. Extraordinary. 11. Amazing. 12. Astonishing. 13. Astounding. 14. Superb. 15. Gorgeous. 16. Grand. 17. Great. 18. Overwhelming. 19. Tireless. 20. Incredible. 21. Corker. 22. Stunning. 23. Ripping. 24. Cyclonic. 25. Crackjack. 26. Devastating. 27. Superlative. 28. Illimitable. 29. Invincible. 30. Scintillating. 31. Irrespressible. 32. Inimitable. 33. Supreme. 34. Greatest. 35. Paramount. 36. Matchless. 37. Unapproachable. 38. Incomparable. 39. World beater. 40. Masterful. 41. Wholesale. 42. Much. 43. More. 44. Most. 45. Towering. 46. Stupendous. 47. Prodigious. 48. Outrageous. 49. Preposterous. 50. Unconscionable. 51. Unique. 52. Colossal. 53. Unlimited. 54. Unutterable. 55. Ineffable. 56. Unspeakable. 57. Machine-like. 58. Miracle. 59. Imperishable. 60. Deathless. 61. Immortal. 62. Illustrious. 63. Radiant. 64. Peerless. 65. Aristocrat. 66. Gentleman. 67. Prince. 68. King of Cricket. 69. Dashing. 70. Clever. 71. Masterly. 72. Beautiful. 73. Artistic. 74. Graceful. 75. Smashing. 76. Vigorous. 77. Surprising. 78. Exquisite. 79. Snodger. 80. Humdinger. 81. Bonzer. 82. Terrific. 83. Unsurpassable. 84. Ingenious. 85. Dazzling. 86. Izzannyplum. 87. Whaddwetellyou. 88. Multiplicationable. 89. Scientist. 90. Heartbreaker. 91. Riotous. 92. Gluttonous. 93. Spontaneous. 94. Marathon. 95. Maestro. 96. Superman. 97. Dynamic. 98. Bobbydazzler. 99. Slang-Wanger. 100. The Little Beaut.

A year later, I landed a job with Reuters, the famous international news agency. And a year after that my brief stint of cricket reporting, suitably exaggerated, landed me the biggest prize of all—an appointment as the Reuter representative for the forthcoming 1932-33 MCC tour of Australia. This involved travelling with the English team throughout the eight-month tour, though not as an official part of it. I have written in another book (*A Cuckoo in the Bodyline Nest*, Kangaroo Press) about my experiences on that historic tour. The title was based on the fact that the Australia-hating English captain, Douglas Jardine, regarded me as a cuckoo in the nest or as an Australian mole in the English camp and ostracised me.

As a reward for my services during the Bodyline War, I was promoted to become the Reuter News Editor for Canada, where I stayed for four years. I liked Canada and the Canadians but, fair dinkum, the winter weather was killing me. Moreover, the tip of the nose of my infant daughter, Carol, became frostbitten because we left her outside in a pram for too long. The Fahrenheit temperature often got down to 25 degrees below zero; if you hung a shirt to dry on the line it would be frozen stiff in half an hour.

Cricket again came to my rescue. The 1936-37 MCC Tour of Australia was coming up, so I wrote an agonised letter to London extolling my services four years earlier and begging for a transfer from Canada before I was frozen to death. It worked and this time the circumstances were somewhat different. Whereas Jardine would not speak to me during my Bodyline War because I was an Australian, 'Gubby' Allen, the new English captain, was under no such restrictions. After all, we had been born within a week of each other in adjoining houses in Sydney; our nappies, so to speak, had hung side by side as children. The reconciliation tour became almost nauseating with goodwill. Some of the English reporters with the team tried to whip up some trouble, but it was no go. Everything was sweetness and light, the word 'bodyline' was as dirty as those four-letter words. On the transcontinental train journey from Perth to Adelaide at the beginning of the tour, Gubby made about nineteen goodwill speeches on railway stations large and small, mere rehearsals of a flood of similar oratory to come in the capital cities. It was a very dull tour in that respect and sometimes I yearned for the sensation-packed Bodyline days.

After the 1936-37 tour I was rewarded again with an appointment as Reuter news editor for Australia, based in Sydney. So you see why I love cricket; it has been good to me. I don't lose much sleep about what is going to happen to the game in the future. I've had my delights in playing and watching it as it was. I remain a Test match traditionalist. I squirm at the cross-bat slogging at the climax of the pyjama games but that is what the huge crowds have paid their big dollars to come and see. It puzzles me, though, how they can remain so patient and uncomplaining at the more orthodox lead-ups to the slogging.

More changes are bound to come to cricket. The game has been changing ever since it started with a crooked stick for a wicket about 800 years ago. For some reason or other, it has aroused violent passions throughout the ages. Oliver Cromwell forbade the playing of 'Krickett' in Ireland in 1656 and ordered 'all sticks and balls' to be burnt by the common hangman. Wild scenes and riots were common at matches in eighteenth-century England, firearms being used, with loss of life. Duels were fought over 'thrown' matches, with fatal results. Frederick, Prince of Wales, died from an abscess caused by a blow from a cricket ball in 1751.

The next change seems certain to be the introduction of white or coloured shorts to summer one-day cricket. This will horrify the purists but I hope Test and other traditional players will stick to the long 'uns. Cricket has already virtually split up in two different games with two different audiences. I hope it continues that way but I have doubts as to whether Test cricket can survive. If cricket goes into shorts, it will be interesting to see whether golf and bowls follow suit. Maybe these all-the-year players will compromise with shorts in the summer and long trousers in the winter.

It is suggested that shorts in one-day cricket would be certain to impress female fans. This does not find favour with Sydney female sports columnist, Debbie Spillane. 'The idea that a bit of Leg Before Trouser activity might attract women to the game sounds as if it's sprung from the mind of the sort of man who thinks females at football matches are obviously there to gaze longingly at muscular male thighs,' Ms Spillane wrote in the *Sun-Herald*. 'Cricket probably boasts more players whose legs I do not wish to see than any other sport in the world.' Ms Spillane went on to express some derogatory remarks about the legs of Merv Hughes, David Boon, Rod Marsh and others. 'Call me a fuddy-fuddy, blame my convent schooling, if you like, but I honestly believe men have a tendency to overrate the impact the male anatomy has on the female sports fan,' she wrote.

I look back with fond memories of what is known as 'social' or 'village' cricket. Village cricket has a certain magic and mystique that sets it apart from all other sports. It will never be obliterated by big-dollar Test and pyjama cricket.

If you think you've seen some exciting one-day cricket, you should have seen the one that took place at Birchgrove Oval in Sydney around about 1955. People seem to think that Kerry Packer invented one-day cricket but it's been around for many years. What Kerry Packer did in 1977 was to purchase the world's best cricket teams, jazz up the rules and regulations of one-day cricket, paint the red balls white, put the players in colourful pyjamas and promote and market it with saturation publicity on television and elsewhere. I imagine that the only reason Mr Packer does not do the same thing to Australian baseball is that, in so doing, it would soon outrate cricket in popularity.

The one-dayer I'm referring to was the result of a dare. The Durban Club Hotel (long since gone) in Hunter Street was a popular watering hole for journalists, especially those from the Golden Ball *Sun* building. The Durban Club boasted the title of the champion cricket team of the ULVA (United Licensed Victuallers' Association, now the Australian Hotels Association). Its cellarman, Geoff Trueman, was the N.S.W. wicket-keeper, and its batsmen included the great all-rounder, Ray Flockton, one of Sydney's most popular traffic cops. Under the influence of a few pints one day at the Durban Club, Alan Hulls, sports editor of the *Daily Telegraph*, said 'You and your champion team! I could pick a team of journos to do you blokes over!' Those were fighting words and the challenge was taken up immediately and Birchgrove Oval booked for a Sunday game. Asked who would be in his team, Alan said airily, 'Oh, old blokes like Gilbert Mant; that's all we need to do you over!'

The great day dawned and I and my fifteen-year-old son, Alistair, were picked up by car by Dick Whitington, the *Telegraph*'s cricket writer. Well, I thought, that's one good cricketer we've got. Dick had been an opening batsman for South Australia in the Sheffield Shield competition. For his provocative statements as a cricket writer, he was known as Contra-Dick. A very cocky Durban Club team was waiting for us at Birchgrove Oval but as cars arrived with members of the Alan Hull's XI, their expressions changed to surprise and consternation. Nobody was more surprised than Dick and I; Alan had kept his selections secret until the very last moments. We had, in fact, five members of the current Australian Test team—Keith Miller, Alan Davidson, Jim Burke, Richie Benaud and Jim De Courcy. The other members of our team included state fast bowler Tom Brooks and Arthur Fagan, soon to be a state player.

Birchgrove Oval is large enough to stage several cricket matches at the same time. I was fielding in the deep not far from a player in a similar position in an adjoining match. As Miller and Davidson opened our bowling, he reacted with astonishment. 'That's Miller, isn't it, mate?' he asked. I explained and the news quickly spread. Players in his match abandoned play for the time being and joined us to watch the great bowlers in action. People walking to catch a ferry at the Birchgrove Wharf stopped to gaze until the ferry gave warning departure hoots on its fog horn. Those were the only people who saw more than 500 runs scored that day. There was no burlesque, it was cricket of the highest order and rich in excitement.

My recollection is that there was a group of houses perched on a high wall or hill at the far end of the ground. I have not been back to check but that was where Keith Miller hit the mightiest six I've seen during more than 70 years of cricket watching and playing. It soared high into the air (we thought it would never come down) and came to rest somewhere in a garden or, perhaps, the roof of a house. We sent out search parties but we never found that ball. Maybe it's still there, awaiting discovery in another age. Now I'll tell you the sort of fellow Keith Miller is—halfway through the game, he noticed my son, Alistair, sitting alone in the grandstand. 'Why don't you go off for a while and let Alistair take your place?' he suggested. And so I did and Alistair (a much better cricketer than I was) was able to tell his school mates next day how he had played with the internationals. You can't say a word against 'Erbar' when I'm around and I'll tell you what that means. Miller was working as a writer with *Sporting Life* magazine at this time. Keith could do anything with a bat or a ball but the writing of short headlines for his stories was completely beyond him. The only type that would accommodate his lengthy headings was a very condensed narrow type named Erbar. He used it in all occasions to the despair of his editor, Syd King, and the amusement of his colleagues. Miller was known as 'Nugget' to cricketers all over the world but to his old journalistic mates he will always be Erbar. I can't remember who won the match. Ron Kissell, of the Durban Club, scored 90-odd and Flocko got his usual bag of runs and wickets. All I know is that it was a grand day of cricket. Top cricketers play hundreds of matches in all parts of the world and memories of some of them fade with the years. But none of the players in that game at Birchgrove Oval that Sunday ever forgot it or Miller's missing sixer.

I played a lot of cricket with the Sydney Journalists' Club team. Our players consisted of journalists, actors and other kindred spirits. We played against various other clubs, business houses and institutions. There was no Sunday hotel trading in those days but we had arrangements with several publicans who would slip a keg or two to us from the back of their pubs. It was the sort of cricket for which a keg of beer was essential equipment and our gallery of spectators consisted mainly of people who knew where they could get 'a drop' on Sunday afternoon.

The most important fixtures on our calendar were the annual series of Sunday 'Test' matches against the Pakistan High Commission to Australia in Sydney. The games had been organised through our journalistic colleague, Ray Watt, the Commission's public relations officer. The Pakistanis took these encounters very seriously, as if their national pride was at stake. With this in mind, they established a sporting auxiliary to the Commission, the members of which included a number of cricketers of the University of Sydney first-grade team.

The venue for the Tests was often the small and picturesque Rushcutters Bay Oval on the shores of Sydney Harbour. The cricket was given international significance by the engagement of George Borwick and Herb Elphingston, two real Test umpires of the day. The Pakistanis were teetotallers (officially at least) but we set up our kegs of beer in the grandstand as usual. Quite a sizeable crowd would turn up for these matches and there was a pleasant picnic atmosphere.

The High Commissioner's household would supply delectable curries for lunch and beautiful Pakistani women in their saris would add colour to the scene.

The cricket was deadly serious and the results of the 'Tests' were never in doubt. The Pakistan team was at times captained by the High Commissioner himself, His Excellency Lieutenant-General Mohammed Yousuf, a very likeable and distinguished man. The wicket-keeper was his English chauffeur, Martin, with English county cricket experience and no slouch with the bat either. There would be a couple of Pakistani members of the Commission and the rest of the team were University of Sydney first-graders. Our team looked smart enough in cream trousers and white cricket boots but we were never in the race. It could have been that a couple of the actors in our team, our main strike bowlers, were suffering hangovers from the night before but that would be unfair to the acting profession. Our performance in the field was often what a cricket writer might describe as 'sluggish'. We accepted our defeats gracefully. After the game there would be the usual speeches, pledging eternal friendship between our two countries. There were congragulatory drinks, in which some of the Pakistanis joined. One of them told me there was an escape clause in the Koran, worded that hard liquor must 'not touch the lips', so that if you swallowed it straight down the mouth and gullet, it was okay. But maybe he manufactured that for his own face-saving conscience and benefit.

I recall one particular incident at Rushcutters Bay when General Yousuf was batting with Martin, the chauffeur. The General hit a ball gently towards point and set off on an impossible run. At the other end, Martin saw the danger and shouted a warning. Now, as any cricketer will tell you, a batsman in this circumstance usually bellows urgently 'Go back!' or 'No!' or 'Stay!' Martin, observing strict protocol, shouted 'Go back, Your Excellency, go back!' By the time His Excellency had received this lengthy message, he was hopelessly out of the crease as point sent in his return.

After a number of humiliating defeats, we decided one year to teach the Pakistanis a lesson and by legitimate means. Richie Benaud, the current Australian captain, and Ian Craig, former Test captain, were both members of the Journalists' Club. They readily agreed to play in our revenge match and I was appointed captain for the day. This was to be a day of glory for me and also my downfall. I was working for the Royal Agricultural Society of New South Wales at the time and my boss, Lieutenant-General Sir Frank Berryman, arranged with Lieutenant-General Sir Reginald Pollard, GOC Eastern Command, to have the match played on the parade ground at Victoria Barracks, where there was a first-class wicket. I think our plan of revenge was leaked to the Pakistanis through diplomatic channels and several more gentlemen were admitted to the Commission's sporting auxiliary. General Yousuf stood down for the day, joining the other two generals among the spectators. The Pakistan team took the field not only with the usual sprinkling of University players but also a couple of Western Suburb stars with Sheffield Shield experience. Never mind, we said confidently, Richie and Ian will give them some curry.

It was the proudest moment of my life when I led out the journos, with an intoxicating sense of power as I imperiously motioned Richie to 'go back a shade' and Ian to 'come in a bit'. Richie opened with a few medium-pacers before switching to his leggies. But even Richie and Ian could not save us that day—the opposition was just too strong. To compound matters, I twisted an ankle in diving for a hot off-dive and hobbled off the field to take no further part in the match. My place was taken by our twelfth man, Michael Baume, later to become a senator. My boss, General Berryman, was not amused. It was the week before the Royal Easter Show, my busiest time of the year, and there was I struggling around the Showground on crutches. The General issued a command that no RAS staff member be permitted to play cricket within one calendar month of the Show. As far as I know, the ban may still be in force.

We had an RAS staff cricket team and played our home games on the main arena of the Showground. The thick kikuyu grass was cut as closely as possible and a mat pitch pegged down. Despite the mat, the ball seldom rose; it was a fast bowlers' graveyard. Boundaries were hard to come by and there were plenty of lofted shots. We had a friendly rivalry with the staff of the Australian Jockey Club who had a splendid turf wicket at Randwick Racecourse. Sam Hordern, our president, was an AJC committeeman and many of our councillors were AJC members. There were reciprocal working arrangements between the two bodies. Some of the top jockeys were members of the AJC cricket team and these diminutive players had wrists of steel able to smite the ball hard and long. The racecourse manager, Geo Rich, was an old schoolfellow of mine and we had some great matches out in the middle of the racecourse.

I remember one match in particular because AJC committeeman, the monocle-wearing Mr Justice Dovey, was one of the umpires. Now, I had taken the judge to the cleaners in my *Sunday Sun* column about ten years previously because of his attitude as an assistant commissioner at the inquiry into the escape of Lieutenant-General Gordon Bennett from Singapore in World War II (see Chapter 3). I think my criticism was justified and I think Dovey, KC, knew it. As I went in to bat, I thought I saw him gazing intently at me.

I had scored twenty or so runs when I went with a cross-bat for my favourite sweep to leg. I missed, the ball thudded on to my leg and there was a concerted howl of 'Howzat?' from jockeys, trainers, groundsmen and other members of the racing fraternity. I was plumb out and I waited for Mr Justice Dovey's hand to go up. Now I'm for it, I thought, and rightly so, and he knows who I am and he has not forgotten. He was a tall and very big man and I was astonished to see him adjust his monocle and rise to his full height. 'NOT OUT!' he declared in his renowned courtroom belligerent voice, glaring at the assembled players and daring them to challenge his judgment. I stayed at the crease to mumbled growls of dissent by the wicket-keeper and nearby fieldsmen and did the decent thing by throwing away my wicket in the next over. As I passed Mr Justice Dovey on the way out he said, 'Now we're square, Mr Mant' and I grinned back at him.

There wasn't much cricket being played in Canada when I worked there as national news editor for Reuters in the mid-1930s. Baseball and ice hockey were the principal summer and winter games. I was stationed in Ottawa and as soon as I arrived I was contacted by local cricketers. There were two reasons for this—(1) it was known that I had travelled with the English team as the Reuter representative during the notorious Bodyline War, and (2) Don Bradman having played with Arthur Mailey's team in Canada in 1932, the assumption was that all Australians must be good cricketers.

There were enough cricketers in the political and diplomatic capital of Ottawa to form four teams. The standard was mediocre and for that reason I performed well enough to be made captain of the Ontario County team in a match against a side from Toronto. I was not puffed up with importance as it would have been the equivalent of being captain of the Wandin Valley second XI in Australia. We played on one of the most delightful cricket grounds in the world, with a first-class wicket, courtesy of the Governor-General of Canada. Rideau Hall was his official residence, a mansion set in magnificent grounds bordered by maples and English oaks and elms. In the 'fall' of autumn, Rideau Hall became a fairyland on a thick carpet of multi-coloured maple leaves. The cricket we played at Rideau Hall was sedate and very English, with occasional polite cries of 'Well played, sir!' from an onlooker. No vulgar kegs of beer or 'barbies' but breaks for lunch and afternoon tea and cakes and scones shared by family groups on rugs laid on the grass. It was the sort of village cricket I loved and still love. I nearly scored a maiden century at Rideau Hall, reaching 87. At this point I missed the ball in attempting a sweep shot to leg, the ball thumped on to my leg pad and bounced up on to my chin. Blood gushed and I was hurried off to a doctor who closed the wound with three stitches. Displaying indomitable Australian courage, I returned to resume my innings, only to discover that I had been given out lbw. That was the closest I ever got to a ton. I've never made a hole-in-one at golf either, but there's still time for that.

The day came when I achieved international status. A team of Bermudan cricketers were touring North America and requested a game against Ottawa, as they wanted to see the Canadian capital. The Bermudians were a very competent side who played regularly against West Indian teams in the Caribbean, so we knew we were in for a hiding. I was appointed captain of an Ottawa Valley team and one local paper promoted the fixture to an international contest, Canada versus Bermuda. It was a great day's cricket and, as expected, we were done like a dinner, but nobody cared. There was a record attendance crowd of about 50, including some French-Canadians from over the river at Hull, curious about the game of cricket, who went away curiouser and curiouser, as Alice would have said. Among the crowd were the Governor-General of Canada, Lord Bessborough, and his French wife, one of the most beautiful women in the world at the time. They brought with them their house guest, a Mr Noel Coward. We were hoping the Bessboroughs would invite us all into Rideau Hall after the game but apparently they felt their presence during the match had been sufficient courtesy to the visiting Bermudans.

During his stay at Rideau Hall the great Noel Coward gave a press conference, which I attended. It was not of much interest as a Reuter news item but I sent a story about it to the *Sydney Mail* to which I had been a contributor for many years. Apparently I had liked Coward, finding him devoid of sham. I wrote: 'He received us with superb self-confidence and farewelled us, one by one, with a theatrical smile and an almost vice-regal handshake. It made me think of Noah saying goodbye to his animals. "So *frightfully* glad you came to see me," he murmured. "*Do* come again, *awfully* soon." He seemed pretty close to the mark when he said, "In a hundred years from now the legitimate theatre will be just as popular as it is today. Mechanised drama will never supersede the flesh-and-blood variety."' The legit. is still doing well, I'm glad to note.

Shortly after I arrived in Canada, Lord Bessborough's term expired and he was succeeded as governor-general by the newly created First Baron Tweedsmuir. He was better known as John Buchan, the Scottish author of bestselling adventure and secret-service thrillers, including *The Thirty-Nine Steps, Greenmantle* and *Prester John*. I had to be very circumspect with the new GG as he was on the board of directors of Reuters. I went to Quebec to meet him when he arrived by steamer and was later summoned on a number of occasions to Rideau Hall, ostensibly to discuss news reporting but really, I think, to be pumped about life in Canada and the reactions to his appointment.

To look at, John Buchan was the last person you would imagine to write exciting cloak-and-dagger stories. A short, gnome-like man with a large head and a somewhat squeaky voice, he did not relate in looks to his tall, handsome upper-class heroes such as Richard Hannay. Buchan wrote more than 50 books, including historical studies, while engaged in politics, diplomacy and as a director of well-known publishers, Thomas Nelson. His novels dealt with international intrigue often involving cross-country chases between spies and counter-spies in the Scottish highlands, the Cotswolds in England and the South African veldt, where he worked for some years. Lord Tweedsmuir was ailing when he went to Canada in 1935 and he died in office in Montreal less than five years later. He came to love Canada and wrote of foreknowledge of his approaching death in his last novel, *Sick Heart River*. It was published in the year following his death and one reviewer said Buchan's foreknowledge of his own death influenced the pity and terror of the novel. I cannot recall whether Richard Hannay played cricket but his creator showed little interest in our games at Rideau Hall. But he was fascinating to talk to and very much the British Empire man. I was very sorry to hear of his passing.

A SAD MOMENT IN CRICKET: There was a Journos' match to be played one Sunday on a wicket on top of Centennial Park near a water tower. The weather was threatening but one of our team drove his station wagon to our black-marketeer in a Paddington back street to pick up a nine-gallon keg of beer. Then the rain came down. It rained and it rained, the match was abandoned and most of the players went home.

The rest of us were left with the keg, the contents of which were unreturnable. There was only one way to solve the problem, but nine gallons were beyond the capacity of our small group of bedraggled cricketers. It was decided to jettison the remaining beer and it led to a poignant scene. Our opening batsman was Don Crosby, to become one of Australia's most distinguished actors. The sight of gallons of the precious amber liquid gushing out of the keg onto the waterlogged grass of Centennial Park was too much for him. Don burst into a flood of tears, which mingled with the water and beer already on the ground. It was a sad moment in cricket to see a grown man break down in such a way.

17

How Being 90 Ruined My Golf

The older one becomes, the quicker the days, weeks, months and years go by. A year is an eternity to a young child wishing that Christmas would come again sooner. When you turn 90, time really becomes a precious commodity. Time does not go by, it flies by.

I reached 90 with a great deal of surprise. I had led a somewhat dissolute young life and had later been led into all sorts of adventures and traumatic experiences when I really did not want to do so. I still eat, drink and do all the wrong things. I follow strictly what I call my 4B Diet—beer, butter, bacon and more beer, with plenty of salt. That's what my stomach wants and that's what my stomach gets. I regard beer as the staff of life, not bread. A lot depends on one's individual stomach when it comes to longevity. I remember as a young reporter interviewing a group of 90-year-olds in a Sydney old men's home, in Petersham, I think. Half the old fellows attributed their longevity to never having smoked or tasted alcohol; the other half attributed it to the fact that they had smoked and drunk alcohol in large quantities with great relish all their lives. The oldest inmate, nudging 99, boasted that not only was he a heavy smoker and drinker but had also enjoyed sexual relations with more than 2,000 women; he bemoaned the fact that he was encountering stiff resistance to his advances from the young nurses at the old men's home. My report was inconclusive as a study of geriatric social and dietary behaviour. I wonder, though, what the result would have been if the stomachs of the old men who smoked and drank had been exchanged with those of the non-smokers and teetotallers? When I worked for the Australian Jersey Herd Society as its publicity officer, I proved conclusively, quoting medical experts, that nobody really knew what cholesterol was and that plenty of rich Jersey milk, cream and butter was good for you. Mind you, if I had been working for the margarine mob, I could have just as conclusively proved, quoting other medical experts, that butter was bad for you. That's what publicity men are for.

Inevitably, a 90-plus-year-old begins to think about death. I do not think about it in a morbid way but more with curiosity. I am not frightened of it, though hoping it will not be too painful; if so, I hope my doctor will pull the plug on me when the time comes. Peter Pan said that to die would be 'an awfully big adventure'. The trouble is there is nobody around to tell you what it is really like up (or down) there, with the possible exception of Shirley Maclaine. J.C. came back for a short while but He did not speak of His experiences. Many believe there will be a Second Coming and we may know then. I have read stories by people claiming to have died briefly, seeing flashing lights and passing into long tunnels, but I do not give that much credence. I do not think I believe in an afterlife but that does not mean I am an agnostic. I wish sometimes that I had the unquestioning faith of a Catholic. There does not seem to me to be enough space up there for the countless billions of people of all religions and denominations who have died; by now satellites and spaceships would surely have found some evidence of them. If it's one's soul that takes on everlasting life, I do not know what a soul looks like or how big it is. If we're not sure about the end of it all, we are also uncertain about the beginning. Scientists talk about the Big Bang that created the universe, but who set it off? That is the question that makes me take an each-way bet in belief in a God of some sort. I go out at night and look at the moon and the stars in wonderment. The conception and birth of a child or an animal are breathtaking miracles. How on earth does a human brain work? Ponder on it next time you're eating crumbed lamb's brains that this soggy mess in a human being's head controls love and hate, genius and idiocy, joy and sorrow. Who contrived the intricacies of a tiny insect with eyes and legs and wings and ability to manoeuvre? To use a popular cliche, it's mind-boggling, if you can comprehend what a mind is.

I've lived from the horse-and-buggy days to the silicone chip. When I was born there was not in general use electricity, wireless, moving pictures, talking pictures, television, motor cars, aeroplanes, household refrigerators, poker machines or video games. Beyond nuclear power and the silicone chip lies what? Maybe there will not be any more need for human beings. It will be back to square one, unless we bring upon ourselves another Big Bang and blow ourselves to smithereens. I'm not losing any sleep over it; that's your worry, mate.

Life was very inconvenient in the Old Australia but I'm glad I lived most of my life in it. I'm all for progress and multiculturalism, if only for the fact that we could not have, morally or physically, kept this island continent to our Anglo-Saxon selves. But we did not have to search for an identity in the Old Australia. We had one. Admittedly, to the outside world we were regarded as a race of insular, isolationist and boastful larrikins. We all looked alike and spoke alike with a Cockney twang. We were unmistakably Australian with an inborn sense of 'mateship' and very sensitive to outside criticism. That's all in the process of change now and I believe it will take another 25 years or more before we can achieve a true national identity. At the moment, we are a nation of different faces, complexions, accents, beliefs and customs. It will require much more inter-communication and inter-marriage before we weld ourselves into recognisable Chip Age Aussies.

In the meantime I remain a Queen's (and the Queen Mum's) man until she abdicates or dies. I have no time for Diana, Fergie & Co., although I have a sneaking admiration for Prince Charles, who is not as silly as he seems at times. I believe an Australian republic is inevitable simply because the old Anglo-Saxon influence will die out or be outnumbered by the people of other ethnic backgrounds. Now is the wrong time for change and the substitution of 'republic' for 'monarchy' is not going to alter our status as an independent nation. A referendum on the subject now would be as divisive as the bitter referendums in World War I and an insult and probable humiliation of the Queen. Besides, the monarchial system in Australia is working very well and the Crown is an attractive-looking logo of our stability. It's the Crown itself, not the Queen's person, that symbolises our nation and I don't see any harm in it. Bob Hawke got it right when he said that the republic should come naturally when all the people wanted it. Mind you, Britain itself set us on the road to a republic by joining the European Common Market and classing us as foreigners. That rankles me considerably.

But I'm a sucker for tradition and pomp and ceremony. I love the drama of it. Republicanism sounds so dull and its Australian leaders seem to be an unsmiling lot, with the exception of Thomas Keneally, who presents a perpetual grin. I worry about what sort of republic we will get—will it be any better than the present system? Asians are dumber than I imagine if they think that because we have a Queen, we are not independent, as Paul Keating would have us believe. They know full well we have long been independent and the anachronism of having a Queen probably tickles their Oriental fancy.

If there are any fairies at the bottom of my garden, I'm sure they've got a beautiful Fairy Queen—it would be ridiculous if they went republican and got a President and Vice-President of the Fairies. If we must have a republic, I think it would be wonderful for Queen Elizabeth to open the Year 2000 Olympic Games in Sydney and abdicate *after* the event; it would be one of the most moving and emotional moments in history, as Australia thanks her in front of the world for her duties as our Queen for more than 40 years. Then bring on the installation of a former High Court judge or a washed-up politician as our first President.

The coming of a republic would result in mixed blessings and disadvantages. The Queen's departure would necessitate the removal of all vestiges of the Queen and the Crown in a multitude of different shapes, sizes and trends. No more king prawns or queen puddings. The royal removal would be a gigantic task over many years in all parts of Australia and would require (which God forbid!) the establishment of a new government department. Unless this is done, we will risk the emergence of dangerous splinter royalist political groups. The word 'royal' will have to be totally and ruthlessly obliterated.

The creation of the Department of the Eradication of All Royal Images and Emblems (DEARIE) would require the recruitment of hordes of public servants to administer it, a splendid start in the reduction of unemployment. Then would come the enlistment of tens of thousands of removalist technicians and tradesmen—paint and varnish removers, metal removers, panel beaters etc.—to deal with the bewildering assortment of images and emblems to be removed. The Royal insignia would have to be removed from our currency, postage stamps, pillar boxes, government stationery, warships and other defence establishments, hotels, banks, golf, bowls, yacht and other clubs, coffee lounges, street names, threatres, laundries, zoos, botanical gardens, mental asylums and more hotels. The scrapping and replacement of letterhead stationery of numerous royal associations and organisations would give a boost to paper manufacturers, stationers and the printing industry. DEARIE would be of special benefit to the teenaged unemployed. Being so adept at the putting on of graffiti of all kinds, they could soon be trained in its removal and take real joy in their work.

The Old Australia still exists in the bush. That's why I live away from the pollution in Port Macquarie. It's not exactly a bush town but twenty minutes down the track you can go into the Wauchope forests and, a bit further on, up amongst the cattle and sheep over the Great Dividing Range. The people of the bush haven't changed much despite multiculturalism, computers and the ubiquitous chip. I could go to this year's Wauchope Show and take photographs of the current Best Uddered Cow and find it much the same as it was twenty years ago. The same sort of faces and clothes and conversation. If the dairy farmers of my day aren't there, their sons will be, with the descendents of the cows I used to photograph. If I turned up with my camera, there would bound to be somebody remarking, 'There's that chap from *The Land*!' They are more sophisticated now—the days when Dad and Dave and other country bumpkins would be conned into buying the Sydney Harbour Bridge are over; today the country bumpkin would be more likely to sell a nonexistent gold mine to an unsuspecting city slicker. The people of the bush are the salt of the earth so far as I am concerned. I feel at ease with them. Yet even in the bush, the way of life has had to change. No longer can you leave your house or car doors unlocked. And if you say 'Hello!' to a little boy or girl in the street, you will be arrested as a paedophile. The children are being trained never to speak to strangers and it's terribly sad such a thing had to happen.

Memories of Gigoomgan and my early years as a jackaroo and other rural pursuits are constantly with me and at intervals I break out into nostalgic verse about it:

> Four and twenty horsemen making down the Bogan,
>   Silver bits a-jingle as they plod across the plain;
> Four and twenty ponies prancing by the river...
>   God! To see the Bogan and the old bush mates again!
>
> Four and twenty horsemen swaying to the saddles,
>   Loping for the wilga in the blazing Western sun;
> Four and twenty horsemen jogging on by starlight,
>   Lifting up their voices when the drowsy day is done.
>
> Four and twenty horsemen making down the Bogan,
>   Phantom riders singing what is music to the brain...
> Four and twenty tramcars crashing over Pitt Street—
>   God! To see the Bogan and the old bush mates again!

The most serious aspect of my passing the 90 milestone is the ruinous effect it has had on my golf. I was never much more than average at it but I loved the game and was pretty good with the irons on occasions. You ask Arthur Thwaite of Port Macquarie about the day I got a birdie on the par-five, 504 metres ninth hole just when he thought he had the game sewn up. I was 86 years old at the time. Aided by a stiff nor'-easter, I took a two-iron from the tee, then two five-irons to the back of the green and a monster putt into the hole. Arthur jumped up and down in disbelief and chagrin and still grizzles about it.

The moment I reached 90 the rot set in. There was a sharp recurrence of the freckles-people-are-looking-at-me syndrome (everything's a syndrome these days). A fellow came up to me after one dreadful round and held out his hand. 'Congratulations, old chap!' 'What for?' I asked. 'I've never played worse.' 'I think it's wonderful that you can still walk around a golf course at your age,' he said. I imagined members pointing me out to visitors: 'See that old bloke over there—he's over ninety'. So that's it, I thought; I've become a Port Macquarie tourist attraction along with the century-old Court House.

The Port Macquarie clubhouse members' lounge faces east towards the South Pacific Ocean and the approach to the ninth hole, protected by three bunkers. On the weekly Veterans' Day, players who have finished their rounds gather in the lounge for drinks and to exchange the usual bad-luck excuses about the game. In between times they idly watch players still on the course advancing up the hill towards the green. This approach has now become a nightmare and an ordeal for me. I imagine hordes of people looking out of the big windows and saying,

'Here comes old Gilbert! Silly old bugger! It's time he gave it up!' I imagine Arthur Thwaite re-telling the story of my birdie at the ninth, with embellishments. I say to myself, 'I'll put this nine-iron into the bunker for sure.' And I lift my head and take my eyes off the ball and into the bunker she goes. 'Silly old bugger! It's time he gave it up!' I hear them say. And, of course, nobody is looking at me at all; they are far more interested in their beer than Old Gilbert, the tourist attraction. I'm still playing with the veterans once a week and my golf is getting worse and worse. It's not because of any physical handicap, it's the freckles syndrome and the inability to keep my head down that are my downfall.

Golf is a game of intense concentration and temperament and keeping your eyes on the ball is a vital part of it, as in all ball games. Lifting the head is a common fault with social golfers who look where the ball is supposed to be going a fraction of a second before hitting it. As a consequence, the ball will be sliced, pulled or missed altogether. I remember once discussing with that great Yorkshire batsman, Maurice Leyland, whether it was easier to hit a cricket ball in flight than a stationary golf ball. I opted for the golf ball because it was not moving. 'Aye,' agreed Maurice, 'but it's such a bluddy little 'un.'

Some of my more sadistic friends urge me to try what golfers know as the Fish Hook Cure but I will have none of it. The equipment for this cure is still used by some insensitive golf clubs as a prize known as the Bradman Trophy, presented to the player with the highest (or worst) stroke score. The cure consists of a length of strong fishing line with a number 7o hook (big enough to catch a fair-sized bream). The line is strung across the player's head with a noose and the fish hook attached to one or both testicles. It is said that if the wearer suddenly lifts his head with this equipment in place, he will never do it again—or anything else, I imagine. I flatly refuse to go to such extremes.

Recently I was honoured to be invited to officially open the Seventh Annual Antique and Old Collectible Fair under the auspices of the Port Macquarie High School. I received some warm and unexpected applause when I pointed out my obvious qualifications for the job. It was, I suppose, my last hurrah as an Old Collectible and in some ways I could echo the words of my kinsman, Adam Lindsay Gordon:

> For good undone and gifts misspent and resolutions vain
> 'Tis somewhat late to trouble. This I know—
> I should live the same life over if I had to live again;
> And the chances are I go where most men go.

THE END

Bibliography

Allen, Frederick Lewis (1931) *Only Yesterday* (Blue Ribbon Books, Inc., New York City)
Angel, Don (1985) *The History of the Journalists' Club* (The Journalists' Club, Sydney)
Bulloch, John Malcolm (1902) *The Gordon Book* (Bazaar of the Fochabers Reading Room, Scotland)
Chronicles of the Twentieth Century (1990); (Chronicle Australia Pty Ltd, Ringwood)
Clark, M.H. *A History of Australia* (Melbourne University Press)
Dusty, Slim and John Lapsley (1979) *Walk a Country Mile* (Rigby, Adelaide)
Edgar, Patricia (1970) *The Politics of the Press* (Sun Books, Melbourne)
Flecker, James Elroy (1936; 1970) *The Collected Poems* (Martin Secker, London)
Hasluck, Paul (1970) *The Government and the People, 1942–45* (Australian War Memorial, Canberra)
Hilvert, John (1984) *Blue Pencil Warriors* (University of Queensland Press, St Lucia)
Lindsay, Jack (1969) *The Roaring Twenties* (The Bodley Head, London)
Luck, Peter (1980) *This Fabulous Century* (Lansdowne Press, Sydney)
Mant, Gilbert (1972) *The Big Show* (Royal Agricultural Society of New South Wales, Sydney)
Mant, Gilbert (1985) *Show People* (Agricultural Societies Council of New South Wales, Sydney)
McCrae, Hugh (1934) *Georgiana's Journal* (Angus & Robertson, Sydney)
McCrae, Hugh (1939) *Poems* (Angus & Robertson, Sydney)
McCrae, Hugh (1948) *Story-Book Only* (Angus & Robertson, Sydney)
McQueen, Humphrey (1977) *Australia's Media Monopolies* (Vasa, Melbourne)
Moloney, Billy (1968) *Memoirs of An Abominable Showman* (Rigby Limited, Adelaide)
Penton, Brian (1947) *Censored!* (Shakespeare Head Press, Sydney)
Triffen, Rodney (1989) *News & Power* (Allen & Unwin, Sydney)

Solution to the Dr Balsam joke in Chapter 3: The boxer had cauliflower ears.

Index

2/19th Battalion, 8th Division, 72, 74
8th Divisions, 23, 73
Aboriginals at Gigoomgan, 36–8, 40
Adelaide Advertiser, 81, 89
Adelaide Establishment, 82
Adelaide News, 81, 89
Agricultural Society Council of NSW, 97, 100
Agricultural Society of NSW, 96, 97
Allen, George Oswald Browning 'Gubby', 27, 151
Alternates in the Bellinger Valley, 146, 147
Ambassadors, The, 48, 49
Anderson, Peter Dalgairns, 29, 40
Anzacs, 76
Arthurs Seat, 128, 129
Associated Newspapers Ltd, 16, 66
Australian Journalists' Association, 55, 92
  women members, 56
Australian soldiers, motivation, 74–6

Balsam jokes, 15, 16
Balsam, Dr Friar, 15, 16, 18, 19, 25, 95, 117, 122, 132–49
Beechwood, 139
Bellbrook, 142, 143
Bellinger Valley, 145–7
Benaud, Richie, 66, 153, 155, 156
Bennett, Lieutenant-General H. Gordon, 23, 24, 94
Berryman, Lieut. Gen. Sir Frank, 94, 109, 155, 156
Bishop-Mant, Ven. Archdeacon Walter, 39
Bodyline Cricket War, 27, 82, 151
Bodyline Tour, 9, 10
Bonney, Edmund Garnet, 81, 87, 88, 90
Bowra Hotel, 144, 145
Bradman, Don, 19, 62, 82, 150
Brennan, John, 68, 69
British Israelites Society, 29, 30
Brodie, Elizabeth (Duchess of Gordon), 124–6, 128, 129
Brown, Jennifer, 29, 131
Buggy, Hugh, 10, 45

Bulletin, 17, 119

Calwell, Arthur Augustus, 87, 88, 90
Censorship, 16, 81–90, 117
  confrontation with the newspapers over, 87–9
Charley, Sir Philip, 110, 111
Chisholm, Alec H., 8, 44, 118
Churchill, Winston, 80
Cinesound, 64
Clark, Manning, 75
Column 8, 17
Columnists
  Sydney post-war, 17
  payola, 17, 18
Commercial Hotel, Krambach, 134, 135
Cosmopolitan Hotel, Taylors Arm, 147, 148
Cousens, Major Charles 'Bill', 22, 23
Coward, Noel, 158
Cowper, Sir Norman, 116, 124
Craig, Ian, 155, 156
Cricket, 150–9
  in Canada in the mid-1930s, 157
  one-day, 152, 153
Curtin, John, 79, 80, 84

Daily Express, 16
Daily Guardian, 150
Daily Mirror, 17, 106
Daily Mirror, London, 19
Daily Telegraph, 17, 44, 84, 87, 88, 106
Daily Telegraph Pictorial, 61
Darwin, Japanese raids on, 84, 85
Davidson, Alan, 9, 153
Deamer, Dulcie, 11, 46
Deamer, Sir, 11, 17
Devine, Matilda (Tilly), 63, 64
Dobell, William, 21, 22
Dorter, Phil, 68, 69
Dovey, W.R. (Bill), 23, 24, 156, 157
Duffell, Gunner John, 9, 76
Dumas, Lloyd, 81, 89
Dusty, Slim, 143, 147, 148

East, Milba, 11, 12

East, Stanley, 11–14
East, Tibby, 11

Fair, Dick, 77, 78
Fairfax, 15, 66, 71
Freud, Sigmund, 42

Gallipoli, 76
Gigoomgan, 29, 30, 34–41
  daily journals, account books, letters, 40
Gilmore, Dame Mary, 21, 114, 119
  Dobell's portrait of her, 21, 22
Gilroy, Cardinal (Sir Norman), 20, 21
Gordon Highlanders, 124, 131
Gordon, Adam Lindsay, 115, 165
Gordon, Duchess of, *see* Brodie, Elizabeth
Gorton, Sir John, 54
Gurr, Tom, 15, 16, 61, 63–6, 91

Hardy, Owen, 11, 12
Harney, W.E. (Bill), 58, 59
Harrington Hotel, 133, 134
Hasluck, Paul, 84, 85
Hastings River, 138, 140
Hilvert, John, 83, 88
Hoey, Tom, 88–90
Hordern, Samuel, 109, 110, 156
Hotel Coopernook, 135, 136

Idriess, Ion 'Jack', 22
Imperial Services Club, 82
Isles, Don, 78

James, Francis, 11, 24
Jamison, Sir John, 96, 97
Jardine, Douglas, 82, 151
Jolliffe, Eric, 58–60
Journalists' Club, The, 55–60, 105
  cricket team, 154, 155
Journalists, Australian journalists in the 1920s and 1930s, 10–14

Keating, Paul, 162
Kendall, Henry, 115, 137
Kilgour, Emily, 30, 32

Krambach, 134, 135

La Trobe, Charles, 128, 129
Lamingtons, 101, 102
Land, The, 7, 15, 95
Leamington sponges, 101–2
Leg-pulls, 19, 20
Leigh, Kate, 63, 64
Leslie, George Farquharson, 29, 40
Ligertwood, Mr Justice George, 23, 62
Lindsay, Jack, 11, 46, 48, 117
Lindsay, Norman, 46, 47, 49, 116
Lindsay, Phillip, 11, 46, 48, 50
Lindsay, Raymond, 11, 46
Lodger, The, 11, 12
Long Flat, 139, 140
Love, Dr Colin, 15, 34
Lower, Lennie, 11, 12

MacArthur, General Douglas, 23, 80, 85
Macdonald, Alex, 11, 56
Macrae, Alexander, 125
Macrae, William, 125
Mant, Alistair, 154
Mant, Barty, 36, 38
Mant, Bessie, 36
Mant, Charles, 35
Mant, Dick, 30, 34
Mant, Frances, 28–30, 33, 34, 118, 119
Mant, George (Grandfather), 29, 30
Mant, George (Uncle), 35–7
Mant, George Joseph, 29, 39, 40
Mant, John, 30–2, 34, 82
Mant, Kath, 39
Reg, 36, 38–40
Mant, Rt Rev. Richard, 39
Mant, Sarah, 39
Mant, William Hall (Billy), 27–9
Marie, 45, 49
Mary, 44, 49
Marylebone Cricket Club, 19
  1932–33 tour of Australiaa, 151
  1936–37 tour of Australia, 151
Master Pastry Cooks' Association of NSW, 101
McCrae homestead, 128, 130
McCrae, Andrew, 125–30
McCrae, George Gordon (grand uncle), 115, 119, 120, 123, 129
McCrae, George Gordon (II), 124, 130
McCrae, Georgiana Huntly, 122–31
McCrae, Hugh Raymond, 34, 47, 49, 113–20, 123, 124, 129, 13
McCrae, Huntley, 116
McCrae, Marjory, 116
McCrae, Rose, 116
Melbourne, early days, 127, 128, 130
Mercier, Emile, 65, 66
Miller, Keith, 153, 154
Monarchy, British, 16, 54, 162

Moore Park, 98, 111, 112
Murdoch, Sir Keith, 79, 91

Namatjira, Albert, 59, 60
Nambucca River, 145
Nambucca Valley, 144

O'Sullivan, Pat, 116
Ogilvy, Clive, 103
Ohamma, 77
Olivier, Laurence, 56
Olsen, John, 48
Olsen, Otto, 79
Outback books, 58, 59
Oxley, John, 140

Packer, Kerry, 24, 152
Packer, Sir Frank, 17, 106, 107
Pakistan High Commission, 154, 155
Parsons, Gordon, 147, 148
Paterson, A.B. 'Banjo', 28
Penton, Brian, 11, 86–8
People, 63, 64
Playford, Thomas, 81, 86
Poetry, 113–15
Pope Paul VI, 56
Port Macquarie, 7, 137, 138
Press and Broadcasting Censorship Order, 89
Pub With No Beer, The, 147, 148
Pubs, local, 132–49

Qantas, 106
Quayle, Jack, 12, 44–6
Quayle, Kit, 12, 44
Quinn, 'Mad' Bill, 45

RAS-Shell Journalists' Tours, 105, 106
Radio Tokyo, 22
Reid, Alan, 79, 80
Republicanism, 162, 163
Rescorl, Jack, 72, 74
Reuters, 73, 79–81
Rideau Hall, 157, 158
Royal Agricultural Society of NSW (RAS), 7, 93–5, 102–11
  Council, 104–07
  cricket team, 156
  RAS/Shell Journalists' Tours, 105, 106
Royal Agricultural Society of Tasmania, 95
Royal Easter Show, 98, 99, 105–9, 112
  financial sponsorship for, 103, 104, 107, 111
  Grand Parade, 107
  showjumping, 108
Royal Show Girl Contest, 106, 107
Ruse, James, 95, 96

Savigny, W.H. ('Sav'), 31, 32
Shell Company of Australia Ltd, 105, 106
Show societies, 95–97, 100, 101
Showground, The, 98
Shows
  Australian pioneer, 100, 101
  agricultural and livestock, 95–102
  country, 7, 95–7, 100
Singapore, 78
  fall of, 77
Slessor, Kenneth, 31, 46–8, 62, 63, 105, 113
Sly-groggers in the Nambucca Valley, 144
Somme, Battles of the, 76
Star, The, 138, 139
Sun, 17
Sun-Herald, 66
Sunday Herald, 66
Sunday Sun, 15, 61–66
Sunday Telegraph, 88, 106
Sydney Grammar School, 30–2
Sydney Morning Herald, 17, 47
Sydney Press Club, 55
Sydney Showground, 111, 112

Taylors Arm, 147, 148
Thomas, Archer, 81, 91
Tobruk, Rats of, 76
Tram to Watsons Bay, 57, 58
Traveller's Rest Hotel, 139, 140
Trueman, Geoff, 153

Ushers, 67

Van Diemen's Land Agricultural Society, 95, 96
Vision, 46–48
Von Barthold, Baron, 101

Watson, 12, 13
Watts, Peggy, 141, 142
Weekend Australian, 17
Weekly News, 53
Whelp, HMS, 55
Who's Who in Australia, 8
Willawarrin, 141, 142
Windsor, Harry, 63
Wireless, 31
Wolfe, Humbert, 54
Woman's Mirror, 43
Workers, The, 21, 93

Yellkow press, 16
Yeo, Frank, 138
Yeomans, John, 60
Yorick Club, 115
Yousuf, Lieutenant-General Mohammed, 155